Praise for Learn Enough Tutorials

"Just started the #100DaysOfCode journey. Today marks day 1. I have completed @mhartl's great Ruby tutorial at @LearnEnough and am looking forward to starting on Ruby on Rails from tomorrow. Onwards and upwards."
—Optimize Prime (@_optimize), Twitter post

"Ruby and Sinatra and Heroku, oh my! Almost done with this live web application. It may be a simple palindrome app, but it's also simply exciting! #100DaysOfCode #ruby @LearnEnough #ABC #AlwaysBeCoding #sinatra #heroku"
—Tonia Del Priore (@toninjaa), Twitter post; Software Engineer for a FinTech Startup for 3+ years

"I have nothing but fantastic things to say about @LearnEnough courses. I am just about finished with the #javascript course. I must say, the videos are mandatory because @mhartl will play the novice and share in the joy of having something you wrote actually work!"
—Claudia Vizena

"I must say, this Learn Enough series is a masterpiece of education. Thank you for this incredible work!"
—Michael King

"I want to thank you for the amazing job you have done with the tutorials. They are likely the best tutorials I have ever read."
—Pedro Iatzky

T0262585

LEARN ENOUGH
PYTHON
TO BE DANGEROUS

Learn Enough Series from Michael Hartl

Visit **informit.com/learn-enough** for a complete list of available publications.

The **Learn Enough** series teaches you the developer tools, Web technologies, and programming skills needed to launch your own applications, get a job as a programmer, and maybe even start a company of your own. Along the way, you'll learn technical sophistication, which is the ability to solve technical problems yourself. And Learn Enough always focuses on the most important parts of each subject, so you don't have to learn everything to get started—you just have to learn enough to be dangerous. The Learn Enough series includes books and video courses so you get to choose the learning style that works best for you.

LEARN ENOUGH PYTHON TO BE DANGEROUS

Software Development, Flask Web Apps, and Beginning Data Science with Python

Michael Hartl

✦ Addison-Wesley

Boston • Columbus • New York • San Francisco • Amsterdam • Cape Town
Dubai • London • Madrid • Milan • Munich • Paris • Montreal • Toronto • Delhi • Mexico City
São Paulo • Sydney • Hong Kong • Seoul • Singapore • Taipei • Tokyo

Cover image: Alexey Boldin/Shutterstock
Figure 1.4: The Pallets Projects
Figures 1.6-1.8, 9.3: Amazon Web Services, Inc.
Figures 1.9, 1.10, 8.2: GitHub, Inc.
Figures 1.11, 1.12, 10.2, 10.3: Fly.io
Figure 2.9: Python Software Foundation
Figures 4.4, 4.5, 4.10, 8.8: Regex101
Figures 5.6, 9.5: Google LLC
Figures 9.4, 9.7: The Wikimedia Foundation
Figures 11.1-11.5, 11.23: Jupyter

For information about buying this title in bulk quantities, or for special sales opportunities (which may include electronic versions; custom cover designs; and content particular to your business, training goals, marketing focus, or branding interests), please contact our corporate sales department at corpsales@pearsoned.com or (800) 382-3419.

For government sales inquiries, please contact governmentsales@pearsoned.com.

For questions about sales outside the U.S., please contact intlcs@pearson.com.

Visit us on the Web: informit.com/aw

Library of Congress Control Number: 2023935869

ISBN-13: 978-0-13-805095-5
ISBN-10: 0-13-805095-3

1 2023

Contents

Preface

Learn Enough Python to Be Dangerous teaches you to write practical and modern programs using the elegant and powerful Python programming language. You'll learn how to use Python for both general-purpose programming and for beginning web-application development. Although mastering Python can be a long journey, you don't have to learn everything to get started . . . you just have to learn enough to be *dangerous*.

You'll begin by exploring the core concepts of Python programming using a combination of the interactive Python interpreter and text files run at the command line. The result is a solid understanding of both *object-oriented programming* and *functional programming* in Python. You'll then build on this foundation to develop and publish a simple self-contained Python package. You'll then use this package in a simple dynamic web application built using the *Flask* web framework, which you'll also deploy to the live Web. As a result, *Learn Enough Python to Be Dangerous* is especially appropriate as a prerequisite to learning web development with Python.

In addition to teaching you specific skills, *Learn Enough Python to Be Dangerous* also helps you develop *technical sophistication*—the seemingly magical ability to solve practically any technical problem. Technical sophistication includes concrete skills like version control and coding, as well as fuzzier skills like Googling the error message and knowing when to just reboot the darn thing. Throughout *Learn Enough Python to Be Dangerous*, we'll have abundant opportunities to develop technical sophistication in the context of real-world examples.

Chapter by Chapter

In order to learn enough Python to be dangerous, we'll begin at the beginning with a series of simple "hello, world" programs using several different techniques (Chapter 1), including an introduction to the Python interpreter, an interactive command-line program for evaluating Python code. In line with the Learn Enough philosophy of always doing things "for real", even as early as Chapter 1 we'll deploy a (very simple) dynamic Python application to the live Web. This chapter also includes pointers to the latest setup and installation instructions via *Learn Enough Dev Environment to Be Dangerous* (https://www.learnenough.com/dev-environment), which is available for free online and as a free downloadable ebook.

After mastering "hello, world", we'll take a tour of some Python *objects*, including strings (Chapter 2), lists (Chapter 3), and other native objects like dates, dictionaries, and regular expressions (Chapter 4). Taken together, these chapters constitute a gentle introduction to *object-oriented programming* with Python.

In Chapter 5, we'll learn the basics of *functions*, an essential subject for virtually every programming language. We'll then apply this knowledge to an elegant and powerful style of coding known as *functional programming*, including an introduction to *comprehensions* (Chapter 6).

Having covered the basics of built-in Python objects, in Chapter 7 we'll learn how to make objects of our own. In particular, we'll define an object for a *phrase*, and then develop a method for determining whether or not the phrase is a *palindrome* (the same read forward and backward).

Our initial palindrome implementation will be rather rudimentary, but we'll extend it in Chapter 8 using a powerful technique called *test-driven development* (TDD). In the process, we'll learn more about testing generally, as well as how to create and publish a Python package.

In Chapter 9, we'll learn how to write nontrivial *shell scripts*, one of Python's biggest strengths. Examples include reading from both files and URLs, with a final example showing how to manipulate a downloaded file as if it were an HTML web page.

In Chapter 10, we'll develop our first full Python web application: a site for detecting palindromes. This will give us a chance to learn about *routes*, *layouts*, *embedded Python*, and *form handling*, together with a second application of TDD. As a capstone to our work, we'll deploy our palindrome detector to the live Web.

Finally, in Chapter 11, we'll get an introduction to Python tools used in the booming field of *data science*. Topics include numerical calculations with NumPy, data visualization with Matplotlib, data analysis with pandas, and machine learning with scikit-learn.

Additional Features

In addition to the main tutorial material, *Learn Enough Python to Be Dangerous* includes a large number of exercises to help you test your understanding and to extend the material in the main text. The exercises include frequent hints and often include the expected answers, with community solutions available by separate subscription at www.learnenough.com.

Final Thoughts

Learn Enough Python to Be Dangerous gives you a practical introduction to the fundamentals of Python, both as a general-purpose programming language and as a specialist language for web development and data science. After learning the techniques covered in this tutorial, and especially after developing your technical sophistication, you'll know everything you need to write shell scripts, publish Python packages, deploy dynamic web applications, and use key Python data-science tools. You'll also be ready for a huge variety of other resources, including books, blog posts, and online documentation.

Learn Enough Scholarships

Learn Enough is committed to making a technical education available to as wide a variety of people as possible. As part of this commitment, in 2016 we created the Learn Enough Scholarship program.[1] Scholarship recipients get free or deeply discounted access to the Learn Enough All Access subscription, which includes all of the Learn Enough online book content, embedded videos, exercises, and community exercise answers.

As noted in a 2019 RailsConf Lightning Talk,[2] the Learn Enough Scholarship application process is incredibly simple: Just fill out a confidential text area telling us a little about your situation. The scholarship criteria are generous and flexible—we understand that there are an enormous number of reasons for wanting a scholarship, from being a student, to being between jobs, to living in a country with an unfavorable

---

1. https://www.learnenough.com/scholarship
2. https://www.learnenough.com/scholarship-talk

exchange rate against the U.S. dollar. Chances are that, if you feel like you've got a good reason, we'll think so, too.

So far, Learn Enough has awarded more than 2,500 scholarships to aspiring developers around the country and around the world. To apply, visit the Learn Enough Scholarship page at www.learnenough.com/scholarship. Maybe the next scholarship recipient could be you!

Acknowledgments

Thanks to Paul Logston, Tom Repetti, and Ron Lee for their helpful comments on drafts of *Learn Enough Python to Be Dangerous*. Thanks also to Prof. Jetson Leder-Luis of Boston University and data scientist Amadeo Bellotti for their helpful feedback and assistance in preparing Chapter 11. Any errors that remain in the text are entirely the fault of these fine gentlemen.

As always, thanks to Debra Williams Cauley for shepherding the production process at Pearson.

About the Author

Michael Hartl (www.michaelhartl.com) is the creator of the *Ruby on Rails*™ *Tutorial* (www.railstutorial.org), one of the leading introductions to web development, and is cofounder and principal author at Learn Enough (www.learnenough.com). Previously, he was a physics instructor at the California Institute of Technology (Caltech), where he received a Lifetime Achievement Award for Excellence in Teaching. He is a graduate of Harvard College, has a Ph.D. in Physics from Caltech, and is an alumnus of the Y Combinator entrepreneur program.

CHAPTER 1

Hello, World!

Welcome to *Learn Enough Python to Be Dangerous*!

This tutorial is designed to get you started writing practical and modern Python programs as fast as possible, with a focus on the real tools used every day by software developers. You'll see how everything fits together by learning skills like testing and test-driven development, publishing packages, beginning web development, and data science. As a result, *Learn Enough Python to Be Dangerous* can serve either as a standalone introduction or as an excellent prerequisite for longer and more syntax-heavy Python tutorials, of which there are many excellent ones.

Python is one of the world's most popular programming languages, and for good reason. Python has a clean syntax, flexible data types, a wealth of useful libraries, and a powerful and elegant design that supports multiple styles of programming. Python has seen particularly robust adoption for command-line programs (also known as *scripting*, as discussed in Chapter 9), web development (via frameworks like *Flask* (Chapter 10) and *Django*), and data science (especially data analysis using *pandas* and machine learning with libraries like *scikit-learn* (Chapter 11)).

Just about the only things Python isn't good for are running inside a web browser (for which JavaScript (https://www.learnenough.com/javascript-tutorial) is necessary) and writing programs where speed is of the essence. And even in the latter case, specialized libraries like NumPy (Section 11.2) can give us the speed of a lower-level language like C with the power and flexibility of a higher-level language like Python.[1]

---

1. "Higher-level" languages like Python, JavaScript, and Ruby generally have greater support for abstraction and perform automatic memory management.

Learn Enough Python to Be Dangerous broadly follows the same structure as *Learn Enough JavaScript to Be Dangerous* (https://www.learnenough.com/javascript) and *Learn Enough Ruby to Be Dangerous* (https://www.learnenough.com/ruby), either of which can be studied either before or after this tutorial. Because many of the examples are the same, the tutorials reinforce each other nicely—there are few things more instructive in computer programming than seeing the same basic problems solved in two or more different languages.[2] As noted in Box 1.1, though, we'll definitely be writing *Python*, not JavaScript or Ruby translated into Python.

Box 1.1: Pythonic programming

More so even than users of other languages, Python programmers—sometimes known as *Pythonistas*—tend to have strongly held opinions on what constitutes proper programming style. For example, as noted by Python contributor Tim Peters in "The Zen of Python" (Section 1.2.1): "There should be one—and preferably only one—obvious way to do it." (This stands in contrast to a famous principle associated with the Perl programming language known as "TMTOWTDI": There's More Than One Way To Do It.)

Code that adheres to good programming practices (as judged by Pythonistas) is known as *Pythonic* code. This includes proper code formatting (especially the practices in PEP 8 – Style Guide for Python Code (https://peps.python.org/pep-0008/)), using built-in Python facilities like `enumerate()` (Section 3.5) and `items()` (Section 4.4.1), and using characteristic idioms like list and dictionary comprehensions (Chapter 6). (As noted in the official documentation (https://peps.python.org/pep-0001/), "PEP stands for Python Enhancement Proposal. A PEP is a design document providing information to the Python community, or describing a new feature for Python or its processes or environment." PEP 8 is the PEP specifically concerned with Python code style and formatting.)

The code in this tutorial generally strives to be as Pythonic as possible given the material introduced at the given point in the exposition. In addition, we will often begin by introducing a series of intentionally *un*Pythonic examples, culminating in a fully Pythonic version. In such cases, the distinction between unPythonic and Pythonic code will be carefully noted.

Pythonistas have been known to be a bit harsh in their judgment of unPythonic code, which can lead beginners to become overly concerned about programming

---

2. See Rosetta Code (https://rosettacode.org/wiki/Rosetta_Code) for a huge compilation of such examples.

Pythonically. But "Pythonic" is a sliding scale, depending on how much experience you have in the language. Moreover, programming is fundamentally about *solving problems*, so don't let worries about programming Pythonically stop you from solving the problems *you* face in your role as a Python programmer and software developer.

There are no programming prerequisites for *Learn Enough Python to Be Dangerous*, although it certainly won't hurt if you've programmed before. What is important is that you've started developing your *technical sophistication* (Box 1.2), either on your own or using the preceding Learn Enough tutorials (https://www.learnenough.com/courses). These tutorials include the following, which together make a good list of prerequisites for this book:

1. *Learn Enough Command Line to Be Dangerous* (https://www.learnenough.com/command-line)

2. *Learn Enough Text Editor to Be Dangerous* (https://www.learnenough.com/text-editor)

3. *Learn Enough Git to Be Dangerous* (https://www.learnenough.com/git)

All of these tutorials are available as print or digital books or online for individual purchase, and we offer a subscription service—the Learn Enough All Access subscription (https://www.learnenough.com/all-access)—with access to all the corresponding online courses.

Box 1.2: Technical sophistication

An essential aspect of using computers is the ability to figure things out and troubleshoot on your own, a skill we at Learn Enough (https://www.learnenough.com/) call *technical sophistication*.

Developing technical sophistication means not only following systematic tutorials like *Learn Enough Python to Be Dangerous*, but also knowing when it's time to break free of a structured presentation and just start Googling around for a solution.

Learn Enough Python to Be Dangerous will give us ample opportunity to practice this essential technical skill.

In particular, as alluded to above, there is a wealth of Python reference material on the Web, but it can be hard to use unless you already basically know what you're doing. One goal of this tutorial is to be the key that unlocks the documentation. This will include lots of pointers to the official Python site.

Especially as the exposition gets more advanced, I'll also sometimes include the web searches you could use to figure out how to accomplish the particular task at hand. For example, how do you use Python to manipulate a Document Object Model (DOM)? Like this: python dom manipulation.

You won't learn everything there is to know about Python in this tutorial—that would take thousands of pages and centuries of effort—but you will learn enough Python to be *dangerous* (Figure 1.1[3]). Let's take a look at what that means.

In Chapter 1, we'll begin at the beginning with a series of simple "hello, world" programs using several different techniques, including an introduction to an inter-active command-line program for evaluating Python code. In line with the Learn Enough philosophy of always doing things "for real", even as early as the first chapter we'll deploy a (very simple) dynamic Python application to the live Web. You'll

Figure 1.1: Python knowledge, like Rome, wasn't built in a day.

---

3. Image courtesy of Kirk Fisher/Shutterstock.

also get pointers to the latest setup and installation instructions via *Learn Enough Dev Environment to Be Dangerous* (https://www.learnenough.com/dev-environment), which is available for free online and as a free downloadable ebook.

After mastering "hello, world", we'll take a tour of some Python *objects*, including strings (Chapter 2), arrays (Chapter 3), and other native objects (Chapter 4). Taken together, these chapters constitute a gentle introduction to *object-oriented programming* with Python.

In Chapter 5, we'll learn the basics of *functions*, an essential subject for virtually every programming language. We'll then apply this knowledge to an elegant and powerful style of coding called *functional programming* (Chapter 6).

Having covered the basics of built-in Python objects, in Chapter 7 we'll learn how to make objects of our own. In particular, we'll define an object for a *phrase*, and then develop a method for determining whether or not the phrase is a *palindrome* (the same read forward and backward).

Our initial palindrome implementation will be rather rudimentary, but we'll extend it in Chapter 8 using a powerful technique called *test-driven development* (TDD). In the process, we'll learn more about testing generally, as well as how to create and publish a self-contained Python package.

In Chapter 9, we'll learn how to write nontrivial *shell scripts*, one of Python's biggest strengths. Examples include reading from both files and URLs, with a final example showing how to manipulate a downloaded file as if it were an HTML web page.

In Chapter 10, we'll develop our first full Python web application: a site for detecting palindromes. This will give us a chance to learn about *routes*, *layouts*, *embedded Python*, and *form handling*. As a capstone to our work, we'll deploy our palindrome detector to the live Web.

Finally, Chapter 11 introduces several core libraries for doing data science in Python, including NumPy, Matplotlib, pandas, and scikit-learn.

By the way, experienced developers can largely skip the first four chapters of *Learn Enough Python to Be Dangerous*, as described in Box 1.3.

Box 1.3: For experienced developers

By keeping a few diffs in mind, experienced developers can skip Chapters 1–4 of this tutorial and start with functions in Chapter 5. They can then move quickly on to functional programming in Chapter 6, consulting earlier chapters as necessary to fill in any gaps.

Here are some of the notable differences between Python and most other languages:

- Use `print` for printing (Section 1.2).

- Use `#!/usr/bin/env python3` for the shebang line in shell scripts (Section 1.4).

- Single- and double-quoted strings are effectively identical (Section 2.1).

- Use formatted strings (f-strings) and curly braces for string interpolation, e.g., `f"foo {bar} baz"` for strings `"foo"` and `"baz"` and variable `bar` (Section 2.2).

- Use `r"..."` for raw strings (Section 2.2.2).

- Python doesn't have an `obj.length` attribute or an `obj.length()` method; instead, use `len(obj)` to calculate object lengths (Section 2.4).

- Whitespace is significant (Section 2.4). Lines are typically ended by newlines or colons, and block structure is indicated using indentation (generally four spaces per block level).

- Use `elif` for `else if` (Section 2.4).

- In a boolean context, all Python objects are `True` except `0`, `None`, "empty" objects (`""`, `[]`, `{}`, etc.), and `False` itself (Section 2.4.2 and later sections).

- Use `[...]` for lists (Chapter 3) and `{key: value, ...}` for hashes (called *dictionaries* in Python) (Section 4.4).

- Python makes extensive use of *namespaces*, so importing a library like `math` leads to accessing methods through a library object by default (e.g., `math.sqrt(2)`) (Section 4.1.1).

1.1 Introduction to Python

Created by Dutch developer Guido van Rossum (Figure 1.2[4]), Python was originally designed as a high-level, general-purpose programming language. The name *Python* is a reference, not directly to the snake of that name, but rather to the British comedy troupe Monty Python. This speaks to a certain lightheartedness at the core of Python, but Python is also an elegant, powerful language useful for serious work. Indeed,

---

4. Image courtesy of Eugene Lazutkin/Getty Images.

Figure 1.2: Guido van Rossum, the creator of Python.

although I am probably better known for my contributions to the Ruby community (especially the *Ruby on Rails Tutorial* (https://www.railstutorial.org/)), Python has long had a special place in my heart (Box 1.4).

Box 1.4: My Python journey

Back in the early days of the World Wide Web, I initially learned Perl and PHP for scripting and web development. When I finally got around to learning Python, I was blown away by how much cleaner and more elegant it was than those languages (in my humble opinion and no offense intended). Although I had programmed in a wide variety of languages by that point—including Basic, Pascal, C, C++, IDL, Perl, and PHP—Python was the first language I really *loved*.

When I was in graduate school, Python played a key role in my doctoral research in theoretical physics, mainly for data processing and as a "glue" language for high-speed simulations written in C and C++. After I graduated, I decided to become an entrepreneur, and I preferred Python so much that I couldn't bring myself to go back to PHP even though at the time the latter had more mature features for web development. Instead, for my first startup I wrote a custom web framework in Python. (Why not just use Django? This was a while ago, and Django hadn't been released yet.)

After Ruby on Rails came out, I ended up getting more involved in the Ruby language (eventually leading to the *Ruby on Rails Tutorial*), but I never lost my interest in Python. I've been impressed by how Python's syntax has continued to mature and become even more elegant, particularly with the advent of Python 3. I was especially pleased to see Python incorporate tau, the mathematical constant I proposed in *The Tau Manifesto* (https://tauday.com/tau-manifesto). Finally, I've watched in amazement as Python's capabilities expanded into areas like numerical computing, plotting, and data analysis (all of which are discussed in Chapter 11), as well as into scientific and mathematical computing (e.g., SciPy and Sage). The power of Python-based systems now genuinely rivals proprietary systems like MATLAB, Maple, and *Mathematica*; especially given Python's open-source nature, it seems likely that this trend will continue.

The future looks bright for Python, and I for one expect to use Python frequently in the years to come. As a result, making this tutorial has been a great opportunity for me to reconnect with my Python roots, and I'm glad you're joining me on the journey.

In order to give you the best broad-range introduction to programming with Python, *Learn Enough Python to Be Dangerous* uses four main methods:

1. An interactive prompt with a Read-Eval-Print Loop (REPL)
2. Standalone Python files
3. Shell scripts (as introduced (https://www.learnenough.com/text-editor-tutorial/advanced_text_editing#sec-writing_an_executable_script) in *Learn Enough Text Editor to Be Dangerous*)
4. Python web applications running in a web server

We'll begin our study of Python with four variations on the time-honored theme of a "hello, world" program, a tradition that dates back to the early days of the C programming language. The main purpose of "hello, world" is to confirm that our system is correctly configured to execute a simple program that prints the string `"hello, world!"` (or some close variant) to the screen. By design, the program is simple, allowing us to focus on the challenge of getting the program to run in the first place.

Because one of the most common applications of Python is writing shell scripts for execution at the command line, we'll start by writing a series of programs to display a greeting in a command-line terminal: first in a REPL; then in a standalone file called **hello.py**; and finally in an executable shell script called **hello**. We'll then write (and deploy!) a simple proof-of-concept web application using the Flask (https://flask.palletsprojects.com) web framework (a lightweight framework that serves as good preparation for a heavier framework like Django).

1.1.1   System Setup and Installation

Throughout what follows, I'll assume that you have access to a Unix-compatible system like macOS or Linux (including the Linux-based Cloud9 IDE (https://www.learnenough.com/dev-environment-tutorial#sec-cloud_ide), as described in the free tutorial *Learn Enough Dev Environment to Be Dangerous*). The cloud IDE is especially well-suited to beginners and is recommended for those looking to streamline their setup process or who run into difficulties configuring their native system.

If you use the cloud IDE, I recommend creating a development environment (https://www.learnenough.com/dev-environment-tutorial#fig-cloud9_page_aws) called **python-tutorial**. The cloud IDE uses the Bash shell program by default; Linux and Mac users can use whichever shell program they prefer—this tutorial should work with either Bash or macOS's default Z shell (Zsh). You can use the following command to figure out which one is running on your system:

```
$ echo $SHELL
```

When updating your system settings (as in Section 1.5.1), be sure to use the profile file corresponding to your shell program (**.bash_profile** or **.zshrc**). See "Using Z Shell on Macs with the Learn Enough Tutorials (https://news.learnenough.com/macos-bash-zshell)" for more information.

This tutorial standardizes on Python 3.10, although the vast majority of code will work with any version after 3.7. You can check to see if Python is already installed by running **python3 --version** at the command line to get the version number (Listing 1.1).[5]

Listing 1.1: Checking the Python version.

```
$ python3 --version
Python 3.10.6
```

---

5. All of the listings in *Learn Enough Python to Be Dangerous* can be found online at github.com/learnenough/learn_enough_python_code_listings.

If instead you get a result like

```
$ python3 --version
-bash: python3: command not found
```

or you get a version number earlier than 3.10 then you should install a more recent version of Python.

The details of installing Python vary by system and can require applying a little technical sophistication (Box 1.2). The different possibilities are covered in *Learn Enough Dev Environment to Be Dangerous*, which you should take a look at now if you don't already have Python on your system. In particular, if you end up using the cloud IDE recommended by *Learn Enough Dev Environment to Be Dangerous*, you can update the Python version as shown in Listing 1.2. Note that the steps in Listing 1.2 should work on any Linux system that supports the APT package manager. On macOS systems, Python can be installed using Homebrew as shown in Listing 1.3.

Listing 1.2: Installing Python on a Linux system like the cloud IDE.

```
$ sudo add-apt-repository -y ppa:deadsnakes/ppa
$ sudo apt-get install -y python3.10
$ sudo apt-get install -y python3.10-venv
$ sudo ln -sf /usr/bin/python3.10 /usr/bin/python3
```

Listing 1.3: Installing Python on macOS using Homebrew.

```
$ brew install python@3.10
```

Whichever way you go, the result should be an executable version of Python (or more specifically, Python 3):

```
$ python3 --version
Python 3.10.6
```

(Exact version numbers may differ.)

For historical reasons, many systems include copies of both Python 3 and an earlier version of Python known as Python 2. You can often get away with using the

python command (without the **3**), especially when working in a virtual environment (Section 1.3). As you level up as a Python programmer, you may find yourself using the plain **python** command more often, secure in the knowledge that the correct version is being used. This route is more error-prone, though, so we'll stick with **python3** in this tutorial since it makes the version number explicit, with negligible risk of accidentally using Python 2.

1.2 Python in a REPL

Our first example of a "hello, world" program involves a Read-Eval-Print Loop, or *REPL* (pronounced "repple"). A REPL is a program that **read**s input, **eval**uates it, **print**s out the result (if any), and then **loop**s back to the read step. Most modern programming languages provide a REPL, and Python is no exception; in Python's case, the REPL is often known as the Python *interpreter* because it directly executes (or "interprets") user commands. (A third common term is the Python *shell*, in analogy with the Bash and Zsh programs used to run command-line shell programs.)

Learning to use the REPL well is a valuable skill for every aspiring Python programmer. As noted Python author David Beazley put it:

> Although there are many non-shell environments where you can code Python, you will be a stronger Python programmer if you are able to run, debug, and interact with Python at the terminal [i.e., the REPL]. This is Python's native environment. If you are able to use Python here, you will be able to use it everywhere else.

The Python REPL can be started with the Python command **python3**, so we can run it at the command line as shown in Listing 1.4.

Listing 1.4: Bringing up the interactive Python prompt at the command line.

```
$ python3
>>>
```

Here **>>>** represents a generic Python prompt waiting for input from the user.

We're now ready to write our first Python program using the **print()** command, as seen in Listing 1.5. (Here **"hello, world!"** is a *string*; we'll start learning more about strings in Chapter 2.)

Listing 1.5: A "hello, world" program in the REPL.

```
>>> print("hello, world!")
hello, world!
```

That's it! That's how easy it is to print "hello, world!" interactively with Python.

If you're familiar with other programming languages (such as PHP or JavaScript), you may have noticed that Listing 1.5 lacks a terminating semicolon to mark the end of the line. Indeed, Python is unusual among programming languages in that its syntax depends on things like newlines (Section 1.2.1) and spaces. We'll see many more examples of Python's unique syntax as this tutorial progresses.

1.2.1 Exercises

1. Box 1.1 references "The Zen of Python" by Tim Peters. Confirm that we can print out the full text of "The Zen of Python" using the command **import this** in the Python REPL (Listing 1.6).

Listing 1.6: "The Zen of Python" by Tim Peters.

```
>>> import this
The Zen of Python, by Tim Peters

Beautiful is better than ugly.
Explicit is better than implicit.
Simple is better than complex.
Complex is better than complicated.
Flat is better than nested.
Sparse is better than dense.
Readability counts.
Special cases aren't special enough to break the rules.
Although practicality beats purity.
Errors should never pass silently.
Unless explicitly silenced.
In the face of ambiguity, refuse the temptation to guess.
There should be one-- and preferably only one --obvious way to do it.
Although that way may not be obvious at first unless you're Dutch.
Now is better than never.
Although never is often better than *right* now.
If the implementation is hard to explain, it's a bad idea.
If the implementation is easy to explain, it may be a good idea.
Namespaces are one honking great idea -- let's do more of those!
```

2. What happens if you use **print("hello,   world!",   end="")** in place
of **print()** by itself? (The **end=""** is known as a *keyword argument* (Section 5.1.2).) How would you change the **end** argument to get the result to match Listing 1.5? *Hint*: Recall (https://www.learnenough.com/command-line-tutorial/basics#sec-exercises_man) that **\n** is the typical way to represent a newline character.

1.3 Python in a File

As convenient as it is to be able to explore Python interactively, most Real Programming™ takes place in text files created with a text editor. In this section, we'll show how to create and execute a Python file with the same "hello, world" program we've discussed in Section 1.2. The result will be a simplified prototype of the reusable Python files we'll start learning about in Section 5.2.

We'll start by creating a directory for this tutorial and a Python file (with a **.py** file extension) for our **hello** program (be sure to exit the interpreter first if you're still in the REPL, which you can do using **exit** or **Ctrl-D**):

```
$ cd     # Make sure we're in the home directory.
$ mkdir -p repos/python_tutorial
$ cd repos/python_tutorial
```

Here the **-p** option to **mkdir** arranges to create intermediate directories if necessary. *Note*: Throughout this tutorial, if you're using the cloud IDE recommended in *Learn Enough Dev Environment to Be Dangerous*, you should replace the home directory ~ with the directory **~/environment**.

Because Python is so widely used, many systems come preinstalled with Python, and default programs often use it extensively. This introduces the possibility of interactions between the version of Python we're using and the versions used by other programs, and the results can be nasty and confusing. To avoid this headache, one common practice is to use self-contained *virtual environments*, which allow us to use the exact version of Python we want, and to install whatever Python packages we want, without affecting the rest of the system.

We'll be using the **venv** package combined with **pip** to install additional packages. This solution is especially suitable for a tutorial like this one because all of the specifics of the setup are contained in a single directory, which can be deleted and recreated if anything goes wrong. There is another powerful solution called Conda, though, which has a large and enthusiastic following among Python programmers. In my experience, Conda is just a little more difficult to use than venv/pip (e.g., the first time I tried using the **conda** utility it took over my system and replaced the default Python, which was tricky to reverse), but as you level up you might find yourself switching over to Conda.[6]

To create a virtual environment, we'll use the **python3** command with **-m** (for "module") and **venv** (the name of the virtual environment module):

```
$ python3 -m venv venv
```

Note that the second occurrence of **venv** is our choice; we could write **python3 -m venv foobar** to create a virtual environment called **foobar**, but **venv** is the conventional choice. N.B. If you ever completely screw up your Python configuration, you can simply remove the venv directory using **rm -rf venv/** and start again (but don't run that command right now or the rest of the chapter might not work!).

Once the virtual environment is installed, we need to *activate* it to use it:

```
$ source venv/bin/activate
(venv) $
```

Note that many shell programs will insert **(venv)** before the prompt **$** to remind us that we're working in a virtual environment. The **activate** step is frequently required when using virtual environments, so I suggest creating a shell alias (https://www.learnenough.com/text-editor-tutorial/vim#sec-saving_and_quitting_files) for it, such as **va**.[7]

To deactivate a virtual environment, use the **deactivate** command:

```
(venv) $ deactivate
$
```

Note that the **(venv)** in front of the prompt disappears upon deactivation.

---

6. Yet another possibility is pipenv, which provides a more structured interface to venv and bears a strong resemblance to the Bundler/**Gemfile** solution used by Ruby.

7. In both Bash and Zsh, this could be accomplished by adding **alias va="source venv/bin/activate"** to your **.bash_profile** or **.zshrc** file and then running **source** on that file. See Saving and quitting files in *Learn Enough Text Editor to Be Dangerous* for more details.

Now let's reactivate the virtual environment and create a file called **hello.py** using the **touch** command (as discussed (https://www.learnenough.com/command-line-tutorial/manipulating_files#sec-listing) in *Learn Enough Command Line to Be Dangerous*):

```
$ source venv/bin/activate
(venv) $ touch hello.py
```

Next, using our favorite text editor, we'll fill the file with the contents shown in Listing 1.7. Note that the code is exactly the same as in Listing 1.5, with the difference that in a Python file there's no command prompt **>>>**.

Listing 1.7: A "hello, world" program in a Python file.
hello.py

```
print("hello, world!")
```

At this point, we're ready to execute our program using the **python3** command we used in Listing 1.1 to check the Python version number. The only difference is that this time we omit the **--version** option and instead include an argument with the name of our file:

```
(venv) $ python3 hello.py
hello, world!
```

As in Listing 1.5, the result is to print "hello, world!" out to the terminal screen, only now it's the raw shell instead of a Python REPL.

Although this example is simple, it's a huge step forward, as we're now in the position to write Python programs much longer than could comfortably fit in an interactive session.

1.3.1   Exercise

1. What happens if you give **print()** two arguments, as in Listing 1.8?

Listing 1.8: Using two arguments.
hello.py

```
print("hello, world!", "how's it going?")
```

1.4 Python in a Shell Script

Although the code in Section 1.3 is perfectly functional, when writing a program to be executed in the command-line shell (https://www.learnenough.com/command-line-tutorial/basics#sec-man_pages) it's often better to use an *executable script* of the sort discussed in *Learn Enough Text Editor to Be Dangerous*.

Let's see how to make an executable script using Python. We'll start by creating a file called **hello**:

```
(venv) $ touch hello
```

Note that we *didn't* include the **.py** extension—this is because the filename itself is the user interface, and there's no reason to expose the implementation language to the user. Indeed, there's a reason not to: By using the name **hello**, we give ourselves the option to rewrite our script in a different language down the line, without changing the command our program's users have to type. (Not that it matters in this simple case, but the principle should be clear. We'll see a more realistic example in Section 9.3.)

There are two steps to writing a working script. The first is to use the same command we've seen before (Listing 1.7), preceded by a "shebang" line telling our system to use Python to execute the script.

Ordinarily, the exact shebang line is system-dependent (as seen with Bash in *Learn Enough Text Editor to Be Dangerous* and with JavaScript (https://www.learnenough.com/javascript-tutorial/hello_world#sec-js_shell) in *Learn Enough JavaScript to Be Dangerous*), but with Python we can ask the shell itself to supply the proper command. The trick is to use the following line to use the **python** executable available as part of the shell's *environment* (env):

```
#!/usr/bin/env python3
```

Using this for the shebang line gives the shell script shown in Listing 1.9.

Listing 1.9: A "hello, world" shell script.
hello

```
#!/usr/bin/env python3

print("hello, world!")
```

We could execute this file directly using the **python** command as in Section 1.3, but a true shell script should be executable without the use of an auxiliary program. (That's what the shebang line is for.) Instead, we'll follow the second of the two steps mentioned above and make the file itself executable using the **chmod** ("change mode") command combined with **+x** ("plus executable"):

```
(venv) $ chmod +x hello
```

At this point, the file should be executable, and we can execute it by preceding the command with **./**, which tells our system to look in the current directory (dot = **.**) for the executable file. (Putting the **hello** script on the PATH (https://www.learnenough.com/text-editor-tutorial/advanced_text_editing#code-export_path), so that it can be called from any directory, is left as an exercise.) The result looks like this:

```
(venv) $ ./hello
hello, world!
```

Success! We've now written a working Python shell script suitable for extension and elaboration. As mentioned briefly above, we'll see an example of a real-life utility script in Section 9.3.

Throughout the rest of this tutorial, we'll mainly use the Python interpreter for initial investigations, but the eventual goal will almost always be to create a file containing Python.

1.4.1 Exercise

1. By moving the file or changing your system's configuration, add the **hello** script to your environment's PATH. (You may find the steps in *Learn Enough Text Editor to Be Dangerous* helpful.) Confirm that you can run **hello** without prepending **./** to the command name. *Note*: If you have a conflicting **hello** program from following *Learn Enough JavaScript to Be Dangerous* or *Learn Enough Ruby to Be Dangerous*, I suggest replacing it—thus demonstrating the principle that the file's name is the user interface, and the implementation can change language without affecting users.

1.5 Python in a Web Browser

Although it wasn't initially designed for web development, Python's elegant and powerful design has led to its widespread use in making web applications. In recognition of this, our final example of a "hello, world" program will be a live web application, written in the simple but powerful *Flask* micro-framework (Figure 1.3[8]). Because of its simplicity, Flask is a perfect introduction to web development with Python while also serving as excellent preparation for a "batteries included" framework like Django.

We'll begin by installing the Flask package using pip (a recursive acronym that stands for "pip installs packages"). The **pip** command comes automatically as part of the virtual environment, so we can access it by typing **pip** at the command line (or **pip3** on some systems—try the latter if the former doesn't work). As a first step, it's a good idea to upgrade pip to ensure we're running the latest version:

```
(venv) $ pip install --upgrade pip
```

Figure 1.3: A traditional drinking-horn flask.

---

8. Image courtesy of Peter Gudella/Shutterstock.

Next, install Flask (Listing 1.10).

Listing 1.10: Installing Flask (with an exact version number).

```
(venv) $ pip install Flask==2.2.2
```

We've included an exact version number in Listing 1.10 in case future versions of Flask don't happen to work with this tutorial; this is similar to our decision to use **python3** instead of plain **python**. As you get more advanced, though, you'll probably just run things like **pip install Flask**, secure in the knowledge that you can figure out what went wrong if the version number doesn't happen to work.

Believe it or not, the one command in Listing 1.10 installs all of the software needed to run a simple but full-strength web application on our local system (where "local" might refer to the cloud if you're using the cloud IDE recommended in *Learn Enough Dev Environment to Be Dangerous*).

Although the code for the "hello, world" web app uses some commands that we haven't covered yet, it's a straightforward adaptation of the example program on the Flask home page (Figure 1.4). Being able to adapt code you don't necessarily understand is a classic hallmark of technical sophistication (Box 1.2).

We'll put our "hello, world" app in a file called **hello_app.py**:

```
(venv) $ touch hello_app.py
```

The code itself closely parallels the program in Figure 1.4, as seen in Listing 1.11.

Listing 1.11: A "hello, world" web app.
python_tutorial/hello_app.py

```python
from flask import Flask

app = Flask(__name__)

@app.route("/")
def hello_world():
    return "<p>hello, world!</p>"
```

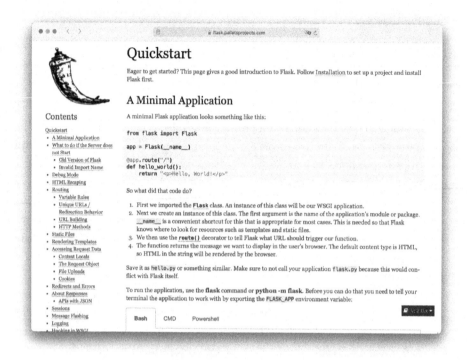

Figure 1.4: A sample program from the Flask home page.

The code in Listing 1.11 defines the behavior for the *root URL* / when responding to an ordinary browser request (known as GET). The response itself is the required "hello, world!" string, which will be returned to the browser as a (very simple) web page.

To run the web application in Listing 1.11, all we need to do is run the **hello_app.py** file using the **flask** command (Listing 1.12). (Do make sure you're running in the virtual environment; weird things can happen if you try running the **flask** command on the default system.) In Listing 1.12, the **--app** option specifies the app and the **--debug** option arranges to update the app when we change the code (which saves us from having to restart the Flask server every time we make a change).

Listing 1.12: Running the Flask app on a local system.

```
(venv) $ flask --app hello_app.py --debug run
 * Running on http://127.0.0.1:5000/
```

At this point, visiting the given URL (which consists of the local address 127.0.0.1 and the port number) shows the application running on the local machine.[9]

If you're using the cloud IDE, the commands are nearly identical to the ones shown in Listing 1.12; the only difference is that you have to include a different port number using the **--port** option (Listing 1.13).

Listing 1.13: Running the Flask app on the cloud IDE.

```
(venv) $ flask --app hello_app.py --debug run --port $PORT
 * Running on http://127.0.0.1:8080/
```

To preview the app and replicate the result shown in Figure 1.5, we have to follow a few more steps. First, we need to preview the app as shown in Figure 1.6.

Figure 1.5: The hello app running locally.

---

9. Many systems configure **localhost** to be a synonym for **127.0.0.1**; with Flask, this can still be arranged, but it requires a little extra configuration, so we'll stick with the raw address in this tutorial.

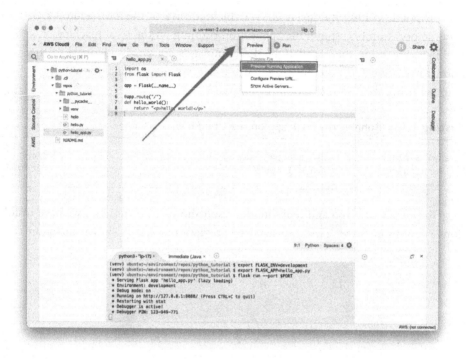

Figure 1.6: The "local" server running on the cloud IDE.

The result typically shows up in a small window inside the IDE (details may vary); by clicking the icon shown in Figure 1.7, we can pop out into a new window. The result should appear as in Figure 1.8 (the only difference with Figure 1.5 is the URL).

Just getting a web app to work, even locally, is a huge accomplishment. But the real *pièce de résistance* is deploying the app to the live Web. This is the goal of Section 1.5.1.

1.5.1 Deployment

Now that we've got our app running locally, we're ready to deploy it to a production environment. This used to be practically impossible to do in a beginning tutorial, but the technology landscape has matured significantly in recent years, to the point where we actually have an abundance of choices. The result will be a production version of the application from Section 1.5.

Figure 1.7: Previewing the hello app.

There's a bit of overhead involved in deploying something the first time, but deploying early and often is a core part of the Learn Enough philosophy of *shipping* (Box 1.5). Moreover, a simple app like "hello, world" is the best kind of app for first-time deployment, because there's so much less that can go wrong.

As with the GitHub Pages deployment option used in previous tutorials (*Learn Enough CSS & Layout to Be Dangerous* (https://www.learnenough.com/css-and-layout) and *Learn Enough JavaScript to Be Dangerous* among them), our first step is to put our project under version control with Git (as covered (https://www.learnenough.com/git-tutorial/getting_started#sec-initializing_the_repo) in *Learn Enough Git to Be Dangerous*). While this is not strictly necessary for the deployment solution used in this section, it's always a good idea to have a fully versioned project so that we can more easily recover from any errors.

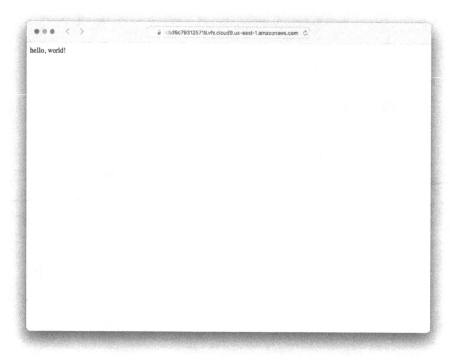

Figure 1.8: The hello app running on the cloud IDE.

Box 1.5: Real artists ship

As legendary Apple cofounder Steve Jobs once said: *Real artists ship.* What he meant was that, as tempting as it is to privately polish in perpetuity, makers must *ship* their work—that is, actually finish it and get it out into the world. This can be scary, because shipping means exposing your work not only to fans but also to critics. "What if people don't like what I've made?" *Real artists ship.*

It's important to understand that shipping is a separate skill from making. Many makers get good at making things but never learn to ship. To keep this from happening to us, we'll follow the practice started in *Learn Enough Git to Be Dangerous* and ship several things in this tutorial. Shipping the "hello, world" app in this section is only the beginning!

Our first step is to create a `.gitignore` file to tell Git to ignore files and directories we don't want to version. Use **touch** `.gitignore` (or any other method you prefer) to create the file and then fill it with the contents shown in Listing 1.14.[10]

Listing 1.14: Ignoring certain files and directories.
.gitignore

```
venv/

*.pyc
__pycache__/

instance/

.pytest_cache/
.coverage
htmlcov/

dist/
build/
*.egg-info/

.DS_Store
```

Next, initialize the repository:

```
(venv) $ git init
(venv) $ git add -A
(venv) $ git commit -m "Initialize repository"
```

It's also a good idea to push any newly initialized repository up to a remote backup. As in previous Learn Enough tutorials, we'll use GitHub for this purpose (Figure 1.9).

Because web apps sometimes include sensitive information like passwords or API keys, I like to err on the side of caution and use a *private* repository. Accordingly, be sure to select the Private option when creating the new repository at GitHub, as shown in Figure 1.10. (By the way, it's still a bad idea to include passwords or API keys, even in a private repo; the best practice is to use environment variables or the like instead.)

---

10. This file is based in part on the example from the Flask documentation itself.

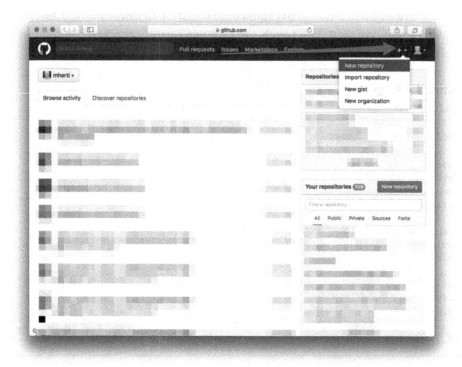

Figure 1.9: Creating a new repository at GitHub.

Next, tell your local system about the remote repository (taking care to fill in **<username>** with your GitHub username) and then push it up:

```
(venv) $ git remote add origin https://github.com/<username>/python_tutorial.git
(venv) $ git push -u origin main
```

The service we'll be using for Flask deployment is Fly.io. We'll start by installing a necessary package and we'll then list the requirements (including Flask) needed to deploy the application. *Note:* The following steps work as of this writing, but deploying to a third-party service is exactly the kind of thing that can change without notice. If that happens, you will likely have an opportunity to apply your technical sophistication (Box 1.2), up to and including finding an alternate service (such as Render) if necessary.

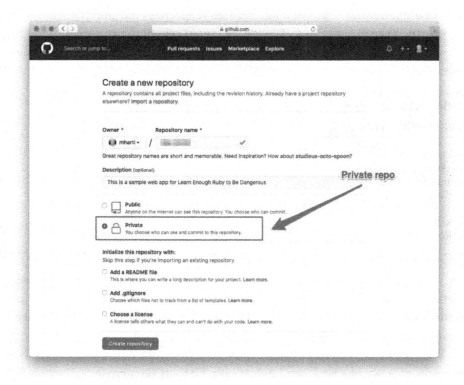

Figure 1.10: Using a private repo.

Our first step is to install a package for Gunicorn, a Python web server:

```
(venv) $ pip install gunicorn==20.1.0
```

Then we need to create a file called **requirements.txt** to tell the deployment host which packages are needed to run our app, which we can do by creating a **requirements.txt** file using

```
$ touch requirements.txt
```

and then filling it with the contents shown in Listing 1.15, which we can figure out using **pip freeze** in a virtual environment where no unneeded packages had been installed. (Some resources recommend redirecting (https://www.learnenough.com/

command-line-tutorial/manipulating_files#sec-redirecting_and_appending) the output of **pip freeze** using **pip freeze > requirements.txt** to create the file
in Listing 1.15, but this approach can lead to unnecessary or invalid packages being
required.)

Listing 1.15: Specifying the requirements for our app.
requirements.txt

```
click==8.1.3
Flask==2.2.2
gunicorn==20.1.0
itsdangerous==2.1.2
Jinja2==3.1.2
MarkupSafe==2.1.1
Werkzeug==2.2.2
```

The current recommended practice for Python package management is to use a
pyproject.toml file to specify the build system for the project. This step is not
required when deploying to Fly.io, but we will follow this practice when we make a
package of our own in Chapter 8.

With the configuration in Listing 1.15, we have set up our system for Fly.io to
detect the presence of a Flask app automatically. Here are the steps for getting started:

1. Sign up (https://fly.io/app/sign–up) for Fly.io. Take care to click the link for the
   free tier, which can be a little tricky to find (Figure 1.11). Free accounts are limited
   to two deployment servers, which is perfect for us since that's the number in this
   tutorial (here and in Chapter 10).

2. Install Fly Control (**flyctl**), a command-line program for interacting with
   Fly.io.[11] Options for macOS and for Linux (including the cloud IDE) are shown in
   Listing 1.16 and Listing 1.17, respectively. For the latter, take care to add any lines
   to your **.bash_profile** or **.zshrc** file as instructed (Listing 1.18), and then run
   source ~/.bash_profile (or **source ~/.zshrc**) to update the configuration.
   Note that the vertical dots in Listing 1.18 indicate omitted lines.

3. Sign in to Fly.io at the command line (Listing 1.19).

---

11. I discovered accidentally that **flyctl** is aliased to **fly**, at least on my system; I suggest seeing if you can
be similarly **fly** on your system as well.

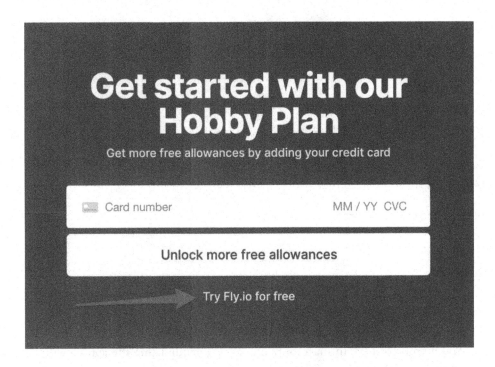

Figure 1.11: The Fly.io free tier.

Listing 1.16: Installing **flyctl** on macOS using Homebrew.

```
(venv) $ brew install flyctl
```

Listing 1.17: Installing **flyctl** on Linux.

```
(venv) $ curl -L https://fly.io/install.sh | sh
```

Listing 1.18: Adding configuration lines for `flyctl`.
`~/.bash_profile or ~/.zshrc`

```
.
.
.
export FLYCTL_INSTALL="/home/ubuntu/.fly"
export PATH="$FLYCTL_INSTALL/bin:$PATH"
```

Listing 1.19: Signing in to Fly.io.[12]

```
(venv) $ flyctl auth login --interactive
```

Once you've signed in to Fly.io, follow these steps to deploy the hello app:

1. Run **flyctl launch** (Listing 1.20) and accept the autogenerated name and the default options (i.e., no database).

2. Edit the generated **Procfile** and fill it with the contents shown in Listing 1.21. You'll probably have to make only one change by updating the app name from **server** to **hello_app**.

3. Deploy the application with **flyctl deploy** (Listing 1.22).[13]

Listing 1.20: "Launching" the app (which is just local configuration).

```
(venv) $ flyctl launch
```

Listing 1.21: *Procfile*

```
web: gunicorn hello_app:app
```

---

12. Listing 1.19 includes the `--interactive` option to prevent **flyctl** from spawning a browser window, which works both on native systems and on the cloud IDE. If you're using a native system, feel free to omit that option.

13. In my testing, **flyctl deploy** fails when running a Virtual Private Network (VPN), so if you use a VPN I suggest you disable it for this step.

Listing 1.22: Deploying the app to Fly.io.

```
(venv) $ flyctl deploy
```

After the deployment step has finished, you can run the command in Listing 1.23 to see the status of the app. (If anything goes wrong, you may find **flyctl logs** helpful in debugging.)

Listing 1.23: Viewing the status of the deployed app.

```
(venv) $ flyctl status     # Details will vary
App
  Name     = restless-sun-9514
  Owner    = personal
  Version  = 2
  Status   = running

  Hostname = crimson-shadow-1161.fly.dev   # Your URL will differ.
  Platform = nomad

Deployment Status
  ID          = 051e253a-e322-4b2c-96ec-bc2758763328
  Version     = v2
  Status      = successful
  Description = Deployment completed successfully
  Instances   = 1 desired, 1 placed, 1 healthy, 0 unhealthy
```

The highlighted line in Listing 1.23 indicates the URL of the live app, which you can open automatically as follows:

```
(venv) $ flyctl open     # won't work on the cloud IDE, so use displayed URL
```

As noted, the **flyctl open** command won't work on the cloud IDE because it needs to spawn a new browser window, but in that case you can just copy and paste the URL from your version of Listing 1.23 into your browser's address bar to obtain the same result.

And that's it! Our hello app is now running in production (Figure 1.12). "It's alive!" (Figure 1.13[14]).

---

14. Image courtesy of Niday Picture Library/Alamy Stock Photo.

Figure 1.12: The hello app running in production.

Figure 1.13: Bringing a site to life is easier than it used to be.

Although there were quite a few steps involved in this section, being able to deploy a site so early is nothing short of miraculous. It may be a simple app, but it's a real one, and being able to deploy it to production is an enormous step.

By the way, you might have noticed that deploying to Fly.io didn't require a Git commit (in contrast to, say, GitHub Pages or a hosting service like Heroku). As a result, it's probably a good idea to make one final commit now and push the result up to GitHub:

```
(venv) $ git add -A
(venv) $ git commit -m "Configure hello app for deployment"
(venv) $ git push
```

1.5.2 Exercises

1. Change "hello, world!" to "goodbye, world!" in **hello_app.py** running locally. Does the updated text display right away? What about after refreshing the browser?

2. Deploy your updated app to Fly.io and confirm that the new text appears as expected.

CHAPTER 2
Strings

Strings are probably the most important data structure for everyday computing. They're used in practically every kind of program imaginable, and are also the raw material of the Web. As a result, strings make an excellent place to start our Python programming journey.

2.1 String Basics

Strings are made up of sequences of characters in a particular order.[1] We've already seen several examples in the context of our "hello, world" programs in Chapter 1. Let's see what happens if we type a string by itself (without **print()**) into the Python REPL:

```
$ source venv/bin/activate
(venv) $ python3
>>> "hello, world!"
'hello, world!'
```

A sequence of characters typed literally is called a *string literal*, which we've created here using the double-quote character **"**. The REPL prints the result of *evaluating* the line, which in the case of a string literal is just the string itself.

A particularly important string is one with no content, consisting simply of two quotes. This is known as an *empty string* (or sometimes *the* empty string):

---

1. Like many other high-level languages, such as JavaScript and Ruby, Python "characters" are just strings of length one. This stands in contrast to lower-level languages like C and Java, which have a special type just for characters.

```
>>> ""
''
```

We'll have more to say about the empty string in Section 2.4.2 and Section 3.1.

Note that the REPL shows the value of the double-quoted strings we entered using single quotes (`'hello, world!'` instead of `"hello, world!"`). This is purely a convention (and indeed may be system-dependent), because single- and double-quoted strings are exactly the same in Python.[2] Well, not *exactly* exactly the same, because a string might contain a literal quote mark (Figure 2.1[3]):

```
>>> 'It's not easy being green'
  File "<stdin>", line 1
    'It's not easy being green'
       ^
SyntaxError: invalid syntax
```

Figure 2.1: Sometimes it's not easy when the REPL generates a syntax error.

---

2. This stands in contrast to Ruby, which uses single-quoted strings for *raw strings*; as noted in Section 2.2.2, Python's convention is to prepend the letter **r** instead.

3. Image courtesy of LorraineHudgins/Shutterstock.

Because the REPL interprets `'It'` as a string, and the final `'` as the *opening* of a *second* string, the result is a syntax error. (Another result, as seen above, is that the syntax highlighting looks odd—a side effect that is frequently useful as a visual hint of a syntax error.)

According to the PEP-8 style guide, the preferred method for including a quote in this manner is simply to use the other kind of quote for defining the string (Listing 2.1).

Listing 2.1: Including a single quote inside a double quote.

```
>>> "It's not easy being green"
"It's not easy being green"
```

Note that the REPL here obeys the same convention we did, switching to double quotes for a string containing a single quote.

Finally, Python is unusual in supporting *triple-quoted strings*:

```
>>> """Return the function value."""
'Return the function value.'
```

When they fit on one line, these strings behave just like single- and double-quoted strings, but we can also add newlines inside them:

```
>>> """This is a string.
...
... We can add newlines inside,
... which is pretty cool.
... """
'This is a string.\nWe can add newlines inside,\nwhich is pretty cool.\n'
```

Triple-quoted strings are notable for their use in *docstrings*, which are special documentation strings used in Python functions (Chapter 5) and classes (Chapter 7). As such, they are used heavily in Python programming.

In general, PEP 8 indicates that single- and double-quoted strings are both acceptable as long as you're consistent, but triple-quoted strings should always use the double-quoted variant:[4]

---

4. The terminology here is standard but a little muddled: "single-quoted" and "double-quoted" refer to the number of quotes in the characters themselves (`'` vs. `"`), whereas "triple-quoted" refers to the number of such characters used on each side when defining a string (`"""`...`"""`).

> In Python, single-quoted strings and double-quoted strings are the same. This PEP does not make a recommendation for this. Pick a rule and stick to it. When a string contains single or double quote characters, however, use the other one to avoid backslashes in the string. It improves readability.
>
> For triple-quoted strings, always use double quote characters to be consistent with the docstring convention in PEP 257.

This tutorial standardizes on double-quoted strings for consistency with this triple-quoted convention and to match the convention used in *Learn Enough JavaScript to Be Dangerous* (https://www.learnenough.com/javascript) and *Learn Enough Ruby to Be Dangerous* (https://www.learnenough.com/ruby), but of course you are free to choose the opposite convention if you like.

2.1.1 Exercises

1. Confirm that we can escape out quotes using a backslash, as in `'It\'s not easy being green'`. This can be convenient if a string contains both single and double quotes (in which case the trick from Listing 2.1 doesn't work). How does the REPL handle `'It\'s not "easy" being green'`?

2. Python supports common special characters such as tabs (`\t`) and newlines (`\n`), which are two different forms of so-called *whitespace*. Show that `\t` and `\n` are interpreted as special characters inside both single- and double-quoted strings. What happens if you put the letter `r` in front of one of the strings? *Hint*: In the REPL, try executing commands like the ones shown in Listing 2.2. We'll learn more about the special `r` behavior in Section 2.2.2.

Listing 2.2: Some strings with special characters.

```
>>> print('hello\tgoodbye')
>>> print('hello\ngoodbye')
>>> print("hello\tgoodbye")
>>> print("hello\ngoodbye")
>>> print(r"hello\ngoodbye")
```

2.2 Concatenation and Interpolation

Two of the most important string operations are *concatenation* (joining strings together) and *interpolation* (putting variable content into strings). We'll start with concatenation, which we can accomplish using the **+** operator:[5]

```
(venv) $ python3
>>> "foo" + "bar"             # String concatenation
'foobar'
>>> "ant" + "bat" + "cat"     # Multiple strings can be concatenated at once.
'antbatcat'
```

Here the result of evaluating **"foo"** plus **"bar"** is the string **"foobar"**. (The meaning of the odd names "foo" and "bar" is discussed (https://www.learnenough.com/command-line-tutorial/manipulating_files#aside-foo_bar) in *Learn Enough Command Line to Be Dangerous* (https://www.learnenough.com/command-line).) Also note the *comments*, indicated using the hash symbol **#**, which you are free to ignore and will be ignored by Python in any case.

Let's take another look at string concatenation in the context of *variables*, which you can think of as named boxes that contain some value (as mentioned (https://www.learnenough.com/css-and-layout-tutorial/templates_and_frontmatter #aside-variable) in *Learn Enough CSS & Layout to Be Dangerous* (https://www. learnenough.com/css-and-layout) and discussed further in Box 2.1).

Box 2.1: Variables and identifiers

If you've never programmed a computer before, you may be unfamiliar with the term *variable*, which is an essential idea in computer science. You can think of a variable as a named box that can hold different (or "variable") content.

As a concrete analogy, consider the labeled boxes that many elementary schools provide for students to store clothing, books, backpacks, etc. (Figure 2.2[6]). The variable is the location of the box, the label for the box is the variable name (also called an *identifier*), and the content of the box is the variable value.

In practice, these different definitions are frequently conflated, and "variable" is often used for any of the three concepts (location, label, or value).

---

5. This use of **+** for string concatenation is common in programming languages, but in one respect it's an unfortunate choice, because addition is the canonical commutative operation in mathematics: $a+b = b+a$. (In contrast, multiplication is in some cases non-commutative; for example, when multiplying matrices it's often the case that $AB \neq BA$.) In the case of string concatenation, though, **+** is most definitely *not* a commutative operation, since, e.g., **"foo"** + **"bar"** is **"foobar"**, whereas **"bar"** + **"foo"** is **"barfoo"**. Partially for this reason, some languages (such as PHP) use a different symbol for concatenation, such as a dot **.** (yielding **"foo"** . **"bar"**).

6. Image courtesy of Africa Studio/Shutterstock.

Figure 2.2: A concrete manifestation of computer variables.

As a concrete example, we can create variables for a first name and a last name using the **=** sign, as shown in Listing 2.3.

Listing 2.3: Using = to assign variables.

```
>>> first_name = "Michael"
>>> last_name = "Hartl"
```

Here **=** associates the identifier **first_name** with the string **"Michael"** and the identifier **last_name** with the string **"Hartl"**.

The identifiers **first_name** and **last_name** in Listing 2.3 are written in so-called snake case,[7] whose name origins are obscure but which is probably the most common convention for Python variable names (Figure 2.3[8]). (In contrast, Python classes use the CamelCase convention, which is described in more detail in Chapter 7.)

---

7. In particular, "snake case" is not a reference to Python itself; snake-case variable names are common in languages whose names, unlike Python's, have nothing to do with snakes, such C, Perl, PHP, JavaScript, and Ruby.

8. Image courtesy of rafaelbenari/123RF.

Figure 2.3: Snake case is the default for Python variable names.

Having defined the variable names in Listing 2.3, we can use them to concatenate the first and last names, while also inserting a space in between (Listing 2.4).

Listing 2.4: Concatenating string variables (and a string literal).

```
>>> first_name + " " + last_name      # Not Pythonic
'Michael Hartl'
```

2.2.1 Formatted Strings

The most Pythonic way (Box 1.1) to build up strings is via *interpolation* using so-called *formatted strings*, or *f-strings*, which combine the letter **f** (for "formatted") and curly braces to insert variable values:

```
>>> f"{first_name} is my first name."    # Pythonic
'Michael is my first name.'
```

Here Python automatically inserts, or *interpolates*, the value of the variable **first_name** into the string at the appropriate place.[9] Indeed, any code inside the curly braces will simply be evaluated by Python and inserted in place.

We can use interpolation to replicate the result of Listing 2.4, as shown in Listing 2.5.

Listing 2.5: Concatenation review, then interpolating.

```
>>> first_name + " " + last_name        # Concatenation (not Pythonic)
'Michael Hartl'
>>> f"{first_name} {last_name}"          # Interpolation (Pythonic)
'Michael Hartl'
```

The two expressions shown in Listing 2.5 are equivalent, but I generally prefer the interpolated version because having to add the single space **" "** in between strings feels a bit awkward (and, as noted, Pythonistas generally agree).

It's worth noting that formatted strings were added in Python 3.6. If for some reason you need to use an earlier version of Python, you can use either **%** formatting or **str.format()** instead. Specifically, the following three lines give the same result:

```
>>> f"First Name: {first_name}, Last Name: {last_name}"
'First Name: Michael, Last Name: Hartl'
>>> "First Name: {}, Last Name: {}".format(first_name, last_name)
'First Name: Michael, Last Name: Hartl'
>>> "First Name: %s, Last Name: %s" % (first_name, last_name)
'First Name: Michael, Last Name: Hartl'
```

Using **format()** in particular has possible advantages that can be useful even when formatted strings are available. See the article "Python 3's f-Strings: An Improved String Formatting Syntax" (https://realpython.com/python-f-strings/) for more information.

2.2.2 Raw Strings

In addition to ordinary strings and formatted strings, Python also supports so-called *raw strings*. For many uses, the two types of strings are effectively identical:

---

9. Programmers familiar with Perl or PHP should compare this to the automatic interpolation of dollar sign variables in expressions like **"Michael $last_name"**.

```
>>> r"foo"
'foo'
>>> r"foo" + r"bar"
'foobar'
```

There are important differences, though. For example, Python won't interpolate into raw strings:

```
>>> r"{first_name} {last_name}"        # No interpolation!
'{first_name} {last_name}'
```

This isn't that surprising, though, since Python won't interpolate into regular strings, either:

```
>>> "{first_name} {last_name}"        # No interpolation!
'{first_name} {last_name}'
```

If regular strings can do everything that raw strings can do, what's the point of raw strings? They are often useful because they are truly literal, containing exactly the characters you type. For example, the "backslash" character is special on most systems, as in the literal newline **\n**. If you want a variable to contain a literal backslash, raw strings make it easier:

```
>>> r"\n"        # A literal 'backslash n' combination
'\\n'
```

Note that Python REPL needs to escape the backslash with an additional backslash; inside regular strings, a literal backslash is represented with *two* backslashes. For a small example like this, there's not much savings, but if there are lots of things to escape it can be a real help:

```
>>> r"Newlines (\n) and tabs (\t) both use the backslash character: \."
'Newlines (\\n) and tabs (\\t) both use the backslash character: \\.'
```

Probably the most common use of raw strings is in defining regular expressions (Section 4.3), but they will also make an appearance when labeling plots in Section 11.3.

The practice of escaping out characters is unnecessary inside raw strings, *except* for quotes of the same kind used to define the string. For example, if you define a raw string using single quotes, ordinarily it works just fine:

```
>>> r'Newlines (\n) and tabs (\t) both use the backslash character: \.'
'Newlines (\\n) and tabs (\\t) both use the backslash character: \\.'
```

As with regular strings, if a raw string defined using single quotes itself contains a single quote, we get a syntax error instead:

```
>>> r'It's not easy being green'
  File "<stdin>", line 1
    'It's not easy being green'
        ^
SyntaxError: invalid syntax
```

2.2.3 Exercises

1. Assign variables **city** and **state** to your current city and state of residence. (If residing outside the U.S., substitute the analogous quantities.) Using interpolation, print a string consisting of the city and state separated by a comma and a space, as in "Los Angeles, CA".

2. Repeat the previous exercise but with the city and state separated by a tab character.

3. Do triple-quoted strings (Section 2.1) support interpolation?

2.3 Printing

As we saw in Section 1.2 and subsequent sections, the Python way to print a string to the screen is to use the **print()** function:

```
>>> print("hello, world!")      # Print output
hello, world!
```

Here **print()** takes in a string as an *argument* and then prints the result to the screen. The **print()** function operates as a *side effect*, which refers to anything a function does other than returning a value. In particular, the expression

```
print("hello, world!")
```

prints the string to the screen and then returns nothing—indeed, it returns a literal Python object called **None**, as we can see here:[10]

```
>>> result = print("hello, world!")
"hello, world"
>>> print(result)
None
```

Here the second instance of **print()** converts **None** to a string representation and prints the result. We can get the string representation directly using the **repr()** ("representation") function:

```
>>> repr(None)
'None'
```

The **repr()** command is frequently useful, especially in the REPL, and works on essentially any Python object.

We saw briefly in Section 1.2.1 that **print()** also accepts a *keyword argument* (Section 5.1.2) called **end** that represents the character used at the end of the string. The default **end** is a newline **\n**, which is why we get a nice break before the next interpreter prompt:

```
>>> print("foo")
foo
>>>
```

We can override this behavior by passing a different string, such as the empty string **""**.

```
>>> print("foo", end="")
foo>>>
```

Note that the prompt now appears immediately after the string. This is potentially useful in a script because it allows us to print out multiple statements without any separation between them.

---

10. Python's **None** is the exact analogue of Ruby's **nil**.

2.3.1 Exercises

1. What is the effect of giving **print()** multiple arguments, as in **print("foo", "bar", "baz")**?

2. What is the effect of running the print test shown in Listing 2.6? *Hint*: You should create and run the file using the same techniques covered in Section 1.3.

Listing 2.6: A test of printing without newlines.
print_test.py

```
print("foo", end="")
print("bar", end="")
print("baz")
```

2.4 Length, Booleans, and Control Flow

One of the most useful built-in Python functions is **len()**, which returns the length of its argument. Among many other things, **len()** works on strings:

```
>>> len("hello, world!")
13
>>> len("")
0
```

This can be a bit of a gotcha for programmers coming from other high-level languages, many of which use **obj.length** (an attribute) or **obj.length()** (a method) to calculate lengths. In Python, **len(obj)** plays this important role instead. (We'll learn more about methods starting in Section 2.5.)

The **len()** function is especially useful in comparisons, such as checking the length of a string to see how it compares to a particular value (note that the REPL supports "up arrow" to retrieve previous lines, just like the command-line terminal):

```
>>> len("badger") > 3
True
>>> len("badger") > 6
False
>>> len("badger") >= 6
```

```
True
>>> len("badger") < 10
True
>>> len("badger") == 6
True
```

The last line uses the equality comparison operator ==, which Python shares with many other languages. (Python also has a comparison operator called **is** that represents a stronger comparison; see Section 3.4.2.)

The return values in the comparisons above, which are always either **True** or **False**, are known as *boolean* values, after mathematician and logician George Boole (Figure 2.4[11]).

Figure 2.4: True or false? This is a picture of George Boole.

---

11. Image courtesy of Yogi Black/Alamy Stock Photo.

Boolean values are especially useful for *control flow*, which lets us take actions based on the result of a comparison (Listing 2.7). In Listing 2.7, the three dots ... are inserted by the Python interpreter and shouldn't be copied literally.

Listing 2.7: Control flow with `if`.

```
>>> password = "foo"
>>> if (len(password) < 6):    # Not fully Pythonic
...     print("Password is too short.")
...
Password is too short.
```

Note in Listing 2.7 that the comparison after **if** is in parentheses, and the **if** statement is terminated by a colon :. The latter is required, but in Python (unlike many other languages) the parentheses are optional, and it's common to leave them off (Listing 2.8).

Listing 2.8: Control flow with `if`.

```
>>> password = "foo"
>>> if len(password) < 6:      # Pythonic
...     print("Password is too short.")
...
Password is too short.
```

Meanwhile, the block structure is indicated by indentation, in this case four spaces before the string **"Password is too short."** (Box 2.2).

Box 2.2: Code formatting

The code samples in this tutorial, including those in the REPL, are designed to show how to format Python in a way that maximizes readability and code comprehension. Unusually among programming languages, Python actually *requires* such formatting, as its block structure is indicated by indentation rather than by curly braces { ... } (as in C/C++, PHP, Perl, JavaScript, etc.) or by a special keyword (e.g., end in Ruby).

While exact styles differ, here are some general guidelines for good code formatting, based in part on PEP 8 – Style Guide for Python Code:

- Indent code to indicate block structure. As noted above, this is required by Python. Python technically allows either spaces or tabs, but tabs are generally considered a Bad Thing, and using spaces (typically via *emulated tabs* (https://www.learnenough.com/text-editor-tutorial/advanced_text_editing#sec-indenting_and_dedenting)) is strongly recommended.

- Use four spaces for indentation. Although some Python style guides, such as Google's Python course, indent two spaces at a time, the official PEP 8 guideline is to use four spaces.

- Add newlines to indicate logical structure. One thing I particularly like to do is add an extra newline after a series of variable assignments, in order to give a visual indication that the setup is done and the real coding can begin. An example appears in Listing 4.12.

- Limit code lines to 79 characters (also called "columns"), and limit comment lines or docstrings to 72 characters. These rules, which are recommended by PEP 8, are even more cautious than the 80-character constraint used in other Learn Enough tutorials and which dates back to the early days of 80-character-width terminals. Many modern developers routinely violate this constraint, considering it outdated, but in my experience using a conservative character limit is a good source of discipline, and will save your neck when using command-line programs like less (or when using your code in a document with more stringent width requirements, such as a book). A line that breaks the character limit is a hint that you should introduce a new variable name, break an operation into multiple steps, etc., to make the code clearer for anyone reading it.

We'll see several examples of more advanced code formatting conventions as we proceed throughout the rest of this tutorial.

We can add a second behavior using **else**, which serves as the default result if the first comparison is **False** (Listing 2.9).

Listing 2.9: Control flow with **if** and **else**.

```
>>> password = "foobar"
>>> if len(password) < 6:
...     print("Password is too short.")
... else:
...     print("Password is long enough.")
...
Password is long enough.
```

The first line in Listing 2.9 *redefines* **password** by assigning it a new value. After reassignment, the **password** variable has length 6, so **len(password) < 6** is **False**. As a result, the **if** part of the statement (known as the **if** *branch*) doesn't get evaluated; instead, Python evaluates the **else** branch, resulting in a message indicating that the password is long enough.

Rather than the more conventional **else if** control flow, Python has a special **elif** keyword that means the same thing, as shown in Listing 2.10 (Figure 2.5[12]).

Figure 2.5: Goldilocks chooses control flow that is just right.

---

12. Image courtesy of Jessie Willcox Smith/Alamy Stock Photo.

Listing 2.10: Control flow with `elif`.

```
>>> password = "goldilocks"
>>> if len(password) < 6:
...     print("Password is too short.")
... elif len(password) < 50:
...     print("Password is just right!")
... else:
...     print("Password is too long.")
...
Password is just right!
```

2.4.1 Combining and Inverting Booleans

Booleans can be combined or inverted using the **and**, **or**, and **not** operators.

Let's start with **and**. When comparing two booleans with **and**, *both* have to be **True** for the combination to be **True**. For example, if I said I wanted both french fries *and* a baked potato, the only way the combination could be true is if I could answer "yes" (true) to both the questions "Do you want french fries?" and "Do you want a baked potato?" If my answer to either of those is false, then the combination must be false as well. The resulting combinations of possibilities are collectively known as a *truth table*; the truth table for **and** appears in Listing 2.11.

Listing 2.11: The truth table for **and**.

```
>>> True and False
False
>>> False and True
False
>>> False and False
False
>>> True and True
True
```

We can apply this to a conditional as shown in Listing 2.12.

Listing 2.12: Using the **and** operator in a conditional.

```
>>> x = "foo"
>>> y = ""
>>> if len(x) == 0 and len(y) == 0:
```

```
...        print("Both strings are empty!")
... else:
...        print("At least one of the strings is nonempty.")
...
At least one of the strings is nonempty.
```

In Listing 2.12, **len(y)** is in fact **0**, but **len(x)** isn't, so the combination is **False** (in agreement with Listing 2.11), and Python evaluates the **else** branch.

In contrast to **and**, **or** lets us take action if *either* comparison (or both) is true (Listing 2.13).

Listing 2.13: The truth table for **or**.

```
>>> True or False
True
>>> False or True
True
>>> True or True
True
>>> False or False
False
```

We can use **or** in a conditional as shown in Listing 2.14.

Listing 2.14: Using the **or** operator in a conditional.

```
>>> if len(x) == 0 or len(y) == 0:
...        print("At least one of the strings is empty!")
... else:
...        print("Neither of the strings is empty.")
...
At least one of the strings is empty!
```

Note from Listing 2.13 that **or** isn't *exclusive*, meaning that the result is true even when *both* statements are true. This stands in contrast to colloquial usage, where a statement like "I want fries or a baked potato" implies that you want either fries *or* a baked potato, but you don't want both (Figure 2.6[13]).

---

13. Image courtesy of Rikaphoto/Shutterstock.

Figure 2.6: Turns out I only wanted fries.

In addition to **and** and **or**, Python supports *negation* via the "not" operator **not**, which just converts **True** to **False** and **False** to **True** (Listing 2.15).

Listing 2.15: The truth table for **not**.

```
>>> not True
False
>>> not False
True
```

We can use **not** in a conditional as shown in Listing 2.16. Note that parentheses *are* required in this case, because otherwise we're asking if **not len(x)** is equal to **0**.

Listing 2.16: Using the **not** operator in a conditional.

```
>>> if not (len(x) == 0):     # Not Pythonic
...     print("x is not empty.")
... else:
...     print("x is empty.")
...
x is not empty.
```

The code in Listing 2.16 is valid Python, as it simply negates the test **len(x)** **==** **0**, yielding **True**:

```
>>> not (len(x) == 0)
True
```

In this case, though, it's more common to use **!=** ("not equals", also read as "bang equals" since **!** is often pronounced "bang"), as seen in Listing 2.17.

Listing 2.17: Using **!=** ("not equals" or "bang equals").

```
>>> if len(x) != 0:          # Not quite Pythonic
...     print("x is not empty.")
... else:
...     print("x is empty.")
...
x is not empty
```

Because we're no longer negating the entire expression, we can omit the parentheses as before. As noted, though, this code would not be considered fully Pythonic; this is because the empty string **""** has a special value in a boolean context (Section 2.4.2).

2.4.2 Boolean Context

Not all booleans are the result of comparisons, and in fact every Python object has a value of either **True** or **False** in a boolean context. We can force Python to use such a boolean context with the **bool()** function. Naturally, both **True** and **False** are just equal to themselves in a boolean context:

```
>>> bool(True)
True
>>> bool(False)
False
```

Using **bool()** allows us to see that a string like **"foo"** is **True** in a boolean context:

```
>>> bool("foo")
True
```

Almost all Python strings are **True** in a boolean context; the only exception is the empty string, which is **False**:[14]

```
>>> bool("")
False
```

Most other things that are "empty" in any sense are **False** in Python. This includes the number **0**:

```
>>> bool(0)
False
```

and **None**:

```
>>> bool(None)
False
```

As we'll see later, empty lists (Chapter 3), empty tuples (Section 3.6), and empty dictionaries (Section 4.4) are also **False**.

It's important to understand that using **bool()** is just for purposes of illustration; in real programs, we'll almost always rely on the presence of a keyword such as **if** or **elif**, which automatically converts all objects to their boolean equivalents. For example, because **""** is **False** in a boolean context, we can replace **len(x) != 0** in Listing 2.17 with **x** itself, as seen in Listing 2.18.

Listing 2.18: Using a string in a boolean context.

```
>>> if x:                    # Pythonic
...     print("x is not empty.")
... else:
...     print("x is empty.")
...
x is not empty.
```

In Listing 2.18, **if x:** converts **x** to **False** if it's the empty string and **True** otherwise.

We can use the same property to rewrite code like Listing 2.12 as shown in Listing 2.19.

---

14. This is the sort of detail that varies from language to language. For example, the empty string is true in Ruby.

Listing 2.19: Using boolean methods.

```
>>> if x or y:
...     print("At least one of the strings is nonempty.")
... else:
...     print("Both strings are empty!")
...
At least one of the strings is nonempty.
```

2.4.3 Exercises

1. If **x** is **"foo"** and **y** is **""** (the empty string), what is the value of **x and y**? Verify using **bool()** that **x and y** is true in a boolean context.

2. Show that we can define a string of length **50** using the convenient code in Listing 2.20, which uses the asterisk ***** to "multiply" the string **"a"** by 50. Go through the steps in Listing 2.10 again with the new password to verify that Python prints out "Password is too long."

Listing 2.20: Defining a password that is too long.

```
>>> password = "a" * 50
>>> password
'aaaaaaaaaaaaaaaaaaaaaaaaaaaaaaaaaaaaaaaaaaaaaaaaaa'
```

2.5 Methods

We saw in Section 2.4 that we can call the **len()** function to get the length of a string. This follows the same basic pattern as the **print()** function discussed in Section 2.3: We type the name of the function with an argument in parentheses.

There is a second important class of functions that are effectively attached to the object under consideration—in the case of this chapter, a string object. Such functions are known as *methods*. In Python (and in many other languages that support object-oriented programming), methods are indicated by typing the object followed by a dot and then the name of the method. For example, Python strings have a method called **capitalize()** that capitalizes the given string:

```
>>> "michael".capitalize()
'Michael'
```

Note that we include parentheses to indicate that **capitalize()** is a method (in this case, with zero arguments). Leaving off the parentheses causes Python to return the raw method:

```
>>> "michael".capitalize
<built-in method capitalize of str object at 0x1014487b0>
```

This is why we generally include parentheses in method names like **capitalize()**.

One important class of methods is *boolean methods*, which return **True** or **False**. In Python, such methods are frequently indicated using the word "is" as the first part of the method:

```
>>> "badger".islower()
True
>>> "BADGER".islower()
False
>>> "bAdGEr".islower()
False
```

Here we see that **islower()** returns **True** if the string is all lowercase and **False** otherwise.

Strings also respond to a wealth of methods that return transformed versions of the string's content. One example is the **capitalize()** method seen above. Strings also have a **lower()** method, which (surprise!) converts the string to all lowercase letters (Figure 2.7[15]):

```
>>> "HONEY BADGER".lower()
'honey badger'
```

Note that the **lower()** method returns a *new* string, without changing (or *mutating*) the original:

```
>>> animal = "HONEY BADGER"
>>> animal.lower()
'honey badger'
```

---

15. Image courtesy of Pavel Kovaricek/Shutterstock.

Figure 2.7: This honey badger used to be a HONEY BADGER, but he don't care.

```
>>> animal
'HONEY BADGER'
```

This is the sort of method that could be useful, for example, when standardizing on lowercase letters in an email address:

```
>>> first_name = "Michael"
>>> username = first_name.lower()
>>> f"{username}@example.com"      # Sample email address
'michael@example.com'
```

As you might be able to guess, Python supports the opposite operation as well; before looking at the example below, see if you can guess the method for converting a string to uppercase (Figure 2.8[16]).

I'm betting you got the right answer (or at least came close):

```
>>> last_name.upper()
'HARTL'
```

---

16. Image courtesy of Arco1/123RF.

Figure 2.8: Early typesetters kept large letters in the "upper case" and small letters in the "lower case".

Being able to guess answers like this is a hallmark of technical sophistication, but as noted in Box 1.2 another key skill is being able to use the documentation. In particular, the Python documentation page on **str** has a long list of useful string methods.[17] Let's take a look at some of them (Figure 2.9).

Inspecting the methods in Figure 2.9, we see one that looks like this:

str.find(sub[, start[, end]])
Return the lowest index in the string where substring *sub* is found within the slice **s[start:end]**. Optional arguments *start* and *end* are interpreted as in slice notation. Return **-1** if *sub* is not found.

---

17. You can find such pages by going directly to the official Python documentation, but the truth is that I nearly always find such pages by Googling things like "python string". Be mindful of the version number—although Python is quite stable at this point, if you notice any discrepancies make sure you're using documentation compatible with your own version of Python.

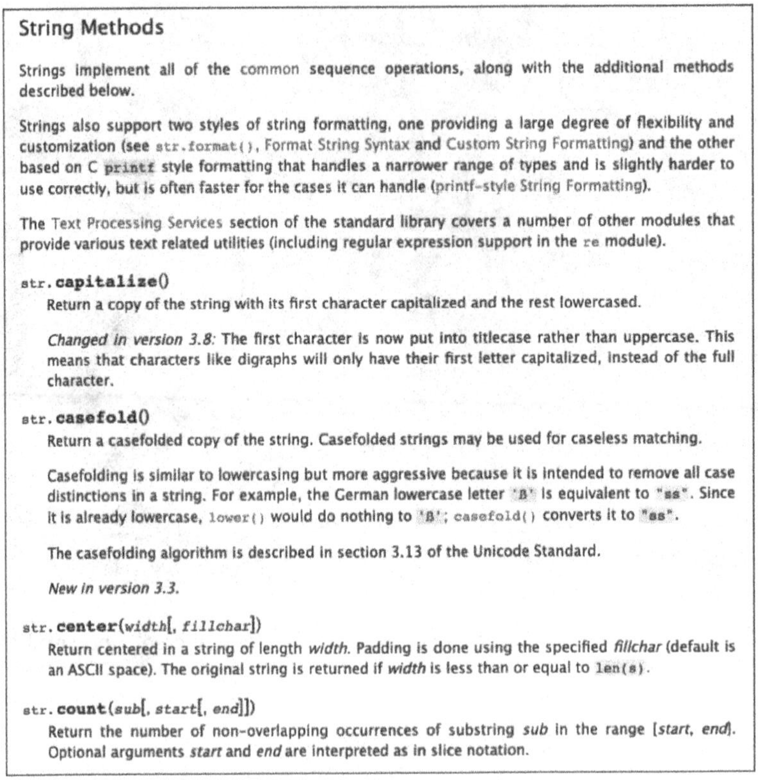

String Methods

Strings implement all of the common sequence operations, along with the additional methods described below.

Strings also support two styles of string formatting, one providing a large degree of flexibility and customization (see `str.format()`, Format String Syntax and Custom String Formatting) and the other based on C `printf` style formatting that handles a narrower range of types and is slightly harder to use correctly, but is often faster for the cases it can handle (printf-style String Formatting).

The Text Processing Services section of the standard library covers a number of other modules that provide various text related utilities (including regular expression support in the `re` module).

`str.`**`capitalize()`**
    Return a copy of the string with its first character capitalized and the rest lowercased.

    Changed in version 3.8: The first character is now put into titlecase rather than uppercase. This means that characters like digraphs will only have their first letter capitalized, instead of the full character.

`str.`**`casefold()`**
    Return a casefolded copy of the string. Casefolded strings may be used for caseless matching.

    Casefolding is similar to lowercasing but more aggressive because it is intended to remove all case distinctions in a string. For example, the German lowercase letter `'ß'` is equivalent to `"ss"`. Since it is already lowercase, `lower()` would do nothing to `'ß'`; `casefold()` converts it to `"ss"`.

    The casefolding algorithm is described in section 3.13 of the Unicode Standard.

    New in version 3.3.

`str.`**`center`**(*width*[, *fillchar*])
    Return centered in a string of length *width*. Padding is done using the specified *fillchar* (default is an ASCII space). The original string is returned if *width* is less than or equal to `len(s)`.

`str.`**`count`**(*sub*[, *start*[, *end*]])
    Return the number of non-overlapping occurrences of substring *sub* in the range [*start*, *end*]. Optional arguments *start* and *end* are interpreted as in slice notation.

Figure 2.9: Some Python string methods.

This indicates that the **find()** method takes an *argument*, **sub**, and returns the location where the substring starts:

```
>>> "hello".find("lo")
3
>>> "hello".find("ol")
-1
```

(Note that **3** corresponds to the *fourth* letter, not the third, a convention known as "zero offset" or "zero-based indexing"; see Section 2.6.)

The result for a nonexistent substring means that we can test whether a string contains a substring by comparing to **-1**:

```
>>> soliloquy = "To be, or not to be, that is the question:"
>>> soliloquy.find("To be") != -1    # Not Pythonic
True
```

The **True** return value indicates that **soliloquy** does contain the substring **"To be"**. But the **find()** documentation also includes an important note:

> The **find()** method should be used only if you need to know the position of *sub*. To check if *sub* is a substring or not, use the **in** operator:
>
> ```
> >>> 'Py' in 'Python'
> True
> ```

Applying this to **soliloquy** yields the results shown in Listing 2.21 (Figure 2.10[18]).

Listing 2.21: Include or does not include? That is the question.

```
>>> soliloquy = "To be, or not to be, that is the question:"  # Just a reminder
>>> "To be" in soliloquy        # Does it include the substring "To be"?
True
>>> "question" in soliloquy     # What about "question"?
True
>>> "nonexistent" in soliloquy  # This string doesn't appear.
False
>>> "TO BE" in soliloquy        # String inclusion is case-sensitive.
False
```

2.5.1 Exercises

1. Write the Python code to test whether the string "hoNeY BaDGer" includes the string "badger" without regard to case.

2. What is the Python method for stripping leading and trailing whitespace from a string? The result should be as shown in Listing 2.22 with **FILL_IN** replaced by the method name.

---

18. Image courtesy of Everett Collection/Shutterstock.

Figure 2.10: Hamlet, Prince of Denmark, asks: "To be, or not to be, that is the question."

Listing 2.22: Stripping whitespace.

```
>>> "   spacious   ".FILL_IN()
'spacious'
```

2.6 String Iteration

Our final topic on strings is *iteration*, which is the practice of repeatedly stepping through an object one element at a time. Iteration is a common theme in computer programming, and we'll get plenty of practice in this tutorial. We'll also see how one sign of your growing power as a developer is learning how to *avoid* iteration entirely (as discussed in Chapter 6 and Section 8.5).

In the case of strings, we'll be learning how to iterate one *character* at a time. There are two main prerequisites to this: First, we need to learn how to access a particular character in a string, and second, we need to learn how to make a *loop*.

We can figure out how to access a particular string character by consulting the Common Sequence Operations (https://docs.python.org/3/library/stdtypes.html

#common-sequence-operations), which indicates that **s[i]** (using square brackets) gives the "*i*th item of *s*, origin 0" for sequences, including strings. (The main sequences listed are lists and tuples, which are covered in Chapter 3, and ranges, which we'll be looking at in just a moment.) Applying this bracket notation to the **soliloquy** string from Section 2.5 lets us see how it works, as shown in Listing 2.23.

Listing 2.23: Investigating the behavior of `str[index]`.

```
>>> soliloquy   # Just a reminder of what the string is
'To be, or not to be, that is the question:'
>>> soliloquy[0]
'T'
>>> soliloquy[1]
'o'
>>> soliloquy[2]
' '
```

We see in Listing 2.23 that Python supports a bracket notation for accessing string elements, so that **[0]** returns the first character, **[1]** returns the second, and so on. (We'll discuss this possibly counterintuitive numbering convention, called "zero offset" or "zero-based indexing", further in Section 3.1.) Each number **0**, **1**, **2**, etc., is called an *index* (plural *indexes* or *indices*).

Now let's look at our first example of a loop. In particular, we'll use a **for** loop that defines an index value **i** and does an operation for each value in the **range()** of length **5** (Listing 2.24).

Listing 2.24: A simple **for** loop.

```
>>> for i in range(5):
...     print(i)
...
0
1
2
3
4
```

Here we've used the **range(5)** function, which as we see creates an object with numbers in the range 0–4.

Listing 2.24 is Python's version of the classic "for loop" that is exceptionally common across an astonishing variety of programming languages, from C and C++ to JavaScript, Perl, and PHP. Unlike those languages, though, which explicitly increment a counter variable, Python defines a range of values directly via a special Range data type.

Listing 2.24 is arguably a little more elegant than the equivalent "classic" **for** loop seen in *Learn Enough JavaScript to Be Dangerous* (Listing 2.25), but it's still not very good Python.

Listing 2.25: A **for** loop in JavaScript.

```
> for (i = 0; i < 5; i++) {
  console.log(i);
}
0
1
2
3
4
```

As a language and as a community, Python is especially vigilant about avoiding plain **for** loops. As computer scientist (and personal friend) Mike Vanier (Figure 2.11[19]) once put it in an email to Paul Graham:

> This [tedious repetition] grinds you down after a while; if I had a nickel for every time I've written "for (i = 0; i < N; i++)" in C I'd be a millionaire.

Figure 2.11: Just a few more **for** loops and Mike Vanier will be a millionaire.

---

19. Image © Mike Vanier.

In order to avoid getting ground down, we'll learn how to use **for** to loop over elements directly. We'll also see how Python lets us avoid loops entirely using functional programming (Chapter 6 and Section 8.5).

For now, though, let's build on Listing 2.24 to iterate through all the characters in the first line of Hamlet's famous soliloquy. The only new thing we need is the index for when the loop should stop. In Listing 2.24, we hard-coded the upper limit (**5**), and we could do the same here if we wanted. The **soliloquy** variable is a bit long to count the characters by hand, though, so let's ask Python to tell us using the **len()** property (Section 2.4):

```
>>> len(soliloquy)
42
```

This exceptionally auspicious result suggests writing code like this:

```
for i in range(42):
    print(soliloquy[i])
```

This code will work, and it is in perfect analogy with Listing 2.24, but it also raises a question: Why hard-code the length when we can just use the **len()** method in the loop itself?

The answer is that we shouldn't. The resulting improved **for** loop appears in Listing 2.26.

Listing 2.26: Combining **range()**, **len()**, and a **for** loop.

```
>>> for i in range(len(soliloquy)):     # Not Pythonic
...     print(soliloquy[i])
...
...
T
o

b
e
.
.
.
t
i
o
n
:
```

Although Listing 2.26 works just fine, it is not Pythonic. Instead, the most Pythonic way to iterate through string characters is to use **for** by itself, because it turns out that the default behavior of **for** applied to a string is simply to consider each character in turn, as seen in Listing 2.27.

Listing 2.27: Looping through a string with **for**.

```
>>> for c in soliloquy:      # Pythonic
...     print(c)
...
T
o

b
e
.
.
.
t
i
o
n
:
```

As noted previously, there are often alternatives to looping, but the **for** style of looping is still an excellent place to start. As we'll see in Chapter 8, one powerful technique is to write a *test* for the functionality we want, then get it passing any way we can, and then *refactor* the code to use a more elegant method. The second step in this process (called *test-driven development*, or TDD) often involves writing inelegant but easy-to-understand code—a task at which the humble **for** loop excels.

2.6.1 Exercises

1. Write a **for** loop that prints out the characters of **soliloquy** in reverse order. *Hint*: What is the effect of the **reversed()** function on a string?

2. One disadvantage of the plain **for** loop in Listing 2.27 is that we no longer have access to the index value itself. We could solve this as in Listing 2.28, but the Pythonic way to do it is to use the **enumerate()** function to gain access to the index and the element at the same time. Confirm that you can use **enumerate()** to obtain the result shown in Listing 2.29.

Listing 2.28: Using an index with string access.

```
>>> for i in range(len(soliloquy)):     # Not Pythonic
...     print(f"Character {i+1} is '{soliloquy[i]}'")
...
Character 1 is 'T'
Character 2 is 'o'
Character 3 is ' '
Character 4 is 'b'
Character 5 is 'e'
Character 6 is ','
Character 7 is ' '
  .
  .
  .
```

Listing 2.29: Iterating through a string with an index.

```
>>> for i, c in enumerate(soliloquy):     # Pythonic
...     print(f"Character {i+1} is '{c}'")
...
Character 1 is 'T'
Character 2 is 'o'
Character 3 is ' '
Character 4 is 'b'
Character 5 is 'e'
Character 6 is ','
Character 7 is ' '
  .
  .
  .
```

CHAPTER 3

Lists

In Chapter 2, we saw that strings can be thought of as sequences of characters in a particular order. In this chapter, we'll learn about the *list* data type, which is the general Python container for a list of arbitrary elements in a particular order. Python lists are similar to the *array* data type in other languages (such as JavaScript and Ruby), so programmers familiar with other languages can probably guess a lot about how Python lists behave. (Although Python does have a built-in array type, in this tutorial "array" always refers to the *ndarray* data type defined by the NumPy library, which is covered in Section 11.2.)

We'll start by explicitly connecting strings and lists via the **split()** method (Section 3.1), and then learn about various other list methods and techniques throughout the rest of the chapter. In Section 3.6, we'll also take a quick look at two closely related data types, Python *tuples* and *sets*.

3.1 Splitting

So far we've spent a lot of time understanding strings, and there's a natural way to get from strings to lists via the **split()** method:

```
$ source venv/bin/activate
(venv) $ python3
>>> "ant bat cat".split(" ")        # Split a string into a three-element list.
['ant', 'bat', 'cat']
```

We see from this result that **split()** returns a list of the strings that are separated from each other by a space in the original string.

Splitting on space is one of the most common operations, but we can split on nearly anything else as well (Listing 3.1).

Listing 3.1: Splitting on arbitrary strings.

```
>>> "ant,bat,cat".split(",")
['ant', 'bat', 'cat']
>>> "ant, bat, cat".split(", ")
['ant', 'bat', 'cat']
>>> "antheybatheycat".split("hey")
['ant', 'bat', 'cat']
```

Many languages support this sort of splitting, but note that Python includes an empty string in the final case illustrated above, which some languages (such as Ruby) trim automatically. We can avoid this extra string in the common case of splitting on newlines using **splitlines()** instead (Listing 3.2).

Listing 3.2: Splitting on newlines vs. **splitlines()**.

```
>>> s = "This is a line.\nAnd this is another line.\n"
>>> s.split("\n")
['This is a line.', 'And this is another line.', '']
>>> s.splitlines()
['This is a line.', 'And this is another line.']
```

Many languages allow us to split a string into its component characters by splitting on the empty string, but this doesn't work in Python:

```
>>> "badger".split("")
"badger".split("")
Traceback (most recent call last):
  File "<stdin>", line 1, in <module>
ValueError: empty separator
```

In Python, the best way to do this is using the **list()** function directly on the string:

```
>>> list("badger")
['b', 'a', 'd', 'g', 'e', 'r']
```

Because Python can naturally iterate over a string's characters, this technique is rarely needed explicitly; instead, we'll typically use *iterators*, which we'll learn about in Section 5.3.

Perhaps the most common use of **split()** is with *no* arguments; in this case, the default behavior is to split on *whitespace* (such as spaces, tabs, or newlines):

```
>>> "ant bat cat".split()
['ant', 'bat', 'cat']
>>> "ant     bat\t\tcat\n    duck".split()
['ant', 'bat', 'cat', 'duck']
```

We'll investigate this case more closely when discussing *regular expressions* in Section 4.3.

3.1.1 Exercises

1. Assign **a** to the result of splitting the string "A man, a plan, a canal, Panama" on comma-space. How many elements does the resulting list have?

2. Can you guess the method to reverse **a** in place? (Google around if necessary.)

3.2 List Access

Having connected strings with lists via the **split()** method, we'll now discover a second close connection as well. Let's start by assigning a variable to a list of characters created using **list()**:

```
>>> a = list("badger")
['b', 'a', 'd', 'g', 'e', 'r']
```

Here we've followed tradition and called the variable **a**, both because it's the first letter of the alphabet and as a nod to the array type that lists so closely resemble.

We can access particular elements of **a** using the same bracket notation we first encountered in the context of strings in Section 2.6, as seen in Listing 3.3.

Listing 3.3: List access with the bracket notation.

```
>>> a[0]
'b'
>>> a[1]
```

```
'a'
>>> a[2]
'd'
```

We see from Listing 3.3 that, as with strings, lists are *zero-offset*, meaning that the "first" element has index **0**, the second has index **1**, and so on. This convention can be confusing, and in fact it's common to refer to the initial element for zero-offset lists as the "zeroth" element as a reminder that the indexing starts at **0**. This convention can also be confusing when using multiple languages (some of which start list indexing at **1**), as illustrated in the xkcd comic strip "Donald Knuth".[1]

So far we've dealt exclusively with lists of characters, but Python lists can contain all types of elements (Listing 3.4).

Listing 3.4: Creating a list with several types of elements.

```
>>> soliloquy = "To be, or not to be, that is the question:"
>>> a = ["badger", 42, "To be" in soliloquy]
>>> a
['badger', 42, True]
>>> a[2]
True
>>> a[3]
Traceback (most recent call last):
  File "<stdin>", line 1, in <module>
IndexError: list index out of range
```

We see here that the square bracket access notation works as usual for a list of mixed types, which shouldn't come as a surprise. We also see that trying to access a list index outside the defined range raises an error if we try to access an element that's out of range.

Another convenient feature of Python bracket notation is supporting *negative* indices, which count from the end of the list:

```
>>> a[-2]
42
```

---

1. This particular xkcd strip takes its name from renowned computer scientist Donald Knuth (pronounced "kuh-NOOTH"), author of *The Art of Computer Programming* and creator of the TEX typesetting system used to prepare many technical documents, including this one.

Among other things, negative indices give us a compact way to select the *last* element in a list. Because **len()** (Section 2.4) works on lists as well as strings, we could do it directly by subtracting **1** from the length (which we have to do because lists are zero-offset):

```
>>> a[len(a) - 1]
True
```

But it's even easier like this:

```
>>> a[-1]
True
```

A final common case is where we want to access the final element and remove it at the same time. We'll cover the method for doing this in Section 3.4.3.

By the way, starting in Listing 3.4, we used a literal square-bracket syntax to define lists by hand. This notation is so natural that you probably didn't even notice it, and indeed it's the same format the REPL uses when printing out lists.

We can use this same notation to define the *empty list* **[]**, which just evaluates to itself:

```
>>> []
[]
```

You may recall from Section 2.4.2 that empty or nonexistent things like **""**, **0**, and **None** are **False** in a boolean context. This pattern holds for the empty list as well:

```
>>> bool([])
False
```

3.2.1 Exercises

1. We've seen that **list(str)** returns a list of the characters in a string. How can we make a list consisting of the numbers in the range 0–4? *Hint*: Recall the **range()** function first encountered in Listing 2.24.

2. Show that you can create a list of numbers in the range 17–41 using **list()** with **range(17, 42)**.

Figure 3.1: Python is unusually good at slicing.

3.3 List Slicing

In addition to supporting the bracket notation described in Section 3.2, Python excels at a technique known as *list slicing* (Figure 3.1[2]) for accessing multiple elements at a time. In anticipation of learning to *sort* in Section 3.4.2, let's redefine our list **a** to have purely numerical elements:

```
>>> a = [42, 8, 17, 99]
[42, 8, 17, 99]
```

One way to slice a list is to use the **slice()** function and provide two arguments corresponding to the index number where the slice should start and where it should end. For example, **slice(2, 4)** lets us pull out the elements with index **2** and **3**, ending at **4**:

```
>>> a[slice(2, 4)]     # Not Pythonic
[17, 99]
```

This can be a little tricky to understand since there is no element with index **4** due to lists being zero-offset. We can understand this better by imagining a pointer that

---

2. Image courtesy of Artjazz/Shutterstock.

moves one element to the right as it creates the slice; it starts at **2**, selects element **2** as it moves to **3**, and then selects element **3** as it moves to **4**.

The explicit **slice()** notation is rarely used in real Python code; far more common is the equivalent notation using colons, like this:

```
>>> a[2:4]     # Pythonic
[17, 99]
```

Note that the index convention is the same: To select elements with indices **2** and **3**, we include a final range that is one *more* than the value of the final index in the slice (in this case, $3 + 1 = 4$).

In the case of our current list, **4** is the length of the list, so in effect we are slicing from the element with index **2** to the end. This is such a common task that Python has a special notation for it—we just leave the second index off entirely:

```
>>> a[2:]     # Pythonic
[17, 99]
```

As you might guess, the same basic notation works to slice from the *front* of the list:

```
>>> a[:2]     # Pythonic
[42, 8]
```

The general pattern here is that **a[start:end]** selects from index **start** to index **end-1**, where either can be omitted to select from the start or to the end. Python also supports an extension to this syntax taking the form **a[start:-end:step]**, which is the same as regular list slicing except taken **step** at a time. For example, we can select numbers from a range **3** at a time as follows:

```
>>> numbers = list(range(20))
>>> numbers
[0, 1, 2, 3, 4, 5, 6, 7, 8, 9, 10, 11, 12, 13, 14, 15, 16, 17, 18, 19]
>>> numbers[0:20:3]      # Not Pythonic
[0, 3, 6, 9, 12, 15, 18]
```

Or we could start at, say, index **5** and end at index **17**:

```
>>> numbers[5:17:3]
[5, 8, 11, 14]
```

As with regular slicing, we can omit values if we want the start or the end:

```
>>> numbers[:10:3]     # Goes from the beginning to 10-1
[0, 3, 6, 9]
>>> numbers[5::3]      # Goes from 5 to the end
[5, 8, 11, 14, 17]
```

We can replicate the result of **numbers[0:20:3]** more Pythonically by omitting both **0** *and* **20**:

```
>>> numbers[::3]       # Pythonic
[0, 3, 6, 9, 12, 15, 18]
```

We can even go backward using a negative step:

```
>>> numbers[::-3]
[19, 16, 13, 10, 7, 4, 1]
```

This suggests a (perhaps too clever) way to *reverse* a list, which is to use a step of **-1**. Applying this idea to our original list looks like this:

```
>>> a[::-1]
[99, 17, 8, 42]
```

You may encounter this **[::-1]** construction in real-life Python code, so it's important to know what it does, but there are more convenient and readable ways to reverse a list, as discussed in Section 3.4.2.

3.3.1 Exercises

1. Define a list with the numbers 0 through 9. Use slicing and **len()** to select the third element through the third-to-last. Accomplish the same task using a negative index.

2. Show that strings also support slicing by selecting just **"bat"** from the string **"ant bat cat"**. (You might have to experiment a little to get the indices just right.)

3.4 More List Techniques

There are many other things we can do with lists other than accessing and selecting elements. In this section we'll discuss element inclusion, sorting and reversing, and appending and popping.

3.4.1 Element Inclusion

As with strings (Section 2.5), lists support testing for element inclusion using the **in** keyword:

```
>>> a = [42, 8, 17, 99]
[42, 8, 17, 99]
>>> 42 in a
True
>>> "foo" in a
False
```

3.4.2 Sorting and Reversing

Python has powerful facilities for *sorting* and *reversing* lists. They come in two general types: *in-place* and *generators*. Let's take a look at some examples to see what this means.

We'll start by sorting a list in place—an excellent trick that in ye olden days of C often required a custom implementation.[3] In Python, we just call **sort()**:

```
>>> a = [42, 8, 17, 99]
>>> a.sort()
>>> a                    # mutated list
[8, 17, 42, 99]
```

As you might expect for a list of integers, **a.sort()** sorts the list numerically (unlike, e.g., JavaScript, which confusingly sorts them "alphabetically", so that 17 comes before 8). We also see that (unlike (https://www.learnenough.com/ruby-tutorial/arrays#sec-more_array_methods) Ruby but *like* (https://www.learnenough.com/javascript-tutorial/arrays#sec-more_array_methods) JavaScript) sorting a list changes, or *mutates*, the list itself. (We'll see in a moment that it returns **None**.)

---

3. This isn't entirely fair to C: Python itself is written in C, so **sort()** actually is just such a "custom implementation"!

We can use **reverse()** to reverse the elements in a list:

```
>>> a.reverse()
>>> a
[99, 42, 17, 8]
```

As with **sort()**, note that **reverse()** mutates the list itself.

Such mutating methods can help demonstrate a common gotcha about Python lists involving list assignment. Suppose we have a list **a1** and want a copy called **a2** (Listing 3.5).

Listing 3.5: A dangerous assignment.

```
>>> a1 = [42, 8, 17, 99]
>>> a2 = a1    # Dangerous!
```

The assignment in the second line is dangerous because **a2** points to the same location in the computer's memory as **a1**, which means that if we mutate **a1** it changes **a2** as well:

```
>>> a1.sort()
>>> a1
[8, 17, 42, 99]
>>> a2
[8, 17, 42, 99]
```

We see here that **a2** has changed even though we didn't do anything to it directly. (You can avoid this using the **list()** function or the **copy()** method, as in **a2 = list(a1)** or **a2 = a1.copy()**.)

Python in-place methods are highly efficient, but usually more convenient are the related **sorted()** and **reversed()** functions. For example, we can obtain a sorted list as follows:

```
>>> a = [42, 8, 17, 99]
>>> sorted(a)    # Pythonic
[8, 17, 42, 99]
>>> a
[42, 8, 17, 99]
```

Here, unlike the case of **sort()**, the original list is unchanged.

Similarly, we can (almost) obtain a reversed list using **reversed( )**:

```
>>> a
[42, 8, 17, 99]
>>> reversed(a)
<list_reverseiterator object at 0x109561910>
```

Unfortunately, the parallel structure with **sorted( )** is slightly broken, at least as of this writing. Rather than returning a list, the **reversed( )** function returns an *iterator*, which is a special type of Python object designed to be (you guessed it) iterated over. This isn't usually a problem because we'll usually be joining or looping over the reversed elements, in which case the generator will serve just fine (Section 5.3), but when we really need a list we can call the **list( )** function directly (Section 3.1):

```
>>> list(reversed(a))
[99, 42, 17, 8]
```

As noted, this minor wart rarely makes a difference since the generator's behavior is effectively identical to the list version when being iterated over.[4]

Comparison
Lists support the same basic equality and inequality comparisons as strings (Chapter 2):

```
>>> a = [1, 2, 3]
>>> b = [1, 2, 3]
>>> a == b
True
>>> a != b
False
```

Python also supports **is**, which tests whether two variables represent the same object. Because **a** and **b**, although they contain the same elements, are not the same object in Python's memory system, **==** and **is** return different results in this case:

```
>>> a == b
True
```

---

4. It's actually even better in certain ways since the generator doesn't require creating the entire list in memory. See Section 5.3 for more information.

```
>>> a is b
False
```

In contrast, the lists **a1** and **a2** from Listing 3.5 are equal using both comparisons:

```
>>> a1 == a2
True
>>> a1 is a2
True
```

The second **True** values follows because **a1** and **a2** truly are the exact same object. This behavior is effectively the same as the **===** syntax supported by many other languages, such as Ruby and JavaScript.

According to the PEP 8 style guide, **is** should always be used when comparing with **None**. For example, we can use **is** to confirm that the list methods for reversing and sorting in place return **None**:

```
>>> a.reverse() == None      # Not Pythonic
True
>>> a.sort() == None         # Not Pythonic
True
>>> a.reverse() is None      # Pythonic
True
>>> a.sort() is None         # Pythonic
True
```

3.4.3 Appending and Popping

One useful pair of list methods is **append()** and **pop()**—**append()** lets us append an element to the end of a list, while **pop()** removes it and returns the value:

```
>>> a = sorted([42, 8, 17, 99])
>>> a
[8, 17, 42, 99]
>>> a.append(6)                        # Appending to a list
>>> a
[8, 17, 42, 99, 6]
>>> a.append("foo")
>>> a
[8, 17, 42, 99, 6, 'foo']
>>> a.pop()                            # Popping an element off
'foo'
```

```
>>> a
[8, 17, 42, 99, 6]
>>> a.pop()
6
>>> a.pop()
99
>>> a
[8, 17, 42]
```

Note that **pop()** returns the value of the final element (while removing it as a side effect), while **append()** returns **None** (as indicated by nothing being printed after an append).

We are now in a position to appreciate the comment made in Section 3.2 about obtaining the last element of the list, as long as we don't mind mutating it:

```
>>> the_answer_to_life_the_universe_and_everything = a.pop()
>>> the_answer_to_life_the_universe_and_everything
42
```

3.4.4 Undoing a Split

A final example of a list method, one that brings us full circle from Section 3.1, is **join()**. Just as **split()** splits a string into list elements, **join()** joins list elements into a string (Listing 3.6).

Listing 3.6: Different ways to join.

```
>>> a = ["ant", "bat", "cat", "42"]
['ant', 'bat', 'cat', '42']
>>> "".join(a)                       # Join on empty space.
'antbatcat42'
>>> ", ".join(a)                     # Join on comma-space.
'ant, bat, cat, 42'
>>> " -- ".join(a)                   # Join on double dashes.
'ant -- bat -- cat -- 42'
```

Note that in all cases shown in Listing 3.6 the lists we're joining consist wholly of strings. What if we wanted a list containing, say, the *number* **42** rather than the string **"42"**? It doesn't work by default:

```
>>> a = ["ant", "bat", "cat", 42]
>>> ", ".join(a)
Traceback (most recent call last):
  File "<stdin>", line 1, in <module>
TypeError: sequence item 3: expected str instance, int found
```

I mention this mainly because many languages, including JavaScript and Ruby, auto-matically convert objects to strings when joining, so this could be considered a minor gotcha in Python for people familiar with such languages.

One solution in Python is to use the **str()** function, which we'll see again in Section 4.1.2:

```
>>> str(42)
'42'
```

Then to complete the **join()** we can use a *generator expression* that returns **str(e)** for each element in the list:

```
>>> ", ".join(str(e) for e in a)
'ant, bat, cat, 42'
```

This somewhat advanced construction is related to *comprehensions*, which we will cover more in Chapter 6.

3.4.5 Exercises

1. To sort a list in reverse order, it's possible to sort and then reverse, but the combined operation is so useful that both **sort()** and **sorted()** support a keyword argument (Section 5.1.2) that does it automatically. Confirm that **a.sort(reverse=True)** and **sorted(a, reverse=True)** both have the effect of sorting and reversing at the same time.

2. Using the list documentation (https://docs.python.org/3/tutorial/datastructures .html), figure out how to insert an element at the beginning of a list.

3. Combine the two lists shown in Listing 3.7 into a single list using the **extend()** method. Does **extend()** mutate **a1**? Does it mutate **a2**?

Listing 3.7: Extending lists.

```
>>> a1 = ["a", "b", "c"]
>>> a2 = [1, 2, 3]
>>> FILL_IN
>>> a1
['a', 'b', 'c', 1, 2, 3]
```

3.5 List Iteration

One of the most common tasks with lists is iterating through their elements and performing an operation with each one. This might sound familiar, since we solved the exact same problem with strings in Section 2.6, and indeed the solution is virtually the same. All we need to do is adapt the **for** loop from Listing 2.27 to lists, i.e., replace **soliloquy** with **a**, as shown in Listing 3.8.

Listing 3.8: Combining list access and a **for** loop.

```
>>> a = ["ant", "bat", "cat", 42]
>>> for i in range(len(a)):     # Not Pythonic
...     print(a[i])
...
ant
bat
cat
42
```

That's convenient, but it's not the best way to iterate through lists, and Mike Vanier still wouldn't be happy (Figure 3.2[5]).

Luckily, looping the Right Way[TM] is easier than it is in most other languages, so we can actually cover it here (unlike in, e.g., *Learn Enough JavaScript to Be Dangerous* (https://www.learnenough.com/javascript), when we had to wait until Chapter 5 (https://www.learnenough.com/javascript-tutorial/functions#sec-iteration_for_each)). The trick is knowing that, as with strings, the default behavior of **for...in** is to return each element in sequence, as shown in Listing 3.9.

---

5. Image © Mike Vanier.

Figure 3.2: Mike Vanier is still annoyed by typing out **for** loops.

Figure 3.3: Avoiding `range(len())` has made Mike Vanier a little happier.

Listing 3.9: Using **for** to iterate over a list the Right Way™.

```
>>> for e in a:      # Pythonic
...     print(e)
...
ant
bat
cat
42
```

Using this style of **for** loop, we can iterate directly through the elements in a list, thereby avoiding having to type out Mike Vanier's *bête noire*, "for (i = 0; i < N; i++)". The result is cleaner code and a happier programmer (Figure 3.3[6]).

By the way, we can use **enumerate()** if for some reason we need the index itself, as shown in Listing 3.10. (If you solved the exercise corresponding to Listing 2.29, the code in Listing 3.10 might look familiar.)

___

6. Image © Mike Vanier.

Listing 3.10: Printing list elements with index.

```
>>> for i, e in enumerate(a):      # Pythonic
...     print(f"a[{i}] = {e}")
...
a[0] = ant
a[1] = bat
a[2] = cat
a[3] = 42
```

Note the final results in Listing 3.10 aren't quite right because we really should show, say, the first element as **"ant"** instead of as **ant**. Fixing this minor blemish is left as an exercise.

Finally, it's possible to break out of a loop early using the **break** keyword (Listing 3.11).

Listing 3.11: Using **break** to interrupt a **for** loop.

```
>>> for i, e in enumerate(a):
...     if e == "cat":
...         print(f"Found the cat at index {i}!")
...         break
...     else:
...         print(f"a[{i}] = {e}")
...
a[0] = ant
a[1] = bat
Found the cat at index 2!
>>>
```

In this case the execution of the loop stops at index 2 and doesn't proceed to any subsequent indices. We'll see a similar construction using the **return** keyword in Section 5.1.

3.5.1 Exercises

1. Use **reversed()** to print out a list's elements in reverse order.

2. We saw in Listing 3.10 that interpolating the values of the list into the string led to printing out, say, **ant** instead of **"ant"**. We could put the quote marks in by hand, but then that would print **42** out as **"42"**, which is also wrong.

Solve this conundrum using the **repr()** function (Section 2.3) to interpolate a representation of each list element, as shown in Listing 3.12.

Listing 3.12: A refinement to Listing 3.10.

```
>>> for i, e in enumerate(a):
...     print(f"a[{i}] = {repr(e)}")
...
???
```

3.6 Tuples and Sets

In addition to lists, Python also supports *tuples*, which are basically lists that can't be changed (i.e., tuples are *immutable*). By the way, I generally say "toople", though you will also hear "tyoople" and "tupple".

We can create literal tuples in much the same way that we created literal lists. The only difference is that tuples use parentheses instead of square brackets:

```
>>> t = ("fox", "dog", "eel")
>>> t
('fox', 'dog', 'eel')
>>> for e in t:
...     print(e)
...
fox
dog
eel
```

We see here that iterating over a tuple uses the same **for...in** syntax used for lists (Listing 3.9).

Because tuples are immutable, trying to change them raises an error:

```
>>> t.append("goat")
Traceback (most recent call last):
  File "<stdin>", line 1, in <module>
AttributeError: 'tuple' object has no attribute 'append'
>>> t.sort()
Traceback (most recent call last):
  File "<stdin>", line 1, in <module>
AttributeError: 'tuple' object has no attribute 'sort'
```

Otherwise, tuples support many of the same operations as lists, such as slicing or non-mutating sorting:

```
>>> t[1:]
('dog', 'eel')
>>> sorted(t)
['dog', 'eel', 'fox']
```

Note in the second case that **sorted()** can take a tuple as an argument but that it returns a list.

By the way, we can also leave off parentheses when defining tuples:

```
>>> u = "fox", "dog", "eel"
>>> u
('fox', 'dog', 'eel')
>>> t == u
True
```

I think this notation is potentially confusing and generally prefer to use parentheses when defining tuples, but you should know about it in case you see it in other people's code. The main exceptions are when simply displaying several variables in the REPL or when doing assignment via so-called *tuple unpacking*, which lets you make multiple assignments at once:

```
>>> a, b, c = t     # Very Pythonic; works for lists, too
>>> a
'fox'
>>> a, b, c         # Tuple to show the variable values
```

Finally, it's worth noting that defining a tuple of one element requires a trailing comma because an object in parentheses alone is just the object itself:

```
>>> ("foo")
'foo'
>>> ("foo",)
('foo',)
```

Python also has native support for *sets*, which correspond closely to the mathematical definition and can be thought of as lists of elements where repeat values are ignored and the order doesn't matter. Sets can be initialized literally using curly braces or by passing a list or a tuple (or in fact any iterable) to the **set()** function:

```
>>> s1 = {1, 2, 3, 4}
>>> s2 = {3, 1, 4, 2}
>>> s3 = set([1, 2, 2, 3, 4, 4])
>>> s1, s2, s3
({1, 2, 3, 4}, {1, 2, 3, 4}, {1, 2, 3, 4})
```

Set equality can be tested with **==** as usual:

```
>>> s1 == s2
True
>>> s2 == s3
True
>>> s1 == s3
True
>>> {1, 2, 3} == {3, 1, 2}
True
```

Sets can also mix types (and can be initialized with a tuple instead of a list):

```
>>> set(("ant", "bat", "cat", 1, 1, "cat"))
{'bat', 'ant', 'cat'}
```

Note that in all cases duplicate values are ignored.

Python sets support many common set operations, such as union and intersection:

```
>>> s1 = {1, 2, "ant", "bat"}
>>> s2 = {2, 3, "bat", "cat"}
>>> s1 | s2    # Set union
{'bat', 1, 2, 'ant', 3, 'cat'}
>>> s1 & s2    # Set intersection
{'bat', 2}
```

See "Sets in Python" (https://realpython.com/python-sets/) for more information.

Because they are unordered, set elements can't be selected directly (how would Python know which set element to pick?) but can be tested for inclusion or iterated over:

```
>>> s = {1, 2, 3, 4}
>>> s[0]
Traceback (most recent call last):
  File "<stdin>", line 1, in <module>
TypeError: 'set' object is not subscriptable
```

```
>>> 3 in s
True
>>> for e in s:
...     print(f"{e} is an element of the set")
...
1 is an element of the set
2 is an element of the set
3 is an element of the set
4 is an element of the set
```

Finally, it's worth noting that, like the empty list, the empty tuple and the empty set are both **False** in a boolean context:

```
>>> bool(())
False
>>> bool(set())
False
```

Note here that, perhaps counterintuitively, we can't use **{}** for the empty set because that combination is reserved for the empty *dictionary*, which we'll discuss in Section 4.4. We also don't have to include a trailing comma in **()**, which is the empty tuple as required.

We can confirm these statements using the **type()** function:

```
>>> type(())
<class 'tuple'>
>>> type({})
<class 'dict'>
>>> type(set())
<class 'set'>
```

Here we see that **()**, **{}**, and **set()** are of class tuple, dictionary, and set, respectively. (We'll discuss more about what a class is in Chapter 7.)

3.6.1 Exercises

1. Confirm the existence of a **tuple()** function by converting **sorted(t)** from a list to a tuple.

2. Create a set with numbers in the range 0–4 by combining **set()** with **range()**. (Recall the use of **range()** in Listing 2.24.) Confirm that the **pop()** method mentioned in Section 3.4.3 allows you to remove one element at a time.

CHAPTER 4

Other Native Objects

Now that we've taken a look at strings and lists (plus tuples and sets), we'll continue with a tour of some other important Python features and objects: math, dates, regular expressions, and dictionaries.

4.1 Math

Like most programming languages, Python supports a large number of mathematical operations:

```
$ source venv/bin/activate
(venv) $ python3
>>> 1 + 1
2
>>> 2 - 3
-1
>>> 2 * 3
6
>>> 10/5
2.0
```

Note that division gives you the answer that you'd expect:

```
>>> 10/4
2.5
>>> 2/3
0.6666666666666666
```

We see here that Python uses *floating-point* division by default. This stands in contrast to some other languages, such as C and Ruby, in which **/** is *integer division* that returns the number of times the denominator goes into the numerator. In other words, **10/4** in a language like C is **2** instead of **2.5**; to perform the same operation in Python, we can use *two* slashes instead of one:

```
>>> 10//4    # Integer division
2
>>> 2//3
0
```

Because of its great numerical capabilities, many programmers, including me, find it convenient to fire up a Python interpreter and use it as a simple calculator when the need arises. It's not fancy, but it's quick and relatively powerful, and the ability to define variables often comes in handy as well.

4.1.1 More Advanced Operations

Python supports more advanced mathematical operations via the **math** object (which is technically a *module*, a special kind of object we'll learn more about starting in Chapter 7). The **math** module has utilities for things like mathematical constants, roots, and trigonometric functions:

```
>>> import math
>>> math.pi
3.141592653589793
>>> math.sqrt(2)
1.4142135623730951
>>> math.cos(0)
1.0
>>> math.cos(2*math.pi)
1.0
```

We see here that the way to use the **math** module is to load it using **import math** and then access the module contents using **math.** (the module name followed by a dot). This is a general pattern with Python modules; the use of the **math.** prefix is known as a *namespace*.

There is one gotcha for those coming from high school (and even college) textbooks that use $\ln x$ for the natural logarithm (base e). Like most other programming languages, Python uses $\log x$ instead:[1]

---

1. It is unclear why introductory math textbooks settled on using $\ln x$ for the natural logarithm when mathematicians generally write it as $\log x$, and even when they write it as $\ln x$ they still often *pronounce* it as "$\log x$".

```
>>> math.log(math.e)
1
>>> math.log(10)
2.302585092994046
```

Mathematicians typically indicate base-ten logarithms using $\log_{10}$, and Python follows suit with **log10**:

```
>>> math.log10(10)
1.0
>>> math.log10(1000000)
6.0
>>> math.log10(1_000_000)
6.0
>>> math.log10(math.e)
0.4342944819032518
```

Note here that we can use underscores in a number as a separator to make it easier to read—thus, **1000000** and **1_000_000** both represent the number one million.

Finally, Python also supports exponentiation via the ****** operator:

```
>>> 2**3
8
>>> math.e**100
2.6881171418161212e+43
```

The final result here, using a number followed by **e+43**, is Python's way of expressing the scientific notation for $e^{100} \approx 2.6881171418161212 \times 10^{43}$.

The **math** documentation (https://docs.python.org/3/library/math.html) includes a more comprehensive list of further operations.

4.1.2 Math to String

We discussed in Chapter 3 how to get from strings to arrays (and vice versa) using **split()** and **join()**. Similarly, Python allows us to convert between numbers and strings.

Probably the most common way to convert from a number to a string is using the **str()** function, which we saw briefly before in Section 3.4.4. For example, Listing 4.1 shows how to use **str()** to convert the circle constant **tau** (Box 4.1 and Figure 4.1) to a string.

Listing 4.1: Using **tau** for the circle constant.

```
>>> math.tau
6.283185307179586
>>> str(math.tau)
'6.283185307179586'
```

Box 4.1: The rise of tau

In the corresponding math sections of *Learn Enough JavaScript to Be Dangerous* (https://www.learnenough.com/javascript) and *Learn Enough Ruby to Be Dangerous* (https://www.learnenough.com/ruby), I had to add the definition of tau by hand, but in Listing 4.1 note that math.tau is part of Python's official math library.

This is a point of particular satisfaction for me, since the use of tau (τ) to represent the circle constant $C/r = 6.283185\ldots$ was proposed in a math essay I published in 2010 called *The Tau Manifesto* (https://tauday.com/tau-manifesto) (which also established the math holiday Tau Day (https://tauday.com/)). Up until that point, the constant C/r had no commonly used name (other than "2π"), but τ has seen increasing adoption over the years, including support in Google's online calculator, Khan Academy, and computer languages such as Microsoft .NET, Julia, and Rust (and of course Python!) (https://tauday.com/state-of-the-tau).

Although adding tau to Python was not without controversy, ultimately it was included in Python 3.6 (and later) as an Easter egg for the kinds of math, science, and computer nerds who enjoy that sort of thing. I hope you might be one of them!

The **str()** function also works on bare numbers:

```
>>> str(6.283185307179586)
'6.283185307179586'
```

To go the other direction, we can use the **int()** ("integer") and **float()** functions:

```
>>> int("6")
6
>>> float("6.283185307179586")
6.283185307179586
```

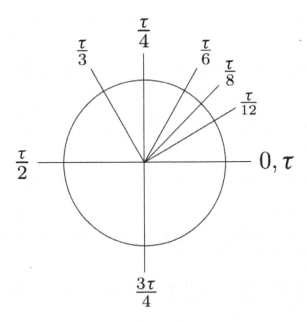

Figure 4.1: Some special angles in terms of $\tau = C/r$.

Be careful not to use **int()** on a string that looks like a **float()**; in many languages, this returns the integer part of the string (so that **"6.28"** and **"6.98"** both yield **6**), but in Python it raises an error:

```
>>> int("6.28")
Traceback (most recent call last):
  File "<stdin>", line 1, in <module>
ValueError: invalid literal for int() with base 10: '6.28'
```

It is valid to call **int()** on a float, though, which has the expected result:

```
>>> int(6.28)
6
>>> int(6.9)
6
```

This means we can convert a string to an integer by calling the two functions in sequence:

```
>>> int(float("6.28"))
6
```

By the way, there's a useful trick to retrieve the result of the previously executed command in the REPL using an underscore _, which represents the value of the previously executed command:

```
>>> float("6.28")
6.28
>>> int(_)
6
```

Finally, it's sometimes convenient to be able to leave off the module name if you're doing lots of calculations with a constant or function. In such cases, you can use the **from <module> import <things>** syntax (Listing 4.2).

Listing 4.2: Importing specific items from a module.

```
>>> from math import sin, cos, tau     # Pythonic
```

This lets us use **sin()**, **cos()**, and **tau** without the **math.** namespace prefix:

```
>>> cos(tau)
1.0
>>> sin(tau/3)
0.8660254037844387
>>> cos(tau/3)
-0.49999999999999983
>>> sin(tau/3)**2 + cos(tau/3)**2
1.0
```

Note that $\cos(\tau/3)$, which is exactly equal to $-\frac{1}{2}$, is displayed as

```
-0.49999999999999983
```

due to numerical roundoff error. (Also, there's nothing special in the last line about $\tau/3$—$\sin^2\theta + \cos^2\theta = 1$ for any angle θ.)

Note: You will sometimes see people import *all* the contents of a module as follows:

```
>>> from math import *    # Dangerous and extremely unPythonic
```

This practice is strongly discouraged because it carries a high risk of *collisions*, where two functions or variables have the same name. Avoiding collisions is part of why, in the words of Tim Peters' "The Zen of Python" (Listing 1.6), "Namespaces are one honking great idea—let's do more of those!"

4.1.3 Exercises

1. What happens when you call **float()** on the string **"1.24e6"**? What about if you call **str()** on the result?

2. Show that **int(6.28)** and **int(6.98)** both equal **6**. This is the same behavior as the *floor function* (written in mathematics as $\lfloor x \rfloor$). Show that Python's **math** module has a **floor()** function with the same effect as **int()**.

4.2 Times and Datetimes

Other frequently used built-in objects are the closely related **time** and **datetime** modules. For example, we can get the current time using the **time()** method:

```
>>> import time
>>> time.time()
1661191145.946213
```

This returns the number of seconds since the *epoch*, defined as January 1, 1970. We can get a more conveniently formatted string using the **ctime()** method (the documentation doesn't say, but this probably stands for "convert time"):

```
>>> time.ctime()
'Mon Aug 22 11:00:32 2022'
```

Python puts a lot of other useful methods in the **datetime** module. As with other Python objects, **datetime** objects include a variety of methods:

```
>>> import datetime
>>> now = datetime.datetime.now()
>>> now.year
```

```
2022
>>> now.month
8
>>> now.day
22
>>> now.hour
16
```

Because many useful methods are defined on the separate **datetime** object within the **datetime** module, it's often more convenient to use **from** to import just that one object (using the same basic syntax seen in Listing 4.2):

```
>>> from datetime import datetime
>>> now = datetime.now()
>>> now.year
2022
>>> now.day
22
>>> now.month
8
>>> now.hour
16
```

This can be a bit confusing, and indeed it's quite unusual for a module to define an object with exactly the same name as the module itself.

It's also possible to initialize **datetime** objects with specific dates and times, such as the first Moon landing (Figure 4.2[2]):

```
>>> moon_landing = datetime(1969, 7, 20, 20, 17, 40)
1969-07-20 20:17:40 -0700
>>> moon_landing.day
20
```

By default, **datetime** uses the local time zone, but this introduces weird location dependence to the operations, so it's a good practice to use UTC instead:[3]

---

2. Image courtesy of Castleski/Shutterstock.

3. For most practical purposes, Coordinated Universal Time (UTC) is the same as Greenwich Mean Time. But why call it UTC? From the NIST Time and Frequency FAQ: **Q:** Why is UTC used as the acronym for Coordinated Universal Time instead of CUT? **A:** In 1970 the Coordinated Universal Time system was devised by an international advisory group of technical experts within the International Telecommunication Union (ITU). The ITU felt it was best to designate a single abbreviation for use in all languages in order to minimize confusion. Since unanimous agreement could not be achieved on using either the English word order, CUT, or the French word order, TUC, the acronym UTC was chosen as a compromise.

Figure 4.2: Buzz Aldrin and Neil Armstrong somehow got to the Moon (and back!) without Python.

```
>>> from datetime import timezone
>>> now = datetime.now(timezone.utc)
>>> print(now)
2022-08-22 18:28:03.943097+00:00
```

To make a **datetime** object for the Moon landing, we need to pass the time zone as a *keyword argument* (first seen in Section 2.3 and discussed further in Section 5.1.2) using **tzinfo** (short for "time zone information"):

```
>>> moon_landing = datetime(1969, 7, 20, 20, 17, 40, tzinfo=timezone.utc)
>>> print(moon_landing)
1969-07-20 20:17:40+00:00
```

Finally, **datetime** objects can be subtracted from each other:

```
>>> print(now - moon_landing)
19390 days, 22:15:36.779053
```

The result here is the number of days, hours, minutes, and seconds since the day and time of the Moon landing. (Your results, of course, will vary, because time marches on, and your value for **datetime.now** will differ.)

You may have noticed that the month and day are returned as *unit-offset* values, which differs from the zero-offset indexing used for lists (Section 3.2). For example, in the eighth month (August), the return value of **now.month()** is **8** rather than **7** (as it would be if months were being treated like indices of a zero-offset list). There is one important value that *is* returned as a zero-offset index, though:

```
>>> moon_landing.weekday()
6
```

Here **weekday** returns the index of the weekday, and because it's zero-offset the **6** index indicates that the Moon landing happened on the seventh day of the week.

We have to be careful here, because in many places (including the United States) day **0** is Sunday, and indeed some programming languages (such as JavaScript and Ruby) follow this convention. But the official international standard is that Monday is the first day, and Python follows this convention instead.

As a result, we can get the name of the day of the week by making a list of strings for the days of the week (assigned to an ALL CAPS identifier, a common Python convention indicating a constant), and then using the return value of **weekday** as an index in the list with the square bracket notation (Section 3.1):

```
>>> DAYNAMES = ["Monday", "Tuesday", "Wednesday",
...             "Thursday", "Friday", "Saturday", "Sunday"]
>>> DAYNAMES[moon_landing.weekday()]
'Sunday'
>>> DAYNAMES[datetime.now().weekday()]
'Monday'
```

(These day names are actually available as part of the **calendar** module via **calendar.day_name**. You just have to run **import calendar** to load the module. See Section 4.2.1 for an example.) Your results for the last line will vary, of course, unless you happen to be reading this on a Monday.

As a final exercise, let's update our Flask hello app from Listing 1.11 with a greeting including the day of the week. The code appears in Listing 4.3, with the result as shown in Figure 4.3. (Refer to Section 1.5 for the commands to run the Flask app.) Note that Listing 4.3 follows the convention of importing system libraries first (e.g., **datetime**), followed by third-party libraries (e.g., **flask**), separated by newlines and followed by two newlines. Fixing the unPythonic location of **DAYNAMES** in Listing 4.3 is left as an exercise (Section 4.2.1).

Listing 4.3: Adding a greeting customized to the day of the week.
hello_app.py

```python
from datetime import datetime

from flask import Flask


app = Flask(__name__)

@app.route("/")
def hello_world():
    # UnPythonic location
```

Figure 4.3: A greeting customized just for today.

```
DAYNAMES = ["Monday", "Tuesday", "Wednesday",
            "Thursday", "Friday", "Saturday", "Sunday"]
dayname = DAYNAMES[datetime.now().weekday()]
return f"<p>Hello, world! Happy {dayname}.</p>"
```

4.2.1 Exercises

1. Use Python to calculate how many seconds after the Moon landing you were born. (Or maybe you were even born *before* the Moon landing—in which case, lucky you! I hope you got to watch it on TV.)

2. Show that Listing 4.3 works even if you pull **DAYNAMES** out of the `hello_world` function, as shown in Listing 4.4. (This is the preferred location for constants in general—under library imports and separated from the rest of the file by two newlines.) Then use the **calendar** module to eliminate the constant entirely (Listing 4.5).

Listing 4.4: Pulling **DAYNAMES** out of the function.
hello_app.py

```
from datetime import datetime

from flask import Flask

DAYNAMES = ["Monday", "Tuesday", "Wednesday",
            "Thursday", "Friday", "Saturday", "Sunday"]


app = Flask(__name__)

@app.route("/")
def hello_world():
    dayname = DAYNAMES[datetime.now().weekday()]
    return f"<p>Hello, world! Happy {dayname}.</p>"
```

Listing 4.5: Using the built-in day names.
hello_app.py

```
from datetime import datetime
import calendar
```

```
from flask import Flask


app = Flask(__name__)

@app.route("/")
def hello_world():
    dayname = calendar.day_name[datetime.now().weekday()]
    return f"<p>Hello, world! Happy {dayname}.</p>"
```

4.3 Regular Expressions

Python has full support for *regular expressions*, often called *regexes* or *regexps* for short, which are a powerful mini-language for matching patterns in text. A full mastery of regular expressions is beyond the scope of this book (and perhaps beyond the scope of human ability), but the good news is that there are many resources available for learning about them incrementally. (Some such resources are mentioned in "Grepping" (https://www.learnenough.com/command-line-tutorial/inspecting_files#sec-grepping) in *Learn Enough Command Line to Be Dangerous* (https://www.learnenough.com/command-line) and "Global find and replace" in *Learn Enough Text Editor to Be Dangerous* (https://www.learnenough.com/text-editor-tutorial/advanced_text_editing#sec-global_find_and_replace).) The most important thing to know about is the general idea of regular expressions; you can fill in the details as you go along.

Regexes are notoriously terse and error-prone; as programmer Jamie Zawinski famously said:

> Some people, when confronted with a problem, think "I know, I'll use regular expressions."
> Now they have two problems.

Luckily, this situation is greatly ameliorated by web applications like regex101, which let us build up regexes interactively (Figure 4.4). Moreover, such resources typically include a quick reference to assist us in finding the code for matching particular patterns (Figure 4.5).

Note that regex101 includes Python-specific regexes (which you can tell has been selected in Figure 4.4 due to the **Python** line having a checkmark next to it). In practice, languages differ little in their implementation of regular expressions, but it's wise to use the correct language-specific settings when available, and always to double-check when moving a regex to a different language.

Figure 4.4: An online regex builder.

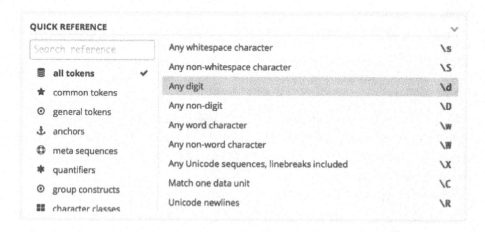

Figure 4.5: A close-up of the regex reference.

Figure 4.6: 90210 (Beverly Hills) is one of the most expensive ZIP codes in America.

Let's take a look at some simple regex matches in Python. A basic regex consists of a sequence of characters that matches a particular pattern. We can create a new regex using a string, which is nearly always a raw string (Section 2.2.2) so that it handles special characters like backslashes automatically. For example, here's a regex that matches standard American ZIP codes (Figure 4.6[4]), consisting of five digits in a row:

```
>>> zip_code = r"\d{5}"
```

If you use regular expressions a lot, eventually you'll memorize many of these rules, but you can always look them up in a quick reference (Figure 4.5).

Now let's see how to tell if a string matches a regex. The way to do this in Python is with the **re** module, which includes a **search** method:

```
>>> import re
>>> re.search(zip_code, "no match")
```

---

4. Image courtesy of 4kclips/123RF.

Here **re.search** returned **None** (which we can infer from the REPL not showing any result), indicating no match. Because **None** is **False** in a boolean context (Section 2.4.2), we can use this result with **if**:

```
>>> if re.search(zip_code, "no match"):
...     print("It's got a ZIP code!")
... else:
...     print("No match!")
...
No match!
```

Now let's take a look at a valid match:

```
>>> re.search(zip_code, "Beverly Hills 90210")
<re.Match object; span=(14, 19), match='90210'>
```

This result is a somewhat cryptic **re.Match** object; in practice, its main use is in boolean contexts as above, like this:

```
>>> if re.search(zip_code, "Beverly Hills 90210"):
...     print("It's got a ZIP code!")
... else:
...     print("No match!")
...
It's got a ZIP code!
```

Another common and instructive regex operation involves creating a list of *all* the matches. We'll start by defining a longer string, one with two ZIP codes (Figure 4.7[5]):

```
>>> s = "Beverly Hills 90210 was a '90s TV show set in Los Angeles."
>>> s += " 91125 is another ZIP code in the Los Angeles area."
>>> s
"Beverly Hills 90210 was a '90s TV show set in Los Angeles. 91125 is another
 ZIP code in the Los Angeles area."
```

You should be able to use your technical sophistication (Box 1.2) to infer what the **+=** operator does here if you haven't seen it before (which might involve doing a quick Google search).

---

5. Image courtesy of Kitleong/123RF.

Figure 4.7: 91125 is a dedicated ZIP code for the campus of the California Institute of Technology (Caltech).

To find out whether the string matches the regex, we can use the **findall()** method to find a list of matches:

```
>>> re.findall(zip_code, s)
['90210', '91125']
```

It's also easy to use a literal regex directly, such as this **findall()** to find all multi-letter words that are in ALL CAPS:

```
>>> re.findall(r"[A-Z]{2,}", s)
['TV', 'ZIP']
```

See if you can find the rules in Figure 4.5 used to make the regex above.

4.3.1 Splitting on Regexes

Our final example of regexes combines the power of pattern matching with the **split** method we saw in Section 3.1. In that section, we saw how to split on spaces, like this:

```
>>> "ant bat cat duck".split(" ")
['ant', 'bat', 'cat', 'duck']
```

We can obtain the same result in a more robust way by splitting on whitespace. Consulting the quick reference (Figure 4.5), we find that the regex for whitespace is **\s**, and the way to indicate "one or more" is with the plus sign **+**. Thus, we can split on whitespace as follows:

```
>>> re.split(r"\s+", "ant bat cat duck")
["ant", "bat", "cat", "duck"]
```

The reason this is so nice is that now we can get the same result if the strings are separated by multiple spaces, tabs, newlines, etc.:

```
>>> re.split(r"\s+", "ant    bat\tcat\nduck")
["ant", "bat", "cat", "duck"]
```

As we saw in Section 3.1, this pattern is so useful that it's actually the default behavior for **split()**. When we call **split()** with zero arguments, Python splits on whitespace automatically:

```
>>> "ant    bat\tcat\nduck".split()
["ant", "bat", "cat", "duck"]
```

4.3.2 Exercises

1. Write a regex that matches the extended-format ZIP code consisting of five digits, a hyphen, and a four-digit extension (such as 10118-0110). Confirm that it works using **re.search()** and the caption in Figure 4.8.[6]

2. Write a regex that splits only on newlines. Such regexes are useful for splitting a block of text into separate lines. In particular, test your regex by pasting the poem in Listing 4.6 into the console and using **sonnet.split(/your regex/)**. What is the length of the resulting list?

Listing 4.6: Some text with newlines.

```
sonnet = """Let me not to the marriage of true minds
Admit impediments. Love is not love
Which alters when it alteration finds,
```

---

6. Image courtesy of Jordi2r/123RF.

Figure 4.8: ZIP code 10118-0110 (the Empire State Building).

```
Or bends with the remover to remove.
O no, it is an ever-fixed mark
That looks on tempests and is never shaken
It is the star to every wand'ring bark,
Whose worth's unknown, although his height be taken.
Love's not time's fool, though rosy lips and cheeks
Within his bending sickle's compass come:
Love alters not with his brief hours and weeks,
But bears it out even to the edge of doom.
    If this be error and upon me proved,
    I never writ, nor no man ever loved."""
```

4.4 Dictionaries

Our final example of a simple Python data type is a *dictionary*, which in most other languages is called a *hash* or an *associative array*. You can think of dictionaries as being like lists but with generic labels rather than integers as indices, so instead of **a[0] = 0** we could have **d["name"] = "Michael"**. Each element is thus a pair of values: a label (the *key*) and an element of any type (the *value*). These elements are also known as *key–value pairs*, much like language dictionaries consist of words (keys) and their associated definitions (values).

The most familiar choice for key labels is strings (Chapter 2); indeed, this is by far the most common choice in languages that support associative arrays. We'll thus focus on creating dictionaries using string keys. As a simple example, let's create an object to store the first and last names of a user, such as we might have in a web application:

```
>>> user = {}                       # {} is an empty dictionary.
>>> user["first_name"] = "Michael"  # Key "first_name", value "Michael"
>>> user["last_name"] = "Hartl"     # Key "last_name", value "Hartl"
```

As you can see, an empty dictionary is represented by curly braces, which is why we needed to use **set()** in Section 3.6 for an empty set. We can also assign values using the same square bracket syntax as for lists. We can retrieve values in the same way:

```
>>> user["first_name"]     # Element access is like lists
'Michael'
>>> user["last_name"]
'Hartl'
>>> user["nonexistent"]
Traceback (most recent call last):
  File "<stdin>", line 1, in <module>
KeyError: 'nonexistent
```

Note in the last example that dictionaries raise an error when the key doesn't exist. This won't generally happen when iterating over keys (Section 4.4.1), but in contexts where you don't know whether the key exists the **get()** method is more convenient:

```
>>> user.get("last_name")
'Hartl'
>>> user.get("nonexistent")
>>> repr(user.get("nonexistent"))
'None'
```

Here we've included a call to **repr()** just to emphasize that the result of **get()** is **None** when the key is nonexistent since the REPL won't generally display it.

If we take a look at how dictionaries are represented, we see that they consist of keys and values separated by colons:

```
>>> user
{'first_name': 'Michael', 'last_name': 'Hartl'}
```

It is possible (and often convenient) to use this syntax to define dictionaries directly:

```
>>> moonman = {"first_name": "Buzz", "last_name": "Aldrin"}
>>> moonman
{'first_name': 'Buzz', 'last_name': 'Aldrin'}
```

Let's take a look at a bigger dictionary consisting of keys equal to prominent moonwalkers and values corresponding to the dates of their first moonwalks:

```
>>> moonwalks = {"Neil Armstrong": 1969,
...              "Buzz Aldrin": 1969,
...              "Alan Shepard": 1971,
...              "Eugene Cernan": 1972,
...              "Michael Jackson": 1983}
```

We can look at the keys and values separately, which (as of Python 3.6 and later) are stored *in order* in special-purpose Python objects:

```
>>> moonwalks.keys()
dict_keys(['Neil Armstrong', 'Buzz Aldrin', 'Alan Shepard',
 'Eugene Cernan', 'Michael Jackson'])
>>> moonwalks.values()
dict_values([1969, 1969, 1971, 1972, 1983])
```

Note that earlier versions of Python didn't order dictionary elements, so you should take care when making any assumptions about ordering.

Like a list index, a dictionary key maps to only one value at a time. This means that we can replace the value corresponding to a key but we can't have two identical keys. As a result, it's sometimes useful to think of dictionary keys as being like an ordered set, since (like sets) they can't have repeated elements. Indeed, the special-purpose **keys()** object mentioned above, technically known as a *view*, can be treated like a set in some contexts; for example, the following code performs a set intersection as in Section 3.6:

```
>>> apollo_11 = {"Neil Armstrong", "Buzz Aldrin"}
>>> moonwalks.keys() & apollo_11
{'Neil Armstrong', 'Buzz Aldrin'}
```

By the way, we can test for the inclusion of a particular dictionary key using the same **in** keyword that works for lists (Section 3.4.1):

```
>>> "Buzz Aldrin" in moonwalks
True
```

Note here that we can omit the **keys()** part and just use **in** with the full dictionary. We'll see another example of this convention in Section 4.4.1.

4.4.1 Dictionary Iteration

As with lists, tuples, and sets, one of the most common dictionary tasks is iterating over the elements. You might be tempted to iterate over the keys as follows:

```
>>> for key in moonwalks.keys():     # Not Pythonic
...     print(f"{key} first performed a moonwalk in {moonwalks[key]}.")
...
Neil Armstrong first performed a moonwalk in 1969
Buzz Aldrin first performed a moonwalk in 1969
Alan Shepard first performed a moonwalk in 1971
Eugene Cernan first performed a moonwalk in 1972
Michael Jackson first performed a moonwalk in 1983
```

As noted in the comment, this isn't Pythonic. The reason is that iterating over the keys is the default:

```
>>> for key in moonwalks:              # Somewhat Pythonic
...     print(f"{key} first performed a moonwalk in {moonwalks[key]}.")
...
Neil Armstrong first performed a moonwalk in 1969
Buzz Aldrin first performed a moonwalk in 1969
Alan Shepard first performed a moonwalk in 1971
Eugene Cernan first performed a moonwalk in 1972
Michael Jackson first performed a moonwalk in 1983
```

This is somewhat Pythonic, but when using both keys and values (as we are here) it's even better to iterate over the dictionary's **items()**:

```
>>> moonwalks.items()
dict_items([('Neil Armstrong', 1969), ('Buzz Aldrin', 1969), ('Alan
Shepard', 1971), ('Eugene Cernan', 1972), ('Michael Jackson', 1983)])
```

This leads to the elegant iteration shown in Listing 4.7.

Listing 4.7: Iterating through a dictionary's `items()`.

```
>>> for name, year in moonwalks.items():   # Pythonic
...     print(f"{name} first performed a moonwalk in {year}")
...
Neil Armstrong first performed a moonwalk in 1969
Buzz Aldrin first performed a moonwalk in 1969
Alan Shepard first performed a moonwalk in 1971
Eugene Cernan first performed a moonwalk in 1972
Michael Jackson first performed a moonwalk in 1983
```

Note that we've also changed to meaningful names in Listing 4.7, using **name, year** in preference to the less specific **key, value**.

4.4.2   Merging Dictionaries

One common operation is *merging* dictionaries, where the elements of two dictionaries are combined into one. For example, consider two dictionaries consisting of academic subjects with corresponding test scores:

```
>>> tests1 = {"Math": 75, "Physics": 99}
>>> tests2 = {"History": 77, "English": 93}
```

It would be nice to be able to create a **tests** dictionary combining all four subject–score combinations.

Older versions of Python didn't natively support merging dictionaries at all, but Python 3.5 added this ****** syntax:

```
>>> {**tests1, **tests2}    # Kind of Pythonic
{'Math': 75, 'Physics': 99, 'History': 77, 'English': 93}
```

That's pretty strange-looking syntax if you ask me, and it's included here mainly because you might encounter it in other people's code. Luckily, as of Python 3.9 there's a great way to merge dictionaries using the pipe operator **|**:

```
>>> tests1 | tests2        # Very Pythonic
{'Math': 75, 'Physics': 99, 'History': 77, 'English': 93}
```

When the dictionaries have no overlapping keys, merging them simply involves combining all key–value pairs. But if the second dictionary does have one or more keys in common, then its values take precedence. In this case, we can think of *updating* the first dictionary with the contents of the second.[7] For example, suppose we combine the tests into a single variable using a merge:

```
>>> test_scores = tests1 | tests2
{'Math': 75, 'Physics': 99, 'History': 77, 'English': 93}
```

Now suppose the student is allowed to retake tests for the two lowest scores:

```
>>> retests = {"Math": 97, "History": 94}
```

At this point, we can update the original test scores with the updated values from the retests (Listing 4.8).

Listing 4.8: Updating a dictionary using a merge.

```
>>> test_scores | retests
{'Math': 97, 'Physics': 99, 'History': 94, 'English': 93}
```

We see that the **"Math"** and **"History"** scores have been updated with the values from the second dictionary.

4.4.3 Exercises

1. Define a dictionary for a **user** with three attributes (keys): **"username"**, **"password"**, and **"password_confirmation"**. How would you test if the password matches the confirmation?

2. We've seen in Listing 2.29 and Listing 3.10 that Python strings and lists support an **enumerate()** function in cases where we need the iteration index. Confirm that we can do the same thing with dictionaries using code like Listing 4.9.

---

7. For this reason, dictionary (or, rather, hash) merges in Ruby use the **update** method.

3. By reversing the elements in Listing 4.8, show that dictionary merges aren't symmetric, so **d1 | d2** is not in general the same as **d2 | d1**. When are they the same?

Listing 4.9: Using **enumerate()** with a dictionary.

```
>>> for i, (name, year) in enumerate(moonwalks.items()):    # Pythonic
...     print(f"{i+1}. {name} first performed a moonwalk in {year}")
...
1. Neil Armstrong first performed a moonwalk in 1969
2. Buzz Aldrin first performed a moonwalk in 1969
3. Alan Shepard first performed a moonwalk in 1971
4. Eugene Cernan first performed a moonwalk in 1972
5. Michael Jackson first performed a moonwalk in 1983
```

4.5 Application: Unique Words

Let's apply the dictionaries from Section 4.4 to a challenging exercise, consisting of our longest program so far. Our task is to extract all the unique words in a fairly long piece of text, and count how many times each word appears.

Because the sequence of commands is rather extensive, our main tool will be a Python file (Section 1.3), executed using the **python3** command. (We're not going to make it a self-contained shell script as in Section 1.4 because we don't intend for this to be a general-purpose utility program.) At each stage, I suggest using Python to execute the code interactively if you have any question about the effects of a given command.

Let's start by creating our file:

```
(venv) $ touch count.py
```

Now fill it with a string containing the text, which we'll choose to be Shakespeare's Sonnet 116[8] (Figure 4.9[9]), as borrowed from Listing 4.6 and shown again in Listing 4.10.

---

8. Note that in the original pronunciation used in Shakespeare's time, words like "love" and "remove" rhymed, as did "come" and "doom".

9. Image courtesy of Psychoshadowmaker/123RF.

Figure 4.9: Sonnet 116 compares love's constancy to the guide star for a wandering bark (ship).

Listing 4.10: Adding some text.

count.py

```
import re


sonnet = """"Let me not to the marriage of true minds
Admit impediments. Love is not love
Which alters when it alteration finds,
Or bends with the remover to remove.
O no, it is an ever-fixed mark
That looks on tempests and is never shaken
It is the star to every wand'ring bark,
Whose worth's unknown, although his height be taken.
Love's not time's fool, though rosy lips and cheeks
Within his bending sickle's compass come:
Love alters not with his brief hours and weeks,
But bears it out even to the edge of doom.
    If this be error and upon me proved,
    I never writ, nor no man ever loved."""
```

Our plan will be to use a dictionary called **uniques** with keys equal to the unique words and values equal to the number of occurrences in the text:

```
uniques = {}
```

For the purposes of this exercise, we'll define a "word" as a run of one or more *word characters* (i.e., letters or numbers, though there are none of the latter in the present text). This match can be accomplished with a regular expression (Section 4.3), which includes a pattern (**\w**) for exactly this case (Figure 4.5):

```
words = re.findall(r"\w+", sonnet)
```

This uses the **findall()** method from Section 4.3 to return a list of all the strings that match "one or more word characters in a row". (Extending this pattern to include apostrophes (so that it matches, e.g., "wand'ring" as well) is left as an exercise (Section 4.5.1).)

At this point, the file should look like Listing 4.11.

Listing 4.11: Adding an object and the matching words.
count.py

```
import re


sonnet = """Let me not to the marriage of true minds
Admit impediments. Love is not love
Which alters when it alteration finds,
Or bends with the remover to remove.
O no, it is an ever-fixed mark
That looks on tempests and is never shaken
It is the star to every wand'ring bark,
Whose worth's unknown, although his height be taken.
Love's not time's fool, though rosy lips and cheeks
Within his bending sickle's compass come:
Love alters not with his brief hours and weeks,
But bears it out even to the edge of doom.
    If this be error and upon me proved,
    I never writ, nor no man ever loved."""

uniques = {}
words = re.findall(r"\w+", sonnet)
```

Now for the heart of our program. We're going to iterate through the **words** list and do the following:

1. If the word already has an entry in the **uniques** object, increment its count by **1**.
2. If the word doesn't have an entry yet in **uniques**, initialize it to **1**.

The result, using the **+=** operator we met briefly in Section 4.3, looks like this:

```
for word in words:
    if word in uniques:
        uniques[word] += 1
    else:
        uniques[word] = 1
```

Finally, we'll print out the result to the terminal:

```
print(uniques)
```

The full program (with added comments) appears as in Listing 4.12.

Listing 4.12: A program to count words in text.

count.py

```
sonnet = """Let me not to the marriage of true minds
Admit impediments. Love is not love
Which alters when it alteration finds,
Or bends with the remover to remove.
O no, it is an ever-fixed mark
That looks on tempests and is never shaken
It is the star to every wand'ring bark,
Whose worth's unknown, although his height be taken.
Love's not time's fool, though rosy lips and cheeks
Within his bending sickle's compass come:
Love alters not with his brief hours and weeks,
But bears it out even to the edge of doom.
    If this be error and upon me proved,
    I never writ, nor no man ever loved."""

# Unique words
uniques = {}
# All words in the text
words = re.findall(r"\w+", sonnet)

# Iterate through `words` and build up a dictionary of unique words.
```

```
for word in words:
    if word in uniques:
        uniques[word] += 1
    else:
        uniques[word] = 1

print(uniques)
```

The result of running **count.py** in the terminal looks something like this:

```
(venv) $ python3 count.py
{'Let': 1, 'me': 2, 'not': 4, 'to': 4, 'the': 4, 'marriage': 1, 'of': 2,
'true': 1, 'minds': 1, 'Admit': 1, 'impediments': 1, 'Love': 3, 'is': 4,
'love': 1, 'Which': 1, 'alters': 2, 'when': 1, 'it': 3, 'alteration': 1,
'finds': 1, 'Or': 1, 'bends': 1, 'with': 2, 'remover': 1, 'remove': 1,
'O': 1, 'no': 2, 'an': 1, 'ever': 2, 'fixed': 1, 'mark': 1, 'That': 1,
'looks': 1, 'on': 1, 'tempests': 1, 'and': 4, 'never': 2, 'shaken': 1,
'It': 1, 'star': 1, 'every': 1, 'wand': 1, 'ring': 1, 'bark': 1, 'Whose': 1,
'worth': 1, 's': 4, 'unknown': 1, 'although': 1, 'his': 3, 'height': 1,
'be': 2, 'taken': 1, 'time': 1, 'fool': 1, 'though': 1, 'rosy': 1, 'lips': 1,
'cheeks': 1, 'Within': 1, 'bending': 1, 'sickle': 1, 'compass': 1, 'come': 1,
'brief': 1, 'hours': 1, 'weeks': 1, 'But': 1, 'bears': 1, 'out': 1, 'even': 1,
'edge': 1, 'doom': 1, 'If': 1, 'this': 1, 'error': 1, 'upon': 1, 'proved': 1,
'I': 1, 'writ': 1, 'nor': 1, 'man': 1, 'loved': 1}
```

This constitutes a good example of a solution "by hand" that is reasonably Pythonic but has a version that is even more Pythonic, though also substantially more advanced (Section 4.5.1). As noted in Box 1.1, "Pythonic" is a sliding scale, and the program in Listing 4.12 is an excellent start.

4.5.1 Exercises

1. Extend the regex used in Listing 4.12 to include an apostrophe, so it matches, e.g., "wand'ring". *Hint*: Combine the first reference regex at regex101 (Figure 4.10) with \w, an apostrophe, and the plus operator **+**.

2. By running the code in Listing 4.13, show that we can effectively replicate the results of Listing 4.12 using the powerful **Counter()** function from the Python **collections** module. See this excellent video (https://www.youtube.com/watch?v=8OKTAedgFYg&t=364s) for more detail on this subject.

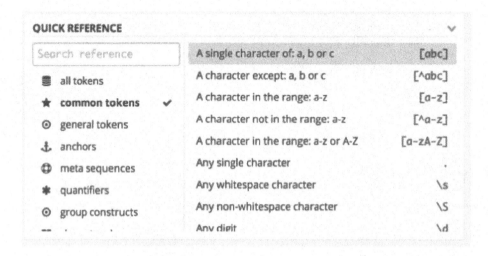

Figure 4.10: An exercise hint.

Listing 4.13: Using the powerful **Counter()** function.

```python
import re

from collections import Counter


sonnet = """Let me not to the marriage of true minds
Admit impediments. Love is not love
Which alters when it alteration finds,
Or bends with the remover to remove.
O no, it is an ever-fixed mark
That looks on tempests and is never shaken
It is the star to every wand'ring bark,
Whose worth's unknown, although his height be taken.
Love's not time's fool, though rosy lips and cheeks
Within his bending sickle's compass come:
Love alters not with his brief hours and weeks,
But bears it out even to the edge of doom.
    If this be error and upon me proved,
    I never writ, nor no man ever loved."""

words = re.findall(r"\w+", sonnet)
print(Counter(words))
```

CHAPTER **5**

Functions and Iterators

So far in this tutorial, we've seen several examples of Python functions, which are one of the most important ideas in Python, and indeed in all of computing. In this chapter, we'll learn how to define functions of our own (Figure 5.1). We'll also learn a bit more about iterators (mentioned briefly in Section 3.4.2), both because Python often uses such objects as the return values of built-in functions and because they're important in their own right.

In case you're not running the Python shell already, you should activate the virtual environment and start the REPL as usual:

```
$ source venv/bin/activate
(venv) $ python3
```

Figure 5.1: Time to level up.

5.1 Function Definitions

As we've seen with functions like **print()** (Section 2.3), **len()** (Section 2.4), and **sorted()** and **reversed()** (Section 3.4.2), function calls in Python consist of a *name* and zero or more arguments in parentheses:

```
print("hello, world!")
```

One of the most important tasks in programming involves defining our own functions, which in Python can be done using the **def** keyword. (As discussed in Section 2.5, functions attached to objects (such as **split()** and **islower()**) are also called *methods*. We'll learn how to define methods of our own in Chapter 7.)

Let's take a look at a simple example of a function definition in the REPL. We'll start with a function that takes a single numerical argument and returns the square, as shown in Listing 5.1.[1]

Listing 5.1: Defining a function.

```
>>> def square(x):
...     return x*x
...
>>> square(10)
100
```

(Here we could also use **x**2**, which would be the same thing.) The function ends with the **return** keyword followed by the return value for the function.

In the case of **square()**, the ending of the function was also the beginning because it's only one line. But, as you might expect, a function can also consist of multiple steps, such as the function shown in Listing 5.2 to return a list of squares from **0** up to **(n-1)**2** (in accordance with the usual behavior of **range()**).

Listing 5.2: Returning a list of squares.

```
>>> def squares_list(n):
...     squares = []
...     for i in range(n+1):
...         squares.append(i**2)
...     return squares
...
>>> squares_list(11)
[0, 1, 4, 9, 16, 25, 36, 49, 64, 81, 100]
```

Listing 5.2 includes a common pattern of initializing a variable, changing it, and then returning the changed value. We'll see how to replace this pattern with a more compact version in Chapter 6.

---

1. Python doesn't have a type mechanism to enforce, say, numerical arguments to functions. There is a **typing** library, though, with support for type hints.

It's worth noting that **return** acts immediately, much like the **break** keyword we saw in Listing 3.11, so we can use it to interrupt a loop. Indeed, **return** interrupts the entire *function*, so as soon as Python sees an occurrence of **return** it leaves the function entirely. For example, we can write a function to return the first number in a list bigger than 10, or **None** if no such number exists, as shown in Listing 5.3.

Listing 5.3: Using **return** to return immediately from a **for** loop.

```
>>> def bigger_than_10(numbers):
...     for n in numbers:
...         if n > 10:
...             return n
...     return None
...
>>> bigger_than_10(squares_list(11))
16
```

Note that we've included an explicit **return None** in Listing 5.3, but in fact returning **None** is the default, so you can actually leave that step off. We'll include it for now but we'll drop it starting in Listing 5.21.

Now that we've seen a few example functions, let's write a function that we'll actually use in an application—in this case, the Flask web app created in Section 1.5. In particular, we'll define a function called **dayname()** that takes a single **datetime** argument (Section 4.2) and returns the day of the week represented by the given time.

Recall from Section 4.2 that a **datetime** object has a method called **weekday()** representing the (zero-offset) index of the day of the week:

```
>>> from datetime import datetime
>>> now = datetime.now()
>>> now.weekday()
3
```

In that same section, we mentioned briefly that the **calendar** library includes an object for the days of the week:

```
>>> import calendar
>>> calendar.day_name
<calendar._localized_day object at 0x100f13910>
>>> list(calendar.day_name)
['Monday', 'Tuesday', 'Wednesday', 'Thursday', 'Friday', 'Saturday', 'Sunday']
```

Here we've used the **list()** function to convert the "localized day" object into a list for easier viewing.

The **day_name** object allows us to find the day of the week as follows:

```
>>> list(calendar.day_name)[0]
'Monday'
```

Here we've used a bracket with an index to access the corresponding element of the list (Section 3.2), but it turns out you can use the same syntax with the "localized day" object directly:

```
>>> calendar.day_name[0]
'Monday'
```

This is exactly the kind of behavior you might not have been able to guess ahead of time, and is a great example of the value of the REPL for experimentation (a key component of technical sophistication (Box 1.2)).

Putting **weekday()** and **day_name** together lets us find the day of the week corresponding to the numerical index:

```
>>> calendar.day_name[datetime.now().weekday()]
'Thursday'
```

This works just fine, but it is getting rather long. It would be convenient to *encapsulate* this definition and logic in a **dayname()** function, so that we could write

```
dayname(datetime.now())
```

By combining the elements above, we can accomplish this as shown in Listing 5.4.

Listing 5.4: Defining **dayname()** in the REPL.

```
>>> def dayname(time):
...     """Return the name of the day of the week for the given time."""
...     return calendar.day_name[time.weekday()]
...
>>>
```

We see in Listing 5.4 that a Python function starts with the **def** keyword followed by the function name and any arguments; next, there's an optional but highly recommended *docstring* (not usually used in the REPL but included here for reasons we'll see in a moment); then, there's the function *body*, which determines the return value of the function using the **return** keyword (which in this case is the *only* line in the body, not counting the docstring); finally, the function is ended by a newline. Note that this final fact contrasts with nearly all other programming languages, which typically end function definitions with a closing curly brace (e.g., C, C++, Perl, PHP, Java, and JavaScript), a closing parenthesis (most varieties of Lisp), or a special keyword like **end** (e.g., Ruby).

We can test the newly defined function as follows:

```
>>> dayname(datetime.now())
'Thursday'
```

This might not seem like a big improvement, but note that it's conceptually simpler because we don't have to think about the implementation (i.e., finding the element of an object corresponding to the value of **weekday()**). This sort of *abstraction layer* between function name and implementation is useful even if the function definition is only one or two lines. (Indeed, I consider one- or two-line functions to be a sign of good program design.) We'll put this function to good use in Section 5.2 to simplify the customized greeting in our hello app (Listing 4.3).

As noted in Section 2.1, including a triple-quoted docstring as in Listing 5.4 is a standard practice with Python functions.[2] In addition to being useful to people reading the code, the docstring itself is available in the REPL via the **help()** function:

```
>>> help(dayname)
```

The result of running **help()** is system-dependent; on my system, running **help(dayname)** in a terminal gives the result shown in Figure 5.2. (This uses the **less** interface covered (https://www.learnenough.com/command-line-tutorial/inspecting_files#sec-less_is_more) in *Learn Enough Command Line to Be Dangerous* (https://www.learnenough.com/command-line), so I typed **q** to quit.)

---

2. Python docstrings typically use the imperative mood, so "Return the name" rather than "Returns the name".

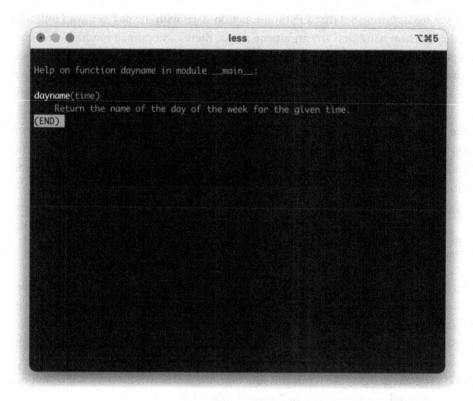

Figure 5.2: The result of running `help(dayname)`.

As previously noted, we wouldn't ordinarily include a docstring in a function defined in the REPL, but we included it in Listing 5.4 so that we could illustrate `help()` as in Figure 5.2. Because built-in Python functions generally define docstrings, using `help()` in the REPL is useful with them as well (Section 5.1.3).

5.1.1 First-Class Functions

One possibly surprising feature of Python functions is that they can be treated as regular variables in many ways (sometimes referred to as *first-class objects*). For example, let's take another look at the `square()` function defined in Listing 5.1:

```
>>> def square(x):
...     return x*x
...
>>> square(10)
100
```

We can actually assign this to a new variable and call it just as before:

```
>>> pow2 = square
>>> pow2(7)
49
```

Perhaps even cooler, we can pass functions as arguments to other functions. For example, we can create a function to apply another function and then add 1 like this:

```
>>> def function_adder(x, f):
...     return f(x) + 1
...
>>>
```

We can then pass **square** as an argument (*without* parentheses, so not **square()**):

```
>>> function_adder(10, square)
101
```

Built-in Python functions work the same way:

```
>>> import math
>>> function_adder(100, math.log10)
3.0
```

This last result follows because $\log_{10} 100 = \log_{10} 10^2 = 2$ and $2 + 1 = 3$. (Why does Python display it as **3.0**?)[3]

5.1.2 Variable and Keyword Arguments

In addition to regular arguments, Python functions support variable-length arguments and keyword arguments. While we won't need to define functions with these sorts

---

3. *Answer*: The **math.log10()** function returns floating-point values rather than integers.

of arguments in this tutorial, we will need them in a few places since many built-in Python functions use them. They are also valuable for more advanced work in Python. Let's take a quick look at how they work.

Suppose we define a function **foo()** with two arguments, **bar** and **baz**:

```
>>> def foo(bar, baz):
...     print((bar, baz))
...
>>> foo("hello", "world")
('hello', 'world')
```

Here we've printed out a tuple (Section 3.6) of the two arguments as a way of showing what their values are.

But what if we didn't know how many arguments we wanted? For example, this won't work:

```
>>> foo("hello", "world", "good day!")
  File "<stdin>", line 1, in <module>
TypeError: foo() takes 2 positional arguments but 3 were given
```

Python supports a variable number of arguments via the special asterisk or "star" syntax ***args** (often pronounced "star args"):[4]

```
>>> def foo(*args):
...     print(args)
...
>>> foo("hello", "world", "good day!")
('hello', 'world', 'good day!')
```

We see here that Python has automatically created a tuple of the arguments, which works for any number:

```
>>> foo("This", "is a bunch", "of arguments", "to the function")
('This', 'is a bunch', 'of arguments', 'to the function')
```

A related construction uses a double-asterisk or double-star syntax for *keywords*, which are key–value pairs separated with an equals sign. The analogue of ***args** in

---

4. You could use ***anything**, but ***args** is conventional.

this case is called ****kwargs** (often pronounced "star star kwargs" or "star star keyword args"); if ***args** results in a tuple, see if you can guess what ****kwargs** does:

```
>>> def foo(**kwargs):
...     print(kwargs)
...
>>> foo(a="hello", b="world", bar="good day!")
{'a': 'hello', 'b': 'world', 'bar': 'good day!'}
```

As you might have guessed, ****kwargs** automatically converts the key–value pairs in the argument into Python's standard data type for such pairs, namely, a dictionary (Section 4.4).

One common pattern is to combine ***args** and ****kwargs**, resulting in the ability to accept a large variety of argument types. A simple example appears in Section 5.1.3.

5.1.3   Exercises

1. Run **help(len)** in the Python interpreter to confirm that **help()** works on built-in functions as well. What is the result of running the command **help(print)**? (The result in this case is called a multi-line docstring.)

2. Define a **deriver()** function as shown in Listing 5.5 that takes in a function and returns how much it changes over a small interval **h**. Confirm that you get the result shown for the **square()** function mentioned at the beginning of Section 5.1.1 (which was first defined in Listing 5.1). What is the result of evaluating **deriver(math.cos, math.tau/2)**?[5]

3. Define a function **foo()** with both ***args** and ****kwargs** as shown in Listing 5.6. What do you get when you execute the function as shown in the final statement of Listing 5.6? (Note that you should not type **. . .** in the call to **foo()**; as we have seen when defining functions, those are continuation characters added automatically by the Python interpreter.)

---

5. Some alert readers may recognize **deriver()** as the quotient that approaches the derivative as $h \to 0$. Since the derivative of $\cos x$ is 0 at $\tau/2$ (corresponding to a minimum), the value of **deriver(math.cos, math.tau/2)** should be close to 0 as well. The derivative of x^2, meanwhile, is $2x$, which accounts for the value shown in Listing 5.5 for the **square()** function when $x = 3$.

Listing 5.5: Deriving the rate of change over a small interval.

```
>>> def deriver(f, x):
...     h = 0.00001
...     return (f(x+h) - f(x))/h
...
>>> deriver(square, 3)
6.000009999951316
```

Listing 5.6: Defining a function with both ***args** and ****kwargs**.

```
>>> def foo(*args, **kwargs):
...     print(args)
...     print(kwargs)
...
>>> foo("This", "is a bunch", "of arguments", "to the function",
...     a="hello", b="world", bar="good day!")
```

5.2 Functions in a File

Although defining functions in a REPL is convenient for demonstration purposes, it's a bit cumbersome, and a better practice is to put them in a file (as we did with the script in Section 4.5). We'll start by moving the function defined in Section 5.1 into **hello_app.py**, and we'll then move it to an even more convenient external file.

Using such an external resource requires the presence of a somewhat mysterious file called **__init__.py**, which causes Python to interpret our project directory as a *package*. The file doesn't have to have any content, though—it just has to *exist*, which we can arrange with **touch**:

```
(venv) $ touch __init__.py
```

(We'll learn a little more about this file requirement when we make a proper package in Chapter 8.) With that, we're ready to run our Flask app at the command line as in Section 1.5:

```
(venv) $ flask --app hello_app.py --debug run
```

Let's recall the current state of our hello application, which looks like Listing 5.7. (This is the same as Listing 4.3; your code may differ if you solved the exercises in Section 4.2.1.)

Listing 5.7: The current state of our hello app.
hello_app.py

```python
from datetime import datetime

from flask import Flask


app = Flask(__name__)

@app.route("/")
def hello_world():
    DAYNAMES = ["Monday", "Tuesday", "Wednesday",
                "Thursday", "Friday", "Saturday", "Sunday"]
    dayname = DAYNAMES[datetime.now().weekday()]
    return f"<p>Hello, world! Happy {dayname}.</p>"
```

Our first step is to put the function definition from Section 5.1 into this file, as shown in Listing 5.8.

Listing 5.8: Adding a function for the day of the week.
hello_app.py

```python
from datetime import datetime
import calendar

from flask import Flask

def dayname(time):
    """Return the name of the day of the week for the given time."""
    return calendar.day_name[time.weekday()]

app = Flask(__name__)

@app.route("/")
def hello_world():
    DAYNAMES = ["Monday", "Tuesday", "Wednesday",
                "Thursday", "Friday", "Saturday", "Sunday"]
    dayname = DAYNAMES[datetime.now().weekday()]
    return f"<p>Hello, world! Happy {dayname}.</p>"
```

Then, we can use the **dayname()** function to delete the unneeded lines and edit the body of **hello_world()** down to a single line, as shown in Listing 5.9. At this point, you should be able to confirm that the app is working, as shown in Figure 5.3.

Listing 5.9: Replacing the greeting.
hello_app.py

```
from datetime import datetime
import calendar

from flask import Flask


def dayname(time):
  """Return the name of the day of the week for the given time."""
  return calendar.day_name[time.weekday()]

app = Flask(__name__)

@app.route("/")
def hello_world():
    return f"<p>Hello, world! Happy {dayname(datetime.now())}.</p>"
```

We can make the code in Listing 5.9 even cleaner by factoring the **dayname()** function into a separate file and then including it into our app. We'll start by cutting the function and pasting it into a new file, **day.py**:

```
(venv) $ touch day.py
```

The resulting files appear as in Listing 5.10 and Listing 5.11.[6] Note that we've slightly updated the greeting in Listing 5.11 so that we can tell our new code is actually working.

Listing 5.10: The **dayname()** function in a file.
day.py

```
import calendar

def dayname(time):
```

---

6. In some editors, you can use Shift-Command-V to paste in a selection using the local indentation level, which saves us the trouble of dedenting it by hand.

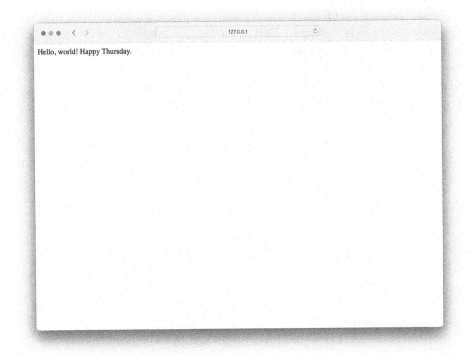
Hello, world! Happy Thursday.

Figure 5.3: The result of a functional greeting.

```
"""Return the name of the day of the week for the given time."""
return calendar.day_name[time.weekday()]
```

Listing 5.11: Our greeting with the function cut.

hello_app.py

```
from datetime import datetime

from flask import Flask


app = Flask(__name__)

@app.route("/")
def hello_world():
    return f"<p>Hello, world! Happy {dayname(datetime.now())} from a file!</p>"
```

As you can verify by reloading the browser, the app doesn't work—it crashes immediately, and all we get is the Flask error page (Figure 5.4), which indicates that there was an *exception* of type **NoMethodError**. (Exceptions are simply a standardized way of indicating particular kinds of errors in a program.) We can find out more about what went wrong by looking at the error message, which indicates that the **dayname()** method isn't defined; zooming in on the message, we see that it even tells us the exact line that has the problem (Figure 5.5).

This practice is a powerful debugging technique: If your Python program crashes, inspecting the error message should be your method of first resort. Moreover, if you can't see right away what went wrong, Googling the error message will often yield useful results (Box 5.1).

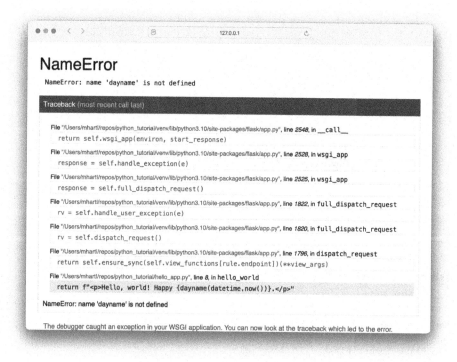

Figure 5.4: A sure sign our app isn't working.

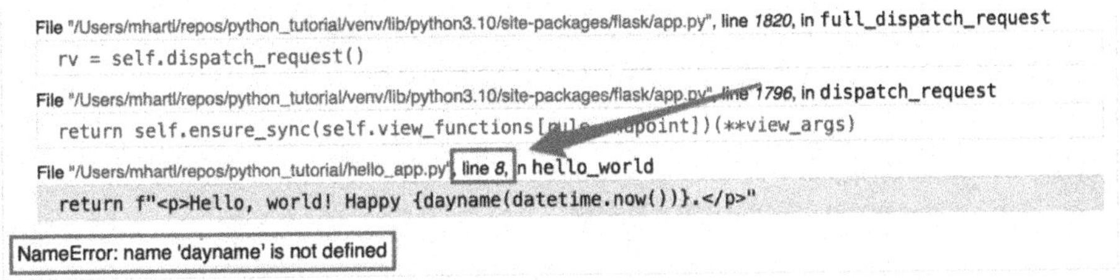

```
File "/Users/mharti/repos/python_tutorial/venv/lib/python3.10/site-packages/flask/app.py", line 1820, in full_dispatch_request
    rv = self.dispatch_request()
File "/Users/mharti/repos/python_tutorial/venv/lib/python3.10/site-packages/flask/app.py", line 1796, in dispatch_request
    return self.ensure_sync(self.view_functions[rule.endpoint])(**view_args)
File "/Users/mharti/repos/python_tutorial/hello_app.py", line 8, in hello_world
    return f"<p>Hello, world! Happy {dayname(datetime.now())}.</p>"
```

```
NameError: name 'dayname' is not defined
```

Figure 5.5: Using the Flask crash page to find an error.

Box 5.1: Debugging Python

One skill that's an essential part of technical sophistication is *debugging*: the art of finding and correcting errors in computer programs. While there's no substitute for experience, here are some techniques that should give you a leg up when tracking down the inevitable glitches in your code:

- *Trace the execution with* `print`. When trying to figure out why a particular program is going awry, it's often helpful to display variable values with temporary `print` statements, which can be removed when the bug is fixed. This technique is especially useful when combined with the `repr()` function, which returns a literal representation of the object (Section 4.3), as in `print(repr(a))`.

- *Comment out code*. It's sometimes a good idea to comment out code you suspect is unrelated to the problem to allow you to focus on the code that isn't working.

- *Use the REPL*. Firing up the Python interpreter and pasting in the problematic code is frequently an excellent way to isolate the problem. When debugging a script, calling it with `python3 -i script.py` will drop you into the REPL when an error is reached. (A more advanced version of the REPL technique is *pdb*, the Python Debugger.)

- *Google it*. Googling error messages or other search terms related to the bug (which often leads to helpful threads at Stack Overflow) is an essential skill for every modern software developer (Figure 5.6).

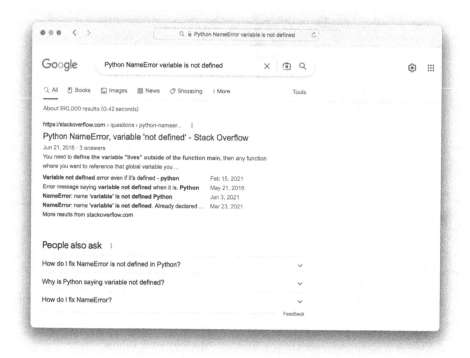

Figure 5.6: How did people ever debug before Google?

The reason for the crash is that we've removed **dayname()** from **hello_app.py**, so naturally our app has no idea what it is. The solution is to import it in much the same way that we imported **flask**, **datetime**, and **calendar**, as shown in Listing 5.12. Note that the import statement in Listing 5.11 includes the current directory (**python_tutorial/day**), which is necessary because our project directory isn't on the Python include path by default.[7] (This is fine for now, but among other things it prevents the app as written from being deployed to production (Section 1.5.1). Utilities intended to be used more often, or in production environments, should be included as *packages*, a subject we'll take up in Chapter 8 and apply in Chapter 9 and Chapter 10.)

It's worth noting at this time that Listing 5.12 includes a full set of imports—modules from the standard library (**datetime**), a third-party library (**flask**), and a

---

7. How would you figure out how to add the current directory to the import path? Here's how I'd do it: python add to import path.

custom library (**python_tutorial.day**)—which by convention are separated from each other by newlines (and from the rest of the file by two newlines).

Listing 5.12: Using a function from an external file.
hello_app.py

```
from datetime import datetime

from flask import Flask

from python_tutorial.day import dayname

app = Flask(__name__)

@app.route("/")
def hello_world():
    return f"<p>Hello, world! Happy {dayname(datetime.now())} from a file!</p>"
```

At this point, the app is working! The result should look something like Figure 5.7.

Figure 5.7: An updated greeting.

5.2.1 Exercise

1. Let's replace the interpolated string in Listing 5.11 with a **greeting()** function in **day.py**. Fill in the code labeled **FILL_IN** in Listing 5.13 to get Listing 5.14 to work.

Listing 5.13: Defining a **greeting()** function.
day.py

```
import calendar


def dayname(time):
  """Return the name of the day of the week for the given time."""
  return calendar.day_name[time.weekday()]

def greeting(time):
  """Return a friendly greeting based on the current time."""
  return FILL_IN
```

Listing 5.14: Importing and using the **greeting()** function.
hello_app.py

```
from datetime import datetime

from flask import Flask

from python_tutorial.day import dayname

app = Flask(__name__)

@app.route("/")
def hello_world():
    return greeting(datetime.now())
```

5.3 Iterators

In this section, we'll start developing the palindrome theme mentioned in the introduction (Chapter 1). Our goal is to write a function called **ispalindrome()** that returns **True** if its argument is the same forward and backward, and **False** otherwise.

We can express the simplest possible definition of a palindrome as "a string is equal to the string reversed." (We'll steadily expand this definition over time.) In order to do this, we need to be able to reverse a string.

One straightforward way to reverse a string would be to combine the **list()** and **join()** functions (Section 3.4.4) with the ability to reverse a list using **reverse()** (Section 3.4.2):

```
>>> s = "foobar"
>>> a = list(s)
>>> a.reverse()
>>> "".join(a)
'raboof'
```

This would work, but a far more elegant method comes from observing that the **reversed()** function, which we saw applied to lists in Section 3.4.2, also works on strings:

```
>>> reversed("foobar")
<reversed object at 0x104858d60>
```

As noted in the Python documentation, **reversed()** returns a reverse *iterator*. An iterator is a powerful Python facility that represents a stream of data—in this case, a string of characters—that gets accessed in sequence. We'll see how to define a special kind of iterator known as a *generator* in Section 5.3.1, and we'll implement a full custom iterator in Section 7.2.

One way to see the result of **reversed()** is to iterate through the reversed object using **for** (Listing 5.15):

Listing 5.15: Using a **for** loop on an iterator.

```
>>> for c in reversed("foobar"):
...     print(c)
...
r
a
b
o
o
f
```

We can also use **list()** to look at the elements directly:

```
>>> list(reversed("foobar"))
['r', 'a', 'b', 'o', 'o', 'f']
```

We see here that **list()** runs through the reversed iterator and gives us the actual list of characters. Note that, unlike the code in Listing 5.15, using **list()** creates the full object in memory. For a small list like the one here it makes little difference, but for large lists the difference could be significant.[8]

We saw in Section 3.4.4 how to use **join()** to combine such a list (in this case, on the empty space **""**):

```
>>> "".join(list(reversed("foobar")))
'raboof'
```

This is excellent progress toward being able to detect palindromes, as we now have a way to find the reverse of a string, but it turns out that **join()** also automatically runs through an iterable object, so we can actually eliminate the intermediate call to **list()**:

```
>>> "".join(reversed("foobar"))
'raboof'
```

At this point, we're in a position to test for a palindrome by comparing a string with its own reverse:

```
>>> "foobar" == "".join(reversed("foobar"))
False
>>> "racecar" == "".join(reversed("racecar"))
True
```

With this technique in our toolkit, we're ready to write the first version of our palindrome method.

Let's put our function for detecting palindromes into its own file, which we'll call **palindrome.py**:

```
(venv) $ touch palindrome.py
```

---

8. Indeed, it's possible to create iterators for *infinite* sets, such as the natural numbers, which can't be instantiated in memory even in principle.

What should we call the palindrome-detecting function? Well, the palindrome detector should take in a string and return **True** when the string is a palindrome and **False** otherwise. This makes it a boolean method. Recall from Section 2.5 that boolean methods in Python generally start with the word "is", which suggests the definition in Listing 5.16. (Actually, for such a *module-level* function, not attached to an object, the snake-case name **is_palindrome** might be more conventional. But we *are* planning to attach it to an object; see Chapter 7.)

Listing 5.16: Our initial **ispalindrome()** function.
palindrome.py

```python
def reverse(string):
    """Reverse a string."""
    return "".join(reversed(string))

def ispalindrome(string):
    """Return True for a palindrome, False otherwise."""
    return string == reverse(string)
```

The code in Listing 5.16 uses the **==** comparison operator (Section 2.4) to return the right boolean value.

We can test the code in Listing 5.16 by importing the palindrome file in the Python interpreter:

```python
>>> import palindrome
```

This makes **ispalindrome()** available through the module name:

```python
>>> palindrome.ispalindrome("racecar")
True
>>> palindrome.ispalindrome("Racecar")
False
```

As seen in the second example, our palindrome detector says "Racecar" isn't a palindrome, so to make our detector a little more general we can use **lower()** to make the string lowercase before the comparison. A working version appears in Listing 5.17.

Listing 5.17: Detecting palindromes independent of case.
palindrome.py

```python
def reverse(string):
    """Reverse a string."""
    return "".join(reversed(string))

def ispalindrome(string):
    """Return True for a palindrome, False otherwise."""
    return string.lower() == reverse(string.lower())
```

Returning to the REPL, we can reload the detector (using the convenient **reload()** function from the **importlib** module)[9] and apply it as follows:

```python
>>> from importlib import reload
>>> reload(palindrome)
>>> palindrome.ispalindrome("Racecar")
True
```

Success!

As a final refinement, let's follow the Don't Repeat Yourself (or "DRY") principle and eliminate the duplication in Listing 5.17. Inspecting the code, we see that **string.lower()** gets used twice, which suggests declaring a variable (which we'll call **processed_content**) to represent the actual string that gets compared to its own reverse (Listing 5.18).

Listing 5.18: Eliminating some duplication.
palindrome.py

```python
def reverse(string):
    """Reverse a string."""
    return "".join(reversed(string))

def ispalindrome(string):
    """Return True for a palindrome, False otherwise."""
    processed_content = string.lower()
    return processed_content == reverse(processed_content)
```

---

9. This is exactly the kind of thing you should think to Google (Box 1.2), using, say, python how to reload a module.

Listing 5.18 eliminates one call to **lower()** at the cost of an extra line, so it's not obviously better than Listing 5.17, but we'll see starting in Chapter 8 that having a separate variable gives us much greater flexibility in detecting more complex palindromes.

As a final step, we should check that the **ispalindrome()** function is still working as advertised:

```
>>> reload(palindrome)
>>> palindrome.ispalindrome("Racecar")
True
>>> palindrome.ispalindrome("Able was I ere I saw Elba")
True
```

As you might guess, confirming such things by hand quickly gets tedious, and we'll see in Chapter 8 how to write *automated tests* to check our code's behavior automatically.

5.3.1   Generators

A *generator*, which we first saw in Section 3.4.2, is a special kind of iterator built using a special operation called **yield**. The effect of **yield** is to produce each element of the sequence in turn.

For example, we can create a string generator by yielding each character in the string:

```
>>> def characters(string):
...     for c in string:
...         yield c
...     return None
...
>>> characters("foobar")
<generator object characters at 0x11f9c1540
```

(We've returned **None** here, but we'll see in Listing 5.21 that we can actually leave off **return** since **None** is the default.)

Now calling **characters()** on a string returns a generator object, which we can iterate over as usual:

```
>>> for c in characters("foobar"):
...     print(c)
...
```

```
f
o
o
b
a
r
```

We can **join()** it as well:

```
>>> "".join(characters("foobar"))
'foobar'
```

Converting a string to an iterator is instructive but not very useful since we can already iterate over regular strings. Let's take a look at a more interesting example that shows off the virtues of generators.

Suppose we wanted to write a function to find numbers that contain all of the digits 0–9.[10] One clever way of doing this is noting that the **set()** function introduced in Section 3.6 can actually take a string as an argument, and returns the set of characters that make up the string:

```
>>> set("1231231234")
{'2', '4', '3', '1'}
```

Note that, as required for sets, repeated elements are simply ignored. (Also recall that the order of the elements doesn't matter.)

This observation suggests that we can detect a number having all ten digits by converting it to a string as in Section 4.1.2 and then comparing it to the set corresponding to all digits:

```
>>> str(132459360782)
'132459360782'
>>> set(str(132459360782))
{'8', '7', '9', '3', '4', '0', '2', '6', '1', '5'}
>>> set(str(130245936782)) == set("0123456789")
True
```

A function to return the first such occurrence then appears in Listing 5.19, with an example showing how it works on a short list of integers. Note that Listing 5.19 uses

---

10. Thanks to Tom Repetti for this example and for his help in preparing this section.

the same technique shown in Listing 5.3 to return from the function immediately once a particular condition is satisfied.

Listing 5.19: Finding a number with all ten digits.

```
>>> def has_all_digits(numbers):
...     for n in numbers:
...         if set(str(n)) == set("0123456789"):
...             return n
...     return None
...
>>> has_all_digits([1424872341, 1236490835741, 12341960523])
1236490835741
```

Now let's use our function to find the first *perfect square* with all of the digits 0–9. One way of doing this is to create a list using all the numbers up to some big number; since we don't know how high to go, let's try a hundred million, or 10^8 (with a +1 because **range(n)** ends at **n-1**, although it doesn't really matter). The result appears in Listing 5.20.

Listing 5.20: Creating a big list of squares.

```
>>> squares = []
>>> for n in range(10**8 + 1):
...     squares.append(n)
...
>>>
```

(We'll see a better way to make this list in Section 6.4.1.) As of this writing, the above code takes a loooong time even on a relatively new computer, to the point where I just hit **Ctrl-C** to break out of the loop. (As it turns out, we don't have to go all the way to 10^8, but we don't know that ahead of time, and this demonstrates the principle.)

The reason the solution in Listing 5.20 takes so long is that the entire range has to be iterated over and the entire list has to be created in memory. A far better solution uses **yield** to create a generator, which supplies the next square only when needed. We can create such a squares generator as shown in Listing 5.21; note that we have left off the **return**, so **None** will be returned by default.

Listing 5.21: A squares generator.

```
>>> def squares_generator():
...     for n in range(10**8 + 1):
...         yield n**2
...
>>> squares = squares_generator()
```

By the way, you may wonder why the call to **range()** in Listing 5.21 doesn't just create exactly the list we're trying to avoid. The answer is that it used to, and you had to use **xrange()** to avoid creating the whole thing in memory. But as of Python 3, the **range()** function does precisely what we want, producing the next element in the range only when needed. This pattern is known as *lazy evaluation*, and indeed is exactly the behavior produced by a generator as well.

With the final assignment in Listing 5.21, we're ready to find the first square containing all the digits:

```
>>> has_all_digits(squares)
1026753849
```

Putting in commas for readability gives the result $1,026,753,849$, and you can confirm using **math.sqrt()** that it is equal to $32,043^2$.

5.3.2 Exercises

1. Using the Python interpreter, determine whether or not your system supports using the **ispalindrome()** function from Listing 5.17 on emojis. (You may find the Emojipedia links to the racing car and fox face emojis helpful.) If your system supports emojis in this context, the result should look something like Figure 5.8. (Note that an emoji is a "palindrome" if it's the same when you flip it horizontally, so the fox-face emoji is a palindrome but the racecar emoji isn't, even though the *word* "racecar" *is* a palindrome.)

2. Using the code in Listing 5.22, show that it's possible to express the **ispalindrome()** function in one line using the advanced slice operator **[::-1]** discussed in Section 3.3. (Some Python programmers may prefer this approach, but I believe the decrease in length doesn't justify the loss in clarity.)

3. Write a generator function that returns the first 50 even numbers.

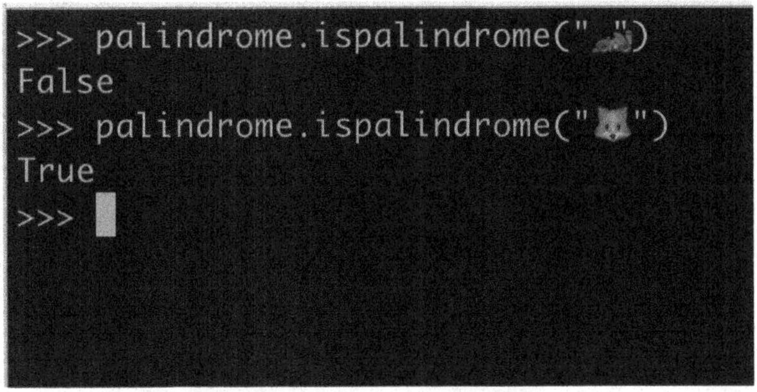

Figure 5.8: Detecting palindromic emojis.

Listing 5.22: A compact but rather obscure version of **ispalindrome()**.
palindrome.py

```python
def ispalindrome(string):
    """Return True for a palindrome, False otherwise."""
    return string.lower() == string.lower()[::-1]
```

CHAPTER 6
Functional Programming

Having learned how to define functions and apply them in a couple of different contexts, now we're going to take our programming to the next level by learning the basics of *functional programming*, a style of programming that emphasizes—you guessed it—functions. As we'll see, functional programming in Python frequently employs a powerful (and very Pythonic) class of techniques called *comprehensions*, which typically involve using functions to conveniently construct Python objects with particular elements. The most common comprehensions are *list comprehensions* and *dictionary comprehensions*, which make lists and dictionaries, respectively. We'll also see an example of how to use *generator comprehensions* to replicate the results of Section 5.3.1, as well as a brief introduction to *set comprehensions*.

This is a challenging chapter, and you may have to get in some reps to fully grok it (Box 6.1), but the rewards are rich indeed.

Box 6.1: Getting in your reps

In contexts ranging from martial arts to chess to language learning, practitioners will reach a point where no amount of analysis or reflection will help them improve— they just need to get in some more repetitions, or "reps".

It's amazing how much you can improve by trying something, kinda-sorta (but maybe not quite) getting it, and then just *doing it again*. In the context of a tutorial like this one, sometimes that means rereading a particularly tricky section or chapter. Some people (including yours truly) will even reread an entire book.

One important aspect of getting in your reps is *suspending self-judgment—* allow yourself not to be good right away. (Many people—including, again, yours

---

truly—often require practice to get good at being okay with not being good right away. Meta-reps, as it were.)

Give yourself a break, get in your reps, and watch your technical sophistication grow by the day.

Our general technique for approaching functional programming will be to perform a task involving a sequence of commands (called "imperative programming",[1] which is what we've mostly been doing so far), and then show how to do the same thing using functional programming.

For convenience, we'll create a file for our explorations, rather than typing everything at the REPL:

```
(venv) $ touch functional.py
```

6.1 List Comprehensions

We begin our study of functional programming with a technique that will give you an Einstein-level comprehension of Python (Figure 6.1[2]). This technique, known as *list comprehensions*, lets us use functions to build up lists using a single command. Its effects are broadly similar to the **map** function covered in *Learn Enough JavaScript to Be Dangerous* (https://www.learnenough.com/javascript) and *Learn Enough Ruby to Be Dangerous* (https://www.learnenough.com/ruby)—indeed, Python itself supports **map**, but list comprehensions are much more Pythonic.

Let's look at a concrete example. Suppose we had a list of mixed-case strings, and we wanted to create a corresponding list of lowercase strings joined on a hyphen (making the result appropriate for use in URLs), like this:

```
"North Dakota" -> "north-dakota"
```

Using previous techniques from this tutorial, we could do this as follows:

1. Define a variable containing a list of strings.

2. Define a second variable (initially empty) for the URL-friendly list of strings.

---

1. From Latin *imperātīvus*, "proceeding from a command."

2. Image courtesy of GL Archive/Alamy.

Figure 6.1: Albert Einstein was a master of comprehensions.

3. For each item in the first list, **append( )** (Section 3.4.3) a lowercase version (Section 2.5) that's been split on whitespace (Section 4.3) and then joined (Section 3.4.4) on hyphens. (You could split on a single space **" "** instead, but splitting on whitespace is so much more robust that it's a good practice to use it by default.)

Let's build this up in the REPL before putting it into our file. We'll start with an example of Step 3 for a single state:

```
(venv) $ python3
>>> state = "North Dakota"
>>> state.lower()
'north dakota'
>>> state.lower().split()
['north', 'dakota']
>>> "-".join(state.lower().split())
'north-dakota'
```

Note the use of the combination **lower().split()**, which applies two methods in succession in a process known as *method chaining*. While not as prevalent in Python as in some other object-oriented languages (due in large part to Python's use of iterators (Section 5.3)), it is still definitely worth knowing.

Combining this **join()** with the other steps outlined above gives us the code shown in Listing 6.1. This is fairly complicated code, so being able to read Listing 6.1 is a good test of your growing technical sophistication. (If it isn't easy to read, firing up the Python interpreter and getting it to work in the REPL is a good idea.)

Listing 6.1: Making URL-appropriate strings from a list.
functional.py

```
states = ["Kansas", "Nebraska", "North Dakota", "South Dakota"]

# urls: Imperative version
def imperative_urls(states):
    urls = []
    for state in states:
      urls.append("-".join(state.lower().split()))
    return urls

print(imperative_urls(states))
```

The result of running Listing 6.1 looks like this:

```
(venv) $ python3 functional.py
['kansas', 'nebraska', 'north-dakota', 'south-dakota']
```

Now let's see how we can do the same thing using a list comprehension. We'll start with a few simpler examples, beginning with one that simply replicates the **list()** function:

```
>>> list(range(10))               # list() function
[0, 1, 2, 3, 4, 5, 6, 7, 8, 9]
>>> [n for n in range(10)]        # List comprehension
[0, 1, 2, 3, 4, 5, 6, 7, 8, 9]
```

The second command—the list comprehension—creates a list consisting of each **n** for **n** in the range 0–9. What makes it more flexible than **list()** is that we can use it with other operations as well, such as squaring:

```
>>> [n*n for n in range(10)]
[0, 1, 4, 9, 16, 25, 36, 49, 64, 81]
```

Applying a similar technique to a list of strings lets us create a list of lowercase versions by calling the **lower()** method (which is just a type of function) on each string in turn:

```
>>> [s.lower() for s in ["ALICE", "BOB", "CHARLIE"]]
['alice', 'bob', 'charlie']
```

Returning to our main example, we can think of the transformation "convert to lowercase then split then join" as a single operation, and use a list comprehension to apply that operation in sequence to each element in the list. The result is so compact that it easily fits in the REPL:

```
>>> states = ["Kansas", "Nebraska", "North Dakota", "South Dakota"]
>>> ["-".join(state.lower().split()) for state in states]
['kansas', 'nebraska', 'north-dakota', 'south-dakota']
```

Pasting this into **functional.py**, we see just how much shorter it is, as shown in Listing 6.2.

Listing 6.2: Adding a functional technique using a list comprehension.
functional.py

```
states = ["Kansas", "Nebraska", "North Dakota", "South Dakota"]

# urls: Imperative version
def imperative_urls(states):
    urls = []
    for state in states:
      urls.append("-".join(state.lower().split()))
    return urls

print(imperative_urls(states))

# urls: Functional version
def functional_urls(states):
    return ["-".join(state.lower().split()) for state in states]

print(functional_urls(states))
```

We can confirm at the command line that the results are the same:

```
(venv) $ python3 functional.py
['kansas', 'nebraska', 'north-dakota', 'south-dakota']
['kansas', 'nebraska', 'north-dakota', 'south-dakota']
```

With Python list comprehensions, we can process those states without a **map** (Figure 6.2[3]).

As a final refinement, let's factor the method chain responsible for making the strings URL-compatible into a separate auxiliary function called **urlify()**:

```
def urlify(string):
    """Return a URL-friendly version of a string.

    Example: "North Dakota" -> "north-dakota"
```

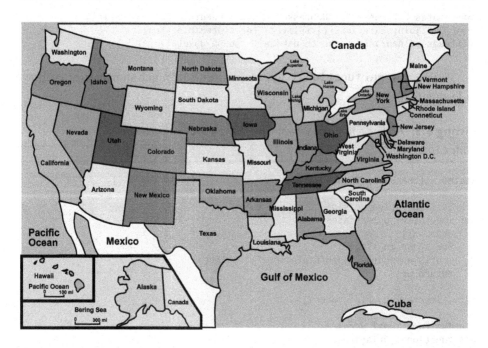

Figure 6.2: Some list comprehensions are equivalent to a **map**.

---

3. Image courtesy of Creative Jen Designs/Shutterstock.

```
    """
    return "-".join(string.lower().split())
```

Note that we've included a multi-line docstring that includes an example of a successful operation. Defining this function in **functional.py** and using it in the imperative and functional versions gives the code in Listing 6.3.

Listing 6.3: Defining an auxiliary function.
functional.py

```
states = ["Kansas", "Nebraska", "North Dakota", "South Dakota"]

def urlify(string):
    """Return a URL-friendly version of a string.

    Example: "North Dakota" -> "north-dakota"
    """
    return "-".join(string.lower().split())

# urls: Imperative version
def imperative_urls(states):
    urls = []
    for state in states:
        urls.append(urlify(state))
    return urls

print(imperative_urls(states))

# urls: Functional version
def functional_urls(states):
    return [urlify(state) for state in states]

print(functional_urls(states))
```

As before, the results are the same:

```
(venv) $ python3 functional.py
['kansas', 'nebraska', 'north-dakota', 'south-dakota']
['kansas', 'nebraska', 'north-dakota', 'south-dakota']
```

Compared to the imperative version, the functional version is a fourth as many lines (1 instead of 4), doesn't mutate any variables (often an error-prone step in

Figure 6.3: Functional programming makes Mike Vanier happiest of all.

imperative programming), and indeed eliminates the intermediate list (**urls**) entirely. This is the sort of thing that makes Mike Vanier very happy (Figure 6.3[4]).

6.1.1 Exercise

1. Using a list comprehension, write a function that takes in the **states** variable and returns a list of URLs of the form **https://example.com/<urlified form>**.

6.2 List Comprehensions with Conditions

In addition to supporting the creation of lists using **for**, Python list comprehensions also support the use of conditions using **if** to select only elements satisfying particular criteria. In this way, list comprehensions with conditions can replicate the behavior of JavaScript's **filter** and Ruby's **select**. (As with **map**, Python actually supports this directly via **filter**; also as with **map**, the comprehension version is far more Pythonic.)

---

4. Last I checked, Mike's favorite language was a "purely functional" language called Haskell. Image © Mike Vanier.

Suppose, for example, that we wanted to select the strings in our **states** list that consist of more than one word, keeping the names that have only one. As in Section 6.1, we'll write an imperative version first:

1. Define a list to store single-word strings.
2. For each element in the list, **append()** it to the storage list if splitting it on whitespace yields a list with length 1.

The result looks like Listing 6.4. Note that in Listing 6.4 and subsequent listings the vertical dots indicate omitted code.

Listing 6.4: Solving a filtering problem imperatively.
functional.py

```
states = ["Kansas", "Nebraska", "North Dakota", "South Dakota"]
.
.
.
# singles: Imperative version
def imperative_singles(states):
    singles = []
    for state in states:
        if len(state.split()) == 1:
            singles.append(state)
    return singles

print(imperative_singles(states))
```

Note in Listing 6.4 the familiar pattern from Listing 6.1: We first define an auxiliary variable in order to maintain state (no pun intended); then loop over the original list, mutating the variable as necessary; then return the mutated result. It's not particularly pretty, but it works:

```
(venv) $ python3 functional.py
['kansas', 'nebraska', 'north-dakota', 'south-dakota']
['kansas', 'nebraska', 'north-dakota', 'south-dakota']
['Kansas', 'Nebraska']
```

Now let's see how to do the same task using a list comprehension. As in Section 6.1, we'll start with a simple numerical example in the REPL. We'll begin by looking at the *modulo operator* **%**, which returns the remainder after dividing an integer by another integer. In other words, **17 % 5** (read "seventeen mod 5") is **2**, because 5 goes into 17 three times (giving 15), with a remainder of $17 - 15 = 2$. In particular, considering integers modulo 2 divides them into two *equivalence classes*: even numbers (remainder 0 (mod 2)) and odd numbers (remainder 1 (mod 2)). In code:

```
>>> 16 % 2  # even
0
>>> 17 % 2  # odd
1
>>> 16 % 2 == 0  # even
True
>>> 17 % 2 == 0  # odd
False
```

We can use **%** in a list comprehension to process a list of numbers and include a number only if it is even:

```
>>> [n for n in range(10) if n % 2 == 0]
[0, 2, 4, 6, 8]
```

This is exactly the same as a regular list comprehension but with an extra **if**.

Using this idea, we see that the functional version of Listing 6.4 is much cleaner—indeed, as in Listing 6.2, it condenses to a single line, as we can see in the REPL:

```
>>> [state for state in states if len(state.split()) == 1]
['Kansas', 'Nebraska']
```

Placing the result in our example file again underscores how much more compact the functional version is than the imperative version (Listing 6.5).

Listing 6.5: Solving a selection problem functionally.
functional.py

```
states = ["Kansas", "Nebraska", "North Dakota", "South Dakota"]
.
.
.
# singles: Imperative version
def imperative_singles(states):
    singles = []
    for state in states:
```

```
    if len(state.split()) == 1:
        singles.append(state)
    return singles

print(imperative_singles(states))

# singles: Functional version
def functional_singles(states):
    return [state for state in states if len(state.split()) == 1]

print(functional_singles(states))
```

As required, the result is the same:

```
(venv) $ python3 functional.py
['kansas', 'nebraska', 'north-dakota', 'south-dakota']
['kansas', 'nebraska', 'north-dakota', 'south-dakota']
['Kansas', 'Nebraska']
['Kansas', 'Nebraska']
```

As compact as list comprehensions can be, it's worth noting that there are limitations to their use. In particular, as the logic inside list comprehensions gets more complicated, they can quickly become unwieldy. It is therefore considered unPythonic to build up complicated list comprehensions; if you find yourself trying to squeeze too much content into a single comprehension, consider using a good old-fashioned **for** loop instead.

6.2.1 Exercise

1. Write two equivalent list comprehensions that return the Dakotas: one using **in** (Section 2.5) to test for the presence of the string "Dakota" and one that tests for the length of the split list being **2**.

6.3 Dictionary Comprehensions

Our next example of functional programming uses *dictionary comprehensions*, giving us functional powers on par with the great lexicographer Dr Samuel Johnson (Figure 6.4[5]). This technique is broadly equivalent to the **reduce** and **inject**

---

5. Image courtesy of Rosenwald Collection. N.B. The omission of the period after "Dr", which is a common British convention, is frequently followed when referring to Dr Johnson.

Figure 6.4: Dr Johnson, master of dictionary comprehensions.

functions introduced in *Learn Enough JavaScript to Be Dangerous* and *Learn Enough Ruby to Be Dangerous*, respectively; readers of the corresponding and rather tricky sections in those tutorials may appreciate how much simpler dictionary comprehensions can be. (Python 2 actually includes a **reduce()** method, but it was removed from default Python 3; it is, however, still available via the **functools** module.)

Our example will build on the list comprehensions from Section 6.1 and Section 6.2 involving the names of a few U.S. states. In particular, we'll make a dictionary that associates state names to the length of each name, with a result that will look like this:[6]

---

6. Note that conventions on formatting dictionaries vary widely, and it's a good idea to pick one and generally stick to it.

```
{
    "Kansas": 6,
    "Nebraska": 8,
    "North Dakota": 12,
    "South Dakota": 12
}
```

We can accomplish this imperatively by initializing a **lengths** object and then iterating through the states, setting **lengths[dictionary]** equal to the corresponding length:

```
lengths[state] = len(state)
```

The full example appears in Listing 6.6.

Listing 6.6: An imperative solution for state–length correspondence.
functional.py

```
        .
        .
        .
# lengths: Imperative version
def imperative_lengths(states):
    lengths = {}
    for state in states:
        lengths[state] = len(state)
    return lengths

print(imperative_lengths(states))
```

If we run the program at the command line, the desired dictionary appears as the final part of the output:

```
(venv) $ python3 functional.py
    .
    .
    .
{'Kansas': 6, 'Nebraska': 8, 'North Dakota': 12, 'South Dakota': 12}
```

The functional version is almost absurdly simple. As with list comprehensions, we use **for** to create an element in the comprehension for each element in the list; for dictionary comprehensions, we just use curly braces instead of square brackets and a key–value pair instead of a single element. In the present case, it looks like this in the REPL:

```
>>> {state: len(state) for state in states}
{'Kansas': 6, 'Nebraska': 8, 'North Dakota': 12, 'South Dakota': 12}
```

Pasting this into our file then yields Listing 6.7.

Listing 6.7: A functional solution for state–length correspondence.
functional.py

```
.
.
.

# lengths: Imperative version
def imperative_lengths(states):
    lengths = {}
    for state in states:
        lengths[state] = len(state)
    return lengths

print(imperative_lengths(states))

# lengths: Functional version
def functional_lengths(states):
    return {state: len(state) for state in states}

print(functional_lengths(states))
```

Running this at the command line yields the expected result:

```
(venv) $ python3 functional.py
.
.
.
{'Kansas': 6, 'Nebraska': 8, 'North Dakota': 12, 'South Dakota': 12}
{'Kansas': 6, 'Nebraska': 8, 'North Dakota': 12, 'South Dakota': 12}
```

As with the examples in Section 6.1 and Section 6.2, the dictionary comprehension condenses the functionality of the imperative version to a single line. This is not *always* the case, but such large compressions are a common feature of functional programming. (This is but one of many reasons why "LOC" or "lines of code" is a dubious metric of program size or programmer productivity.)

6.3.1 Exercise

1. Using a dictionary comprehension, write a function that associates each element in **states** with its URL-compatible versions. *Hint*: Reuse the **urlify()** function defined in Listing 6.3.

6.4 Generator and Set Comprehensions

In this section, we'll replicate the result from Section 5.3.1 using comprehensions, starting with a list comprehension and then using a *generator comprehension*. We'll also include a brief example of *set comprehensions*.

6.4.1 Generator Comprehensions

Recall from Section 5.3.1 that we defined a function to find a number containing all digits 0–9, as reproduced in Listing 6.8.

Listing 6.8: Finding a number with all ten digits (again).

```
>>> def has_all_digits(numbers):
...     for n in numbers:
...         if set(str(n)) == set("0123456789"):
...             return n
...     return None
```

In Listing 5.20, we used an imperative solution to build up a list of *perfect squares*, but gave up because it was taking too long. With the techniques in Section 6.1, we're now in a position to create the same list using a list comprehension:

```
>>> squares = [n**2 for n in range(10**8 + 1)]
```

Unfortunately, although syntactically nicer, this code still has to iterate over the entire range and create the entire list in memory. As in Section 5.3.1, I lost patience and hit Ctrl-C to interrupt the execution before it was finished.

Now for the analogue of Listing 5.21, which used **yield** to yield each squared number in turn. We can create this behavior even more conveniently using a generator comprehension, which looks just like a list comprehension except with parentheses instead of square brackets:

```
>>> squares = (n**2 for n in range(10**8 + 1))
```

As with the generator in Listing 5.21, this supplies the next number only when required, which means we can find the first perfect squares with all ten digits as we did in Section 5.3.1:

```
>>> has_all_digits(squares)
1026753849
```

This is the same answer of $1,026,753,849 = 32,043^2$ that we got in Section 5.3.1, but with *much* less code.

6.4.2 Set Comprehensions

Set comprehensions can be used to quickly make sets if the rules can be specified simply. The syntax both without and with conditions is nearly identical to the syntax for list comprehensions in Section 6.1 and Section 6.2, just with curly braces in place of square brackets.

For example, we can make a set of all the numbers between 5 and 20 as follows:

```
>>> {n for n in range(5, 21)}
{5, 6, 7, 8, 9, 10, 11, 12, 13, 14, 15, 16, 17, 18, 19, 20}
```

And we can make a set of the even numbers greater than 0 like this:

```
>>> {n for n in range(10) if n % 2 == 0}
{0, 2, 4, 6, 8}
```

Set operations such as intersection (**&**) work as usual:

```
>>> {n for n in range(5, 21)} & {n for n in range(10) if n % 2 == 0}
{8, 6}
```

6.4.3 Exercise

1. Write a generator comprehension that returns the first 50 even numbers.

6.5 Other Functional Techniques

Although comprehensions are among the most common and powerful functional techniques in Python, the language includes many other techniques as well. One example is summing the elements in a list (or range), which we can do iteratively using the code in Listing 6.9. Note the familiar pattern of initializing a variable (in this case, **total**) and then adding to it in some way (in this case, literally adding a number).[7]

Listing 6.9: An imperative solution for summing integers.
functional.py

```
.

.

.
numbers = range(1, 101)      # 1 up to 100

# sum: Imperative solution
def imperative_sum(numbers):
    total = 0
    for n in numbers:
      total += n
    return total

print(imperative_sum(numbers))
```

The result is 5050 as required:

```
(venv) $ python3 functional.py
.

.

.
5050
```

The functional (and very Pythonic) solution is to use the built-in **sum()** function:

```
>>> sum(range(1, 101))
5050
```

---

7. Because it's conventional to speak of summing the numbers between 1 and 100—rather than the numbers between 0 and 100—Listing 6.9 uses **range(1, 101)** to generate the number range 1–100, but of course the answer would be the same if we used **range(101)** since adding 0 doesn't change the sum.

Using this in our functional file gives us the one additional line shown in Listing 6.10.

Listing 6.10: A fully Pythonic solution for summing integers.
functional.py

```
.
.
.
numbers = range(1, 11)  # 1 up to 10

# sum: Imperative solution
def imperative_sum(numbers):
    total = 0
    for n in numbers:
      total += n
    return total

print(imperative_sum(numbers))
print(sum(numbers))
```

We can confirm at the command line that the results agree:

```
(venv) $ python3 functional.py
.
.
.
5050
5050
```

A similar facility is the **prod()** function in the **math** module, which returns the product of the list elements. The **itertools** module includes a large variety of similar tools.

6.5.1 Functional Programming and TDD

In many cases, the imperative approach offers the most straightforward solution to a problem, which can make imperative solutions a good place to start even though they are usually longer than their functional counterparts. Indeed, we might not even know the latter exists; a common situation is to write an imperative solution for a particular task, such as the sum shown in Listing 6.9, only to discover later on that there's a functional way to do it (in this case, using the built-in **sum()** function). But making changes to working code can be risky, which might make us understandably reluctant to change to the functional version.

My favorite technique for managing this challenge is *test-driven development* (TDD), which involves writing an *automated test* that captures the desired behavior in code. We can then get the test to pass using any method we want, including an ugly but easy-to-understand imperative solution. At that point, we can *refactor* the code—changing its form but not its function—to use a more concise functional solution. As long as the test still passes, we can be confident that the code still works.

In Chapter 8, we'll apply this exact technique to the principal object developed in Chapter 7. In particular, we'll use TDD to implement a fancy extension to the **is-palindrome()** function first seen in Section 5.3, one that detects such complicated palindromes as "A man, a plan, a canal—Panama!" (Figure 6.5[8]).

Figure 6.5: Teddy Roosevelt was a man with a plan.

---

8. Image courtesy of Everett Collection Historical/Alamy Stock Photo.

6.5.2 Exercise

1. Use **math.prod()** to find the product of the numbers in the range 1–10. How does this compare to **math.factorial(10)**?

CHAPTER 7

Objects and Classes

So far in this tutorial, we've seen many examples of Python objects. In this chapter, we'll learn how to use Python *classes* to make objects of our own, which have both data (attributes) and functions (methods) attached to them. We'll also learn how to define a custom iterator for our class. Finally, we'll learn how to reuse functionality with *inheritance*.

7.1 Defining Classes

Classes are a way of organizing data and functions into a single convenient object. In Python, we can create a class of our own using two basic elements:

1. Use the **class** keyword to define the class.
2. Use the special **__init__** method (often called an *initializer function*) to specify how to initialize a class.

Our concrete example will be a **Phrase** class with a **content** attribute, which we'll put in **palindrome.py** (last seen in Section 5.3). Let's build it up piece by piece (for simplicity we'll omit the **reverse()** and **ispalindrome()** functions for the moment). The first element is the **class** itself (Listing 7.1).

Listing 7.1: Defining a **Phrase** class.
palindrome.py

```
class Phrase:
    """A class to represent phrases."""
```

```
if __name__ == "__main__":
    phrase = Phrase()
    print(phrase)
```

In Listing 7.1, we've created an *instance* (particular object) of the **Phrase** class using

```
phrase = Phrase()
```

which automatically calls **__init__** under the hood. The strange-looking syntax

```
if __name__ == "__main__":
```

arranges to execute the subsequent code if the file is run at the command line but not when the class is loaded into other files. This convention is very much Pythonic but can seem a bit obscure; most Python developers just learn this trick by example, but see the official documentation (https://docs.python.org/3/library/__main__.html) if you're interested in an explanation.

Meanwhile, the final **print()** in Listing 7.1 lets us see some concrete (if not especially instructive) results at the command line:

```
$ source venv/bin/activate
(venv) $ python3 palindrome.py
<__main__.Phrase object at 0x10267afa0>
```

This shows Python's abstract internal representation of a bare instance of the **Phrase** class. (Should your results match exactly?) We also see where the value **"__main__"** comes from in **if __name__ == "__main__"**—it's the "top-level code environment", which is the environment (containing classes, functions, variables, etc.) in which Python shell scripts are executed.

We'll start filling in Listing 7.1 in a moment, but before moving on we should note that, unlike variables and methods, Python classes use *CamelCase* (with a leading capital) instead of snake_case (Section 2.2). CamelCase, which is named for the resemblance of the capital letters to humps of a camel (Figure 7.1[1]), involves separating words using capitalization rather than with underscores. It's hard to tell with **Phrase**,

---

1. Image courtesy of Utsav Academy and Art Studio. Pearson India Education Services Pvt. Ltd.

Figure 7.1: The origin of CamelCase.

since it's only a single word, but we'll see the principle more clearly illustrated in Section 7.3, which defines a class called **TranslatedPhrase**.

Eventually, we'll use **Phrase** to represent a phrase like "Madam, I'm Adam." that can qualify as a palindrome even if it's not literally the same forward and backward. At first, though, all we'll do is define a **Phrase** initializer function that takes in an argument (the **content**) and sets a *data attribute* called **content**.[2] As we'll see, we can access an object's attributes using the same dot notation used for methods.

In order to add the attribute, we first need to define the **__init__** method that gets called when we initialize an object using **Phrase()** (Listing 7.2). The use of double underscores is a convention in Python used to indicate "magic" methods used internally for defining object behavior. We'll see a couple more examples of such magic or "dunder" (**d**ouble-**under**score) methods in Section 7.2. (Underscores, both double and single, have special meaning for Python attributes and methods; see Section 7.4.1 for more.)

---

2. Python data attributes correspond to Ruby *instance variables* and JavaScript *properties*. Where Ruby uses the @ symbol and JavaScript uses **this** (followed by a dot), Python uses **self** (followed by a dot).

Listing 7.2: Defining __init__.

palindrome.py

```python
class Phrase:
    """A class to represent phrases."""

    def __init__(self, content):
        self.content = content

if __name__ == "__main__":
    phrase = Phrase("Madam, I'm Adam.")
    print(phrase.content)
```

Listing 7.2 initializes a data attribute called **content**, which is distinguished by being attached to the **self** object and inside the class represents the object itself.[3] Note that calling them both **content** is just a convention; we could have written this as well:

```python
def __init__(self, foo):
    self.bar = foo
```

That would probably be confusing to human readers but wouldn't bother Python one bit.

With the definition in Listing 7.2, we now have a working example:

```
(venv) $ python3 palindrome.py
Madam, I'm Adam.
```

We can also now assign directly to **content** using the dot notation, as seen in Listing 7.3.

Listing 7.3: Assigning to an object attribute.

palindrome.py

```python
class Phrase:
    """A class to represent phrases."""

    def __init__(self, content):
        self.content = content
```

---

3. If you ever find yourself writing classes with a large number of attributes, take a look at the **dataclasses** module. Data classes use a special *decorator* called **@dataclass** to create methods like __init__ automatically, saving you the trouble of typing out a bunch of **self.<something> = <something>** initializations.

```
if __name__ == "__main__":
    phrase = Phrase("Madam, I'm Adam.")
    print(phrase.content)

    phrase.content = "Able was I, ere I saw Elba."
    print(phrase.content)
```

The result is as you probably can guess:

```
(venv) $ python3 palindrome.py
Madam, I'm Adam.
Able was I, ere I saw Elba.
```

At this point, we're ready to restore the **reverse()** and **ispalindrome()** functions in our initial definition of **Phrase**, as shown in Listing 7.4 (which also deletes the calls to **print()** and related lines, though you are welcome to keep them if you like since they will be executed only when the file is run as a script due to the **if __name__ == "__main__"** trick).

Listing 7.4: Our initial **Phrase** class definition.
palindrome.py

```
class Phrase:
    """A class to represent phrases."""

    def __init__(self, content):
        self.content = content

def reverse(string):
    """Reverse a string."""
    return "".join(reversed(string))

def ispalindrome(string):
    """Return True for a palindrome, False otherwise."""
    processed_content = string.lower()
    return processed_content == reverse(processed_content)
```

Just as a reality check, it's a good idea to run it in the REPL to catch any syntax errors, etc.:

```
(venv) $ source venv/bin/activate
(venv) $ python3
```

```
>>> import palindrome
>>> phrase = palindrome.Phrase("Racecar")
>>> phrase.content
'Racecar'
>>> palindrome.ispalindrome(phrase.content)
True
```

As a next step, we'll move the **ispalindrome()** function into the **Phrase** object itself, adding it as a method. (Because **reverse()** is of potentially general utility, we'll leave it outside the class. Note that it is available inside the class even if placed after the class definition.) The only things we need to do are (1) change the method to take zero arguments and (2) use the **Phrase** content instead of the variable **string**. Exactly how to do this second step is shown in Listing 7.5.

Listing 7.5: Moving **ispalindrome()** into the **Phrase** class.
palindrome.py

```
class Phrase:
    """A class to represent phrases."""

    def __init__(self, content):
        self.content = content

    def ispalindrome(self):
        """Return True for a palindrome, False otherwise."""
        processed_content = self.content.lower()
        return processed_content == reverse(processed_content)

def reverse(string):
    """Reverse a string."""
    return "".join(reversed(string))
```

As with the assignment in Listing 7.2, Listing 7.5 shows that inside the **ispalindrome()** method we can access the value of **content** through **self**.

The result of Listing 7.5 is that we can now call **ispalindrome()** directly on a phrase instance. After reloading the **palindrome** module as in Section 5.3, we can confirm in the REPL:

```
>>> from importlib import reload
>>> reload(palindrome)
>>> phrase = palindrome.Phrase("Racecar")
```

Figure 7.2: A Formula One palindrome.

```
>>> phrase.ispalindrome()
True
```

It worked! A **phrase** instance initialized with the string "Racecar" knows that it's a palindrome (Figure 7.2[4]).

The palindrome detector in Listing 7.5 is fairly rudimentary, but we now have a good foundation for building (and testing) a more sophisticated palindrome detector in Chapter 8.

7.1.1 Exercises

1. By filling in the code in Listing 7.6, add a **louder** method to the **Phrase** object that returns a LOUDER (all-caps) version of the content. Confirm in the REPL that the result appears as in Listing 7.7. *Hint*: Use the appropriate string method from Section 2.5.

2. Restore the **if __name__ == "__main__"** material from Listing 7.3 and confirm that it is *not* run when importing **palindrome.py**.

---

4. Image courtesy of Msyaraafiq/Shutterstock.

Listing 7.6: Making the content LOUDER.
palindrome.py

```python
class Phrase:
    """A class to represent phrases."""

    def __init__(self, content):
        self.content = content

    def ispalindrome(self):
        """Return True for a palindrome, False otherwise."""
        processed_content = self.content.lower()
        return processed_content == reverse(processed_content)

    def louder(self):
        """Make the phrase LOUDER."""
        # FILL IN

def reverse(string):
    """Reverse a string."""
    return "".join(reversed(string))
```

Listing 7.7: Using `louder()` in the REPL.

```python
>>> reload(palindrome)
>>> p = palindrome.Phrase("yo adrian!")
>>> p.louder()
'YO ADRIAN!'
```

7.2 Custom Iterators

Previously in this tutorial, we've seen how to iterate through several different Python objects, including strings (Section 2.6), lists (Section 3.5), and dictionaries (Section 4.4.1). We also encountered iterators directly in Section 5.3. In this section, we'll learn how to add an iterator to a custom class as well.

Using the class defined in Listing 7.5, we can iterate through the content directly (since it's just a string):

```python
>>> phrase = palindrome.Phrase("Racecar")
>>> for c in phrase.content:
```

```
...     print(c)
...
R
a
c
e
c
a
r
```

This is roughly analogous to iterating through the keys of a dictionary using

```
for key in dictionary.keys():     # Not Pythonic
    print(key)
```

But recall from Section 4.4.1 that this works without calling the **keys()** method:

```
for key in dictionary:            # Pythonic
    print(key)
```

It would be nice if we could do the same thing with a **Phrase** instance, like this:

```
phrase = palindrome.Phrase("Racecar")
for c in phrase:
    print(c)
```

We can do this with a custom iterator. The general requirements for an iterator are twofold:

1. An **__iter__** method that does any necessary setup and then returns **self**
2. A **__next__** method that returns the next element in the sequence

Note that, as with **__init__**, the methods to perform iteration use the double-underscore convention to indicate that they are magic (dunder) methods used to define the behavior of Python objects.

In our particular case, we also need the **iter()** function, which turns an ordinary object into an iterator. We can see how this works with a string in the REPL:

```
>>> phrase_iterator = iter("foo")     # makes a string iterator
>>> type(phrase_iterator)             # use type() to find the type
```

```
<class 'str_iterator'>
>>> next(phrase_iterator)
'f'
>>> next(phrase_iterator)
'o'
>>> next(phrase_iterator)
'o'
>>> next(phrase_iterator)
Traceback (most recent call last):
  File "<stdin>", line 1, in <module>
StopIteration
```

We see from the **type()** function that **iter()** takes in a string and returns a string iterator. Calling **next()** on the iterator yields the next element in the sequence until it reaches the end, as indicated by the special **StopIteration** exception.

Our strategy for adding an iterator to the **Phrase** class looks like this:

1. In **__iter__**, create a phrase iterator based on the **content** attribute using **iter()**, and then return **self** as required by the way Python iterators work.

2. In **__next__**, call **next()** on the phrase iterator and return the result.

Converting these steps to code gives the result in Listing 7.8.

Listing 7.8: Adding an iterator to the **Phrase** class.

palindrome.py

```
class Phrase:
    """A class to represent phrases."""

    def __init__(self, content):
        self.content = content

    def ispalindrome(self):
        """Return True for a palindrome, False otherwise."""
        processed_content = self.content.lower()
        return processed_content == reverse(processed_content)

    def __iter__(self):
        self.phrase_iterator = iter(self.content)
        return self

    def __next__(self):
        return next(self.phrase_iterator)
```

```
def reverse(string):
    """Reverse a string."""
    return "".join(reversed(string))
```

With the code in Listing 7.8, we can reload the **palindrome** module to see if it worked:

```
>>> reload(palindrome)
>>> phrase = palindrome.Phrase("Racecar")
>>> for c in phrase:
...     print(c)
R
a
c
e
c
a
r
```

Yup! We can now iterate through a **Phrase** object without having to specify the **content** attribute explicitly.

7.2.1   Exercise

1. Using the REPL, determine if **list(phrase)** works after the custom iterator has been defined as in Listing 7.8. What about joining on the empty string using **"".join(phrase)**?

7.3   Inheritance

When learning about Python classes, it's useful to investigate the *class hierarchy* using the **__class__** and **__mro__** attributes, where the latter stands for *method resolution order*, which turns out to print the exact hierarchy we need.

Let's look at an example of what this means in the case of a familiar type of object, a string:

```
>>> s = "foobar"
>>> type(s)        # one way to get the class
<class 'str'>
>>> s.__class__    # another way to get the class
<class 'str'>
```

```
>>> s.__class__.__mro__
(<class 'str'>, <class 'object'>)
```

What this tells us is that a string is of class **str**, which in turn is of type **object**. The latter is known as a *superclass* because it is usually thought of as being "above" the **str** class.

A diagram of the resulting class hierarchy appears in Figure 7.3. We see here that the superclass of **str** is **object**, which is where the hierarchy ends. This pattern is true of every Python object: Trace back the class hierarchy far enough and you'll always reach **object**, which has no superclass itself.

The way Python's class hierarchy works is that each class *inherits* the attributes and methods of classes further up in the hierarchy. For example, we've just seen how to find the class of an object of type **str**:

```
>>> "honey badger".__class__
<class 'str'>
```

But where does the **__class__** attribute come from? The answer is that **str** inherits **__class__** from **object** itself:

```
>>> object().__class__
<class 'object'>
```

The class of each object with **object** as superclass stores its class name in **__class__**.

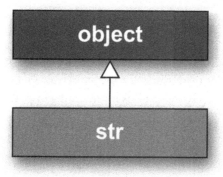

Figure 7.3: The inheritance hierarchy for the **str** class.

Let's return now to the **Phrase** class we defined in Section 7.1. As presently defined, **Phrase** *has a* **content** attribute, which in the terminology of object-oriented programming is known as a *has-a* relationship. Such a design is known as *composition*, where a **Phrase** is composed of a **content** attribute (possibly among other things). Another way of looking at the situation is to say that a **Phrase** *is a* string, which is known as an *is-a relationship*. In this case, we could arrange for the **Phrase** class to inherit from Python's native string class, called **str**, using code as in Listing 7.9.[5] A visual representation of the corresponding class hierarchies appears in Figure 7.4 and Figure 7.5 (with **Phrase** in place of **palindrome.Phrase** for brevity).

Listing 7.9: Inheriting from **str**.
palindrome.rb

```
class Phrase(str):
    """A class to represent phrases."""
    .
    .
    .
```

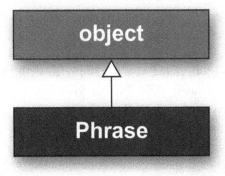

Figure 7.4: The class hierarchy for the **Phrase** class with composition.

---

5. As we'll see in Section 7.4, the way to implement inheritance in Python is simply to include the superclass as an argument (in this case, **str**).

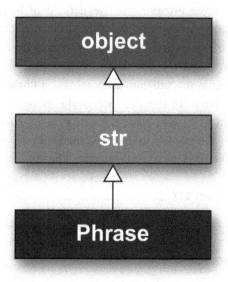

Figure 7.5: The class hierarchy for the **Phrase** class with inheritance from **str**.

Which design to adopt depends on our preferences as programmers and the general practices of the corresponding programming community. In particular, different language communities vary in their enthusiasm for inheriting from built-in objects like **str**. For example, such a practice is common in the Ruby community, even to the point of adding methods to the base **String**[6] class itself.

In contrast, many members of the Python community prefer to use composition in this case. In my survey of Pythonistas, some considered inheriting from **str** to be fine, but a majority considered it to be unPythonic, with one even stating that it seemed like a "Ruby developer writing Python." Perhaps the best test is that I actually implemented it when preparing this chapter; having **Phrase** inherit from **str** was fairly straightforward, but having **TranslatedPhrase** inherit from **Phrase** (Section 7.4) was *extremely* tricky (whereas the Ruby and even JavaScript versions were much easier). In order to avoid this complexity, and in accordance with my perception of generally preferred Python practices, this chapter uses composition instead of inheritance.

---

6. **String** is the Ruby analogue of Python's **str** class.

7.3.1 Exercise

1. What are the class hierarchies for lists and dictionaries?

7.4 Derived Classes

Let's build on the techniques in Section 7.3 to make a class that inherits from **Phrase**, which we'll call **TranslatedPhrase**. The purpose of this so-called *derived class* (or *subclass*) is to reuse as much of **Phrase** as possible while giving us the flexibility to, say, test if a *translation* is a palindrome.

We'll start by factoring **processed_content()** into a separate method, as shown in Listing 7.10. We'll see in a moment why this is useful in the current context, though it's a nice refinement in any case. Note that Listing 7.10 also eliminates the custom iterator from Section 7.2 for brevity, though you are welcome to retain it.

Listing 7.10: Factoring **processed_content()** into a method.
palindrome.py

```python
class Phrase:
    """A class to represent phrases."""

    def __init__(self, content):
        self.content = content

    def ispalindrome(self):
        """Return True for a palindrome, False otherwise."""
        return self.processed_content() == reverse(self.processed_content())

    def processed_content(self):
        """Process content for palindrome testing."""
        return self.content.lower()

def reverse(string):
    """Reverse a string."""
    return "".join(reversed(string))
```

Now we're ready to inherit from **Phrase**. We'll start by including the name of the superclass as an argument to the *derived* class:

```python
class TranslatedPhrase(Phrase):
    """A class to represent phrases with translation."""
    pass
```

Our plan is to use **TranslatedPhrase** like this:

```
TranslatedPhrase("recognize", "reconocer")
```

where the first argument is the **Phrase** content and the second argument is the translation. As a result, a **TranslatedPhrase** instance needs a **translation** attribute, which we'll create using **__init__** as with **content** in Listing 7.2:

```
class TranslatedPhrase(Phrase):
    """A class to represent phrases with translation."""

    def __init__(self, content, translation):
        # Handle content here.
        self.translation = translation
```

Note that **__init__** takes *two* arguments, **content** and **translation**. We've handled **translation** like a normal attribute, but what to do about **content**? The answer is a special Python function called **super()**:

```
class TranslatedPhrase(Phrase):
    """A class to represent phrases with translation."""

    def __init__(self, content, translation):
        super().__init__(content)
        self.translation = translation
```

This calls the **__init__** method for the superclass—in this case, **Phrase**. The result is that the **content** attribute gets set as in Listing 7.10.

Putting everything together gives the **TranslatedPhrase** class shown in Listing 7.11.

Listing 7.11: Defining **TranslatedPhrase**.
palindrome.py

```
class Phrase:
    """A class to represent phrases."""

    def __init__(self, content):
        self.content = content

    def ispalindrome(self):
        """Return True for a palindrome, False otherwise."""
        return self.processed_content() == reverse(self.processed_content())
```

```
    def processed_content(self):
        return self.content.lower()

class TranslatedPhrase(Phrase):
    """A class to represent phrases with translation."""

    def __init__(self, content, translation):
        super().__init__(content)
        self.translation = translation

def reverse(string):
    """Reverse a string."""
    return "".join(reversed(string))
```

Because **TranslatedPhrase** inherits from the **Phrase** object, an instance of **Trans-latedPhrase** automatically has all the methods of a **Phrase** instance, including **ispalindrome()**. Let's create a variable called **frase** (pronounced "FRAH-seh", Spanish for "phrase") to see how it works (Listing 7.12).

Listing 7.12: Defining a **TranslatedPhrase**.

```
>>> reload(palindrome)
>>> frase = palindrome.TranslatedPhrase("recognize", "reconocer")
>>> frase.ispalindrome()
False
```

We see that **frase** has an **ispalindrome()** method as claimed, and that it returns **False** because "recognize" isn't a palindrome.

But what if we wanted to use the *translation* instead of the content for determining whether the translated phrase is a palindrome or not? Because we factored **processed_content()** into a separate method (Listing 7.10), we can do this by *overriding* the **processed_content()** method in **TranslatedPhrase**, as seen in Listing 7.13.

Listing 7.13: Overriding a method.
palindrome.py

```
class Phrase:
    """A class to represent phrases."""

    def __init__(self, content):
        self.content = content
```

```
    def processed_content(self):
        """Process the content for palindrome testing."""
        return self.content.lower()

    def ispalindrome(self):
        """Return True for a palindrome, False otherwise."""
        return self.processed_content() == reverse(self.processed_content())

class TranslatedPhrase(Phrase):
    """A class to represent phrases with translation."""

    def __init__(self, content, translation):
        super().__init__(content)
        self.translation = translation

    def processed_content(self):
        """Override superclass method to use translation."""
        return self.translation.lower()

def reverse(string):
    """Reverse a string."""
    return "".join(reversed(string))
```

The key point in Listing 7.13 is that we're using **self.translation** in the **TranslatedPhrase** version of **processed_content()**, so Python knows to use that one instead of the one in **Phrase**. Because the translation "reconocer" *is* a palindrome, we get a different result from the one we got in Listing 7.12, as shown in Listing 7.14.

Listing 7.14: Calling **ispalindrome()** after overriding **processed_content()**.

```
>>> reload(palindrome)
>>> frase = palindrome.TranslatedPhrase("recognize", "reconocer")
>>> frase.ispalindrome()
True
```

The resulting inheritance hierarchy appears as in Figure 7.6.

This practice of overriding gives us great flexibility. We can trace the execution of **frase.ispalindrome()** for the two different cases:

Case 1: Listing 7.11 and Listing 7.12

      1. **frase.ispalindrome()** calls **ispalindrome()** on the **frase** instance, which is a **TranslatedPhrase**. Since there is no **ispalindrome()** method in the **TranslatedPhrase** object, Python uses the one from **Phrase**.

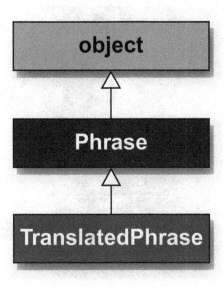

Figure 7.6: The inheritance hierarchy for the `TranslatedPhrase` class.

2. The **ispalindrome()** method in **Phrase** calls the **processed_content** method. Since there is no **processed_content()** method in the **Trans-latedPhrase** object, Python uses the one from **Phrase**.

3. The result is to compare the processed version of the **TranslatedPhrase** instance with its own reverse. Since "recognize" isn't a palindrome, the result is **False**.

Case 2: Listing 7.13 and Listing 7.14

1. **frase.ispalindrome()** calls **ispalindrome()** on the **frase** instance, which is a **TranslatedPhrase**. As in Case 1, there is no **ispalindrome()** method in the **TranslatedPhrase** object, so Python uses the one from **Phrase**.

2. The **ispalindrome()** method in **Phrase** calls the **processed_content** method. Since there now *is* a **processed_content()** method in the **TranslatedPhrase** object, Python uses the one from **TranslatedPhrase** instead of the one in **Phrase**.

Figure 7.7: Narciso se reconoce. (Narcissus recognizes himself.)

3. The result is to compare the processed version of **self.translation** with its own reverse. Since "reconocer" *is* a palindrome, the result is **True**.

¿Puedes «reconocer» un palíndromo en español? (Can you "reconocer" [recognize] a palindrome in Spanish?) (See Figure 7.7.[7])

7.4.1 Exercises

1. You may have noticed that the **processed_content()** method is only used internally to the classes. Many object-oriented languages have a way of designating such methods as *private*, a practice known as *encapsulation*. Python doesn't have truly private methods, but it does have a convention for indicating them using a leading underscore. Confirm that the classes still work after changing **processed_content()** to **_processed_content()** as shown in Listing 7.15.

---

7. John William Waterhouse, "Echo and Narcissus", 1903 (detail). Image courtesy of Archivart/Alamy Stock Photo.

Listing 7.15: Using a convention for private methods.

palindrome.py

```python
class Phrase:
    """A class to represent phrases."""

    def __init__(self, content):
        self.content = content

    def _processed_content(self):
        """Process the content for palindrome testing."""
        return self.content.lower()

    def ispalindrome(self):
        """Return True for a palindrome, False otherwise."""
        return self._processed_content() == reverse(self._processed_content())

class TranslatedPhrase(Phrase):
    """A class to represent phrases with translation."""

    def __init__(self, content, translation):
        super().__init__(content)
        self.translation = translation

    def _processed_content(self):
        """Override superclass method to use translation."""
        return self.translation.lower()

def reverse(string):
    """Reverse a string."""
    return "".join(reversed(string))
```

Note: Python has a second convention, known as *name mangling*, that uses *two* leading underscores. With this convention, Python automatically changes the name of the method in a standard way so that it can't be easily accessed through an object instance.

2. It might make sense when iterating over a **TranslatedPhrase** to use the translation instead of the untranslated content. Arrange for this by overriding the **__iter__** method in the derived class (Listing 7.16). Confirm using the Python interpreter that the updated iterator works as expected. (Note that Listing 7.16 incorporates the private method convention from the previous exercise.)

Listing 7.16: Overriding the **__iter__** method.

palindrome.py

```python
class Phrase:
    """A class to represent phrases."""
    .
    .
    .
    def __iter__(self):
        self.phrase_iterator = iter(self.content)
        return self

    def __next__(self):
        return next(self.phrase_iterator)

class TranslatedPhrase(Phrase):
    """A class to represent phrases with translation."""

    def __init__(self, content, translation):
        super().__init__(content)
        self.translation = translation

    def _processed_content(self):
        """Override superclass method to use translation."""
        return self.translation.lower()

    def __iter__(self):
        self.phrase_iterator = FILL_IN
        return self

def reverse(string):
    """Reverse a string."""
    return "".join(reversed(string))
```

CHAPTER 8

Testing and Test-Driven Development

Although rarely covered in introductory programming tutorials, *automated testing* is one of the most important subjects in modern software development. Accordingly, this chapter includes an introduction to testing in Python, including a first look at *test-driven development*, or TDD.

Test-driven development came up briefly in Section 6.5.1, which promised that we would use testing techniques to add an important capability to finding palindromes, namely, being able to detect complicated palindromes such as "A man, a plan, a canal—Panama!" (Figure 6.5) or "Madam, I'm Adam." (Figure 8.1[1]). This chapter fulfills that promise.

As it turns out, learning how to write Python tests will also give us a chance to learn how to create (and publish!) a Python package, another exceptionally useful Python skill rarely covered in introductory tutorials.

Here's our strategy for testing the current palindrome code and extending it to more complicated phrases:

1. Set up our initial package (Section 8.1).

2. Write automated tests for the existing **ispalindrome()** functionality (Section 8.2).

3. Write a *failing* test for the enhanced palindrome detector (RED) (Section 8.3).

---

1. "The Temptation of Adam" by Tintoretto. Image courtesy of Album/Alamy Stock Photo.

Figure 8.1: The Garden of Eden had it all—even palindromes.

4. Write (possibly ugly) code to get the test *passing* (GREEN) (Section 8.4).

5. *Refactor* the code to make it prettier, while ensuring that the test suite stays GREEN (Section 8.5).

8.1 Package Setup

We saw as early as Section 1.5 that the Python ecosystem includes a large number of self-contained software packages. In this section, we'll create a package based on the palindrome detector developed in Chapter 7. As part of this, we'll set up the beginnings of a *test suite* to test our code.

Python packages have a standard structure that can be visualized as shown in Listing 8.1 (which contains both generic elements like **pyproject.toml** and non-generic elements like **palindrome_YOUR_USERNAME_HERE**). The structure includes some configuration files (discussed in just a moment) and two directories: a **src** (source) directory and a **tests** directory. The **src** directory in turn contains a directory for the palindrome package, which includes a special required file called **__init__.py**

and the **palindrome_YOUR_USERNAME_HERE** module itself.[2] (It is possible to flatten
the directory structure by eliminating the package directory, but the structure in
Listing 8.1 is fairly standard and is designed to mirror the official Packaging Python
Projects documentation.) The result of the structure in Listing 8.1 will be the ability
to include the **Phrase** class developed in Chapter 7 using the code

```
from palindrome_mhartl.phrase import Phrase
```

Listing 8.1: File and directory structure for a sample Python package.

```
python_package_tutorial/
├── LICENSE
├── pyproject.toml
├── README.md
├── src/
│   └── palindrome_YOUR_USERNAME_HERE/
│       ├── __init__.py
│       └── phrase.py
└── tests/
    └── test_phrase.py
```

We can create the structure in Listing 8.1 by hand using a combination of **mkdir**
and **touch**, as shown in Listing 8.2.

Listing 8.2: Setting up a Python package.

```
$ cd ~/repos     # Use ~/environment/repos on Cloud9
$ mkdir python_package_tutorial
$ cd python_package_tutorial
$ touch LICENSE pyproject.toml README.md
$ mkdir -p src/palindrome_YOUR_USERNAME_HERE
$ touch src/palindrome_YOUR_USERNAME_HERE/__init__.py
$ touch src/palindrome_YOUR_USERNAME_HERE/phrase.py
$ mkdir tests
$ touch tests/test_phrase.py
```

---

2. Technically, there are various distinctions between *packages* and *modules* in Python, but they are
rarely important. See this Stack Overflow comment (https://stackoverflow.com/questions/7948494/whats-
the-difference-between-a-python-module-and-a-python-package/49420164#49420164) for some of the
minutiae on the subject.

At this point, we'll fill in a few of the files with more information, including the project configuration file **pyproject.toml** (Listing 8.3), a README file **README.md** (Listing 8.4), and a **LICENSE** file (Listing 8.5).[3] Some of these files are only templates, so you should replace things like **<username>** in **pyproject.toml** with your own username, the **url** field with the planned URL for your project, etc. (Being able to do things like this is an excellent application of technical sophistication.) To see a concrete example of the files in this section, see the GitHub repo (https://github.com/mhartl/python_package_tutorial) for my version of this package.

Listing 8.3: The project configuration for a Python package.
~/python_package_tutorial/project.toml

```
[build-system]
requires = ["hatchling"]
build-backend = "hatchling.build"

[project]
name = "example_package_YOUR_USERNAME_HERE"
version = "0.0.1"
authors = [
  { name="Example Author", email="author@example.com" },
]
description = "A small example package"
readme = "README.md"
requires-python = ">=3.7"
classifiers = [
    "Programming Language :: Python :: 3",
    "License :: OSI Approved :: MIT License",
    "Operating System :: OS Independent",
]

[project.urls]
"Homepage" = "https://github.com/pypa/sampleproject"
"Bug Tracker" = "https://github.com/pypa/sampleproject/issues"
```

---

3. Don't worry about the details of files like **pyproject.toml**; I don't understand them either. I just copied them from the documentation (Box 1.2).

Listing 8.4: A README file for the package.
~/python_package_tutorial/README.md

```
# Palindrome Package

This is a sample Python package for
[*Learn Enough Python to Be Dangerous*](https://www.learnenough.com/python)
by [Michael Hartl](https://www.michaelhartl.com/).
```

Listing 8.5: A license template for a Python package.
~/python_package_tutorial/LICENSE

```
Copyright (c) YYYY Your Name

Permission is hereby granted, free of charge, to any person obtaining a copy
of this software and associated documentation files (the "Software"), to deal
in the Software without restriction, including without limitation the rights
to use, copy, modify, merge, publish, distribute, sublicense, and/or sell
copies of the Software, and to permit persons to whom the Software is
furnished to do so, subject to the following conditions:

The above copyright notice and this permission notice shall be included in all
copies or substantial portions of the Software.

THE SOFTWARE IS PROVIDED "AS IS", WITHOUT WARRANTY OF ANY KIND, EXPRESS OR
IMPLIED, INCLUDING BUT NOT LIMITED TO THE WARRANTIES OF MERCHANTABILITY,
FITNESS FOR A PARTICULAR PURPOSE AND NONINFRINGEMENT. IN NO EVENT SHALL THE
AUTHORS OR COPYRIGHT HOLDERS BE LIABLE FOR ANY CLAIM, DAMAGES OR OTHER
LIABILITY, WHETHER IN AN ACTION OF CONTRACT, TORT OR OTHERWISE, ARISING FROM,
OUT OF OR IN CONNECTION WITH THE SOFTWARE OR THE USE OR OTHER DEALINGS IN THE
SOFTWARE.
```

With all that configuration done, we're now ready to configure the environment for development and testing. As in Section 1.3, we'll use **venv** for the virtual environment. We'll also be using **pytest** for testing, which we can install using **pip**. The resulting commands are shown in Listing 8.6.

Listing 8.6: Setting up the package environment (including testing).

```
$ deactivate      # just in case a virtual env is already active
$ python3 -m venv venv
$ source venv/bin/activate
(venv) $ pip install --upgrade pip
(venv) $ pip install pytest==7.1.3
```

At this point, as in Section 1.5.1, it's a good idea to create a **.gitignore** file (Listing 8.7), put the project under version control with Git (Listing 8.8), and create a repository at GitHub (Figure 8.2). This last step will also give you URLs for the configuration file in Listing 8.3.

Listing 8.7: Ignoring certain files and directories.
.gitignore

```
venv/

*.pyc
__pycache__/

instance/

.pytest_cache/
.coverage
htmlcov/

dist/
build/
*.egg-info/

.DS_Store
```

Listing 8.8: Initializing the package repository.

```
$ git init
$ git add -A
$ git commit -m "Initialize repository"
```

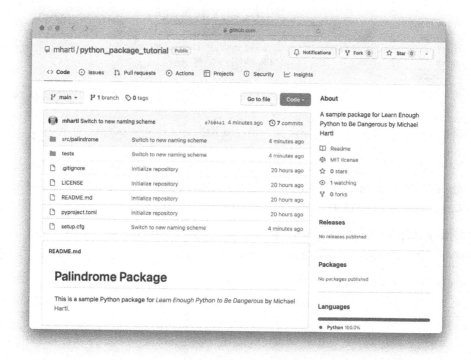

Figure 8.2: The package repository and README at GitHub.

8.1.1 Exercise

1. If you haven't already, update Listing 8.3 with the right package name and fill the **url** and **Bug Tracker** fields with the corresponding GitHub URLs (the tracker URL is just the base URL plus **/issues**). Likewise, update the license template in Listing 8.5 with your name and the current year. Commit and push your changes up to GitHub.

8.2 Initial Test Coverage

Now that we've set up our basic package structure, we're ready to get started testing. Because the necessary **pytest** package has already been installed (Listing 8.6), we can actually run the (nonexistent) tests immediately:

```
(venv) $ pytest
============================= test session starts ==============================
platform darwin -- Python 3.10.6, pytest-7.1.3, pluggy-1.0.0
rootdir: /Users/mhartl/repos/python_package_tutorial
collected 0 items

=========================== no tests ran in 0.00s ==============================
```

Exact details will differ (and will be omitted in future examples for that reason), but your results should be similar.

Now let's write a minimal failing test and then get it to pass. Because we've already created a **tests** directory with the test file **test_phrase.py** (Listing 8.2), we can begin by adding the code shown in Listing 8.9.

Listing 8.9: The initial test suite. RED

test/test_phrase.py

```
def test_initial_example():
    assert False
```

Listing 8.9 defines a function containing one *assertion*, which asserts that something has a boolean value of **True**, in which case the assertion passes, and fails otherwise. Because Listing 8.9 literally asserts that **False** is **True**, it fails by design:

Listing 8.10: RED

```
(venv) $ pytest
============================= test session starts ==============================
collected 1 item

tests/palindrome_test.py F                                             [100%]

=================================== FAILURES ===================================
_____ test_non_palindrome _____

    def test_non_palindrome():
>       assert False
E       assert False

tests/palindrome_test.py:4: AssertionError
=========================== short test summary info ============================
FAILED tests/palindrome_test.py::test_non_palindrome - assert False
============================== 1 failed in 0.01s ===============================
```

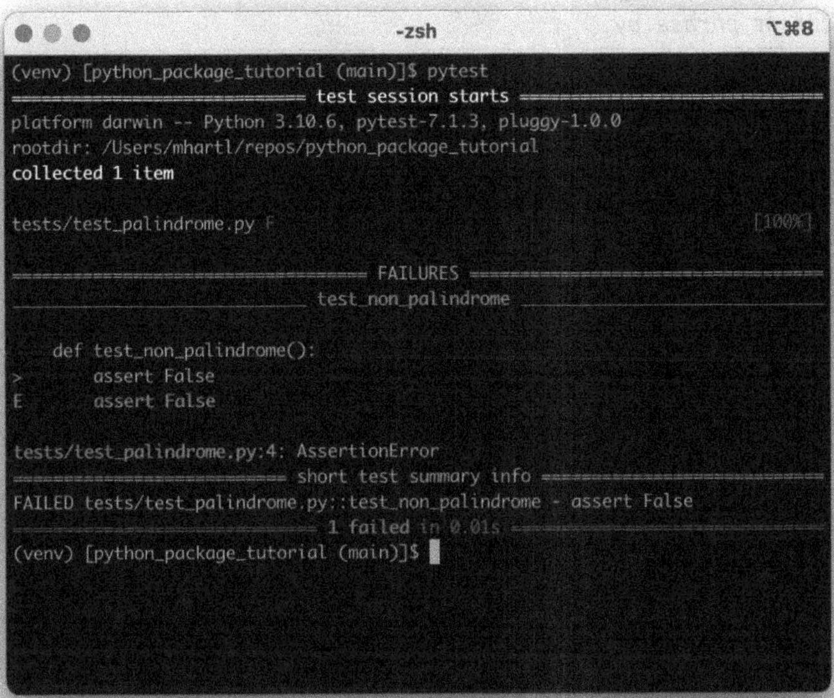

Figure 8.3: The RED state of the initial test suite.

By itself, this test isn't useful, but it demonstrates the concept, and we'll add a useful test in just a moment.

Many systems, including mine, display failing tests in the color red, as shown in Figure 8.3. Because of this, a failing test (or collection of tests, known as a *test suite*) is often referred to as being RED. To help us keep track of our progress, the captions of code listings corresponding to a failing test suite are labeled RED, as seen in Listing 8.9 and Listing 8.10.

To get from a failing to a passing state, we can change **False** to **True** in Listing 8.9, yielding the code in Listing 8.11.

Listing 8.11: A passing test suite. GREEN

test/test_phrase.py

```
def test_initial_example():
    assert True
```

As expected, this test passes:

Listing 8.12: GREEN

```
(venv) $ pytest
============================== test session starts ===============================
collected 1 item

tests/test_phrase.py .                                                     [100%]

=============================== 1 passed in 0.00s ================================
```

Because many systems display passing tests using the color green (Figure 8.4), a passing test suite is often referred to as GREEN. As with RED test suites, the captions of code listings corresponding to passing tests will be labeled GREEN (as seen in Listing 8.11 and Listing 8.12).

In addition to asserting that true things are **True**, it is often convenient to assert that false things are *not* **False**, which we can accomplish using **not** (Section 2.4.1), as shown in Listing 8.13.

Listing 8.13: A different way to pass. GREEN

test/test_phrase.py

```
def test_initial_example():
    assert not False
```

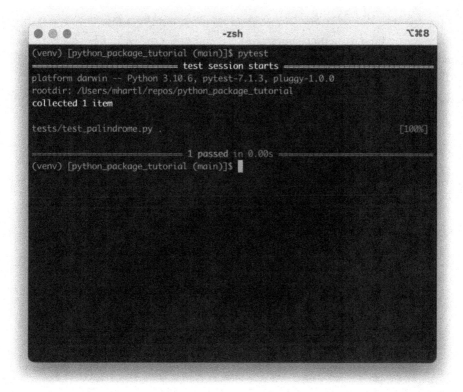

Figure 8.4: A GREEN test suite.

As before, this test is GREEN:

Listing 8.14: GREEN

```
(venv) $ pytest
============================ test session starts ============================
collected 1 item

tests/test_phrase.py .                                                [100%]

============================ 1 passed in 0.00s =============================
```

8.2.1   A Useful Passing Test

Having learned the basic mechanics of GREEN and RED tests, we're now ready to write our first useful test. Because we mainly want to test the **Phrase** class, our first step is to fill in **phrase.py** with the source code for defining phrases. We'll start with just **Phrase** itself (without **TranslatedPhrase**), as shown in Listing 8.15. Note that for brevity we've also omitted the iterator code from Section 5.3.

Listing 8.15: Defining **Phrase** in a package.
~/src/palindrome/phrase.py

```python
class Phrase:
    """A class to represent phrases."""

    def __init__(self, content):
        self.content = content

    def processed_content(self):
        """Process the content for palindrome testing."""
        return self.content.lower()

    def ispalindrome(self):
        """Return True for a palindrome, False otherwise."""
        return self.processed_content() == reverse(self.processed_content())

def reverse(string):
    """Reverse a string."""
    return "".join(reversed(string))
```

At this point, we're ready to try importing **Phrase** into our test file. With the package structure as in Listing 8.1, the **Phrase** class should be importable from the **palindrome** package, which in turn should be available using **palindrome.-phrase**.[4] The result appears in Listing 8.16, which also replaces the example test from Listing 8.13.

---

4. You wouldn't necessarily have been able to guess this; it's just the way Python packages work based on the directory structure shown in Listing 8.1 (i.e., the **phrase.py** file is in a directory called **palindrome**).

Listing 8.16: Importing the **palindrome** package. RED
test/test_phrase.py

```
from palindrome_mhartl.phrase import Phrase
```

Unfortunately, the test suite doesn't pass even though there's no longer even a test that could fail:

Listing 8.17: RED

```
(venv) $ pytest
============================= test session starts ==============================
collected 0 items / 1 error

==================================== ERRORS ====================================
_____ ERROR collecting tests/test_phrase.py _____
ImportError while importing test module
'/Users/mhartl/repos/python_package_tutorial/tests/test_phrase.py'.
Hint: make sure your test modules/packages have valid Python names.
Traceback:
lib/python3.10/importlib/__init__.py:126: in import_module
    return _bootstrap._gcd_import(name[level:], package, level)
tests/test_phrase.py:1: in <module>
    from palindrome_mhartl.phrase import Phrase
E   ImportError: cannot import name 'Phrase' from 'palindrome.palindrome'
(/Users/mhartl/repos/python_package_tutorial/src/palindrome/phrase.py)
=========================== short test summary info ============================
ERROR tests/test_phrase.py
!!!!!!!!!!!!!!!!!!!!!! Interrupted: 1 error during collection !!!!!!!!!!!!!!!!!!!!!!
============================== 1 error in 0.03s ===============================
```

The issue is that our package needs to be installed in the local environment in order to perform the **import** in Listing 8.16. Because it hasn't been installed yet, the test suite is in an error state. Although this is technically not the same as a failing state, an error state is still often called RED.

To fix the error, we need to install the **palindrome** package locally, which we can do using the command shown in Listing 8.18.

Listing 8.18: Installing an editable package locally.

```
(venv) $ pip install -e .
```

As you can learn from running **pip install --help** (or by viewing the **pytest** documentation), the **-e** option installs the package in **e**ditable mode, so it will update automatically when we edit the files. The location of the installation is in the current directory, as indicated by the **.** (dot).

At this point, the test suite should be, if not quite GREEN, at least no longer RED:

```
(venv) $ pytest
=========================== test session starts ===========================
collected 0 items

=========================== no tests ran in 0.00s ===========================
```

Now we're ready to start making some tests to check that the code in Listing 8.15 is actually working. We'll start with a negative case, checking that a non-palindrome is correctly categorized as such:

```
def test_non_palindrome():
    assert not Phrase("apple").ispalindrome()
```

Here we've used **assert** to assert that **"apple"** should *not* be a palindrome (Figure 8.5[5]).

In similar fashion, we can test a literal palindrome (one that's literally the same forward and backward) with another **assert**:

```
def test_literal_palindrome():
    assert Phrase("racecar").ispalindrome()
```

Combining the code from the above discussion gives us the code shown in Listing 8.19.

Listing 8.19: An actually useful test suite.
test/test_phrase.py

```
from palindrome_mhartl.phrase import Phrase


def test_non_palindrome():
    assert not Phrase("apple").ispalindrome()
```

---

5. Image courtesy of Glayan/Shutterstock.

Figure 8.5: The word "apple": not a palindrome.

```
def test_literal_palindrome():
    assert Phrase("racecar").ispalindrome()
```

Now for the real test (so to speak):

Listing 8.20: GREEN

```
(venv) $ pytest
============================== test session starts ==============================
platform darwin -- Python 3.10.6, pytest-7.1.3, pluggy-1.0.0
rootdir: /Users/mhartl/repos/python_package_tutorial
collected 2 items

tests/test_phrase.py ..                                          [100%]

=============================== 2 passed in 0.00s ===============================
```

The tests are now GREEN, indicating that they are in a passing state. That means our code is working!

8.2.2 Pending Tests

Before moving on, we'll add a couple of *pending* tests, which are placeholders/reminders for tests we want to write. The way to write a pending test is to use the **skip()** function, which we can include directly from the **pytest** package, as shown in Listing 8.21.

Listing 8.21: Adding two pending tests. YELLOW
test/test_phrase.py

```
from pytest import skip

from palindrome_mhartl.phrase import Phrase


def test_non_palindrome():
    assert not Phrase("apple").ispalindrome()

def test_literal_palindrome():
    assert Phrase("racecar").ispalindrome()

def test_mixed_case_palindrome():
    skip()

def test_palindrome_with_punctuation():
    skip()
```

We can see the result of Listing 8.21 by rerunning the test suite:

Listing 8.22: YELLOW

```
(venv) $ pytest
============================== test session starts ==============================
collected 4 items

tests/test_phrase.py ..ss                                                [100%]

========================== 2 passed, 2 skipped in 0.00s ==========================
```

Note how the test runner displays the letter **s** for each of the two "skips". Sometimes people speak of a test suite with pending tests as being YELLOW, in analogy with the

Figure 8.6: A YELLOW (pending) test suite.

red-yellow-green color scheme of traffic lights (Figure 8.6), although it's also common to refer to any non-RED test suite as GREEN.

Filling in the test for a mixed-case palindrome is left as an exercise (with a solution shown in Listing 8.25), while filling in the second pending test and getting it to pass is the subject of Section 8.3 and Section 8.4.

8.2.3 Exercises

1. By filling in the code in Listing 8.23, add a test for a mixed-case palindrome like "RaceCar". Is the test suite still GREEN (or YELLOW)?

2. In order to make 100% sure that the tests are testing what we *think* they're testing, it's a good practice to get to a failing state (RED) by intentionally *breaking* the tests. Change the application code to break each of the existing tests in turn, and then confirm that they are GREEN again once the original code has been restored. An example of code that breaks the test in the previous exercise (but not the other tests) appears in Listing 8.24. (One advantage of writing the tests *first* is that this RED–GREEN cycle happens automatically.)

Listing 8.23: Adding a test for a mixed-case palindrome.
test/test_phrase.py

```
from pytest import skip

from palindrome_mhartl.phrase import Phrase


def test_non_palindrome():
    assert not Phrase("apple").ispalindrome()

def test_literal_palindrome():
    assert Phrase("racecar").ispalindrome()

def test_mixed_case_palindrome():
    FILL_IN

def test_palindrome_with_punctuation():
    skip()
```

Listing 8.24: Intentionally breaking a test. RED
src/palindrome/phrase.py

```
class Phrase:
    """A class to represent phrases."""

    def __init__(self, content):
        self.content = content

    def processed_content(self):
        """Process the content for palindrome testing."""
        return self.content#.lower()
```

```
    def ispalindrome(self):
        """Return True for a palindrome, False otherwise."""
        return self.processed_content() == reverse(self.processed_content())

def reverse(string):
    """Reverse a string."""
    return "".join(reversed(string))
```

8.3 Red

In this section, we'll take the important first step toward being able to detect more complex palindromes like "Madam, I'm Adam." and "A man, a plan, a canal—Panama!". Unlike the previous strings we've encountered, these phrases—which contain both spaces and punctuation—aren't strictly palindromes in a literal sense, even if we ignore capitalization. Instead of testing the strings as they are, we have to figure out a way to select only the letters, and then see if the resulting letters are the same forward and backward.

The code to do this is fairly tricky, but the tests for it are simple. This is one of the situations where test-driven development particularly shines (Box 8.1). We can write our simple tests, thereby getting to RED, and then write the application code any way we want to get to GREEN (Section 8.4). At that point, with the tests protecting us against undiscovered errors, we can change the application code with confidence (Section 8.5).

Box 8.1: When to test

When deciding when and how to test, it's helpful to understand *why* to test. In my view, writing automated tests has three main benefits:

1. Tests protect against *regressions*, where a functioning feature stops working for some reason.
2. Tests allow code to be *refactored* (i.e., changing its form without changing its function) with greater confidence.
3. Tests act as a *client* for the application code, thereby helping determine its design and its interface with other parts of the system.

Although none of the above benefits *require* that tests be written first, there are many circumstances where test-driven development (TDD) is a valuable tool to have in your kit. Deciding when and how to test depends in part on how comfortable you are writing tests; many developers find that, as they get better at writing tests, they are more inclined to write them first. It also depends on how difficult the test is relative to the application code, how precisely the desired features are known, and how likely the feature is to break in the future.

In this context, it's helpful to have a set of guidelines on when we should test first (or test at all). Here are some suggestions based on my own experience:

- When a test is especially short or simple compared to the application code it tests, lean toward writing the test first.

- When the desired behavior isn't yet crystal clear, lean toward writing the application code first, then write a test to codify the result.

- Whenever a bug is found, write a test to reproduce it and protect against regressions, then write the application code to fix it.

- Write tests before refactoring code, focusing on testing error-prone code that's especially likely to break.

We'll start by writing a test for a palindrome with punctuation, which just parallels the tests from Listing 8.19:

```
def test_palindrome_with_punctuation():
    assert palindrome.ispalindrome("Madam, I'm Adam.")
```

The updated test suite appears in Listing 8.25, which also includes the solution to a couple of exercises in Listing 8.23 (Figure 8.7[6]).

Listing 8.25: Adding a test for a punctuated palindrome. RED
test/test_phrase.py

```
from pytest import skip

from palindrome_mhartl.phrase import Phrase


def test_non_palindrome():
    assert not Phrase("apple").ispalindrome()
```

---

6. Image courtesy of Msyaraafiq/Shutterstock.

Figure 8.7: "RaceCar" is still a palindrome (ignoring case).

```
def test_literal_palindrome():
    assert Phrase("racecar").ispalindrome()

def test_mixed_case_palindrome():
    assert Phrase("RaceCar").ispalindrome()

def test_palindrome_with_punctuation():
    assert Phrase("Madam, I'm Adam.").ispalindrome()
```

As required, the test suite is now RED (output somewhat streamlined):

Listing 8.26: RED

```
(venv) $ pytest
============================ test session starts ===============================
collected 4 items

tests/test_phrase.py ...F                                                  [100%]

==================================== FAILURES ==================================
_____ test_palindrome_with_punctuation _____

    def test_palindrome_with_punctuation():
>       assert Phrase("Madam, I'm Adam.").ispalindrome()
E       assert False
```

```
tests/test_phrase.py:14: AssertionError
=========================== short test summary info ============================
FAILED tests/test_phrase.py::test_palindrome_with_punctuation - assert False
========================== 1 failed, 3 passed in 0.01s =========================
```

At this point, we can start thinking about how to write the application code and get to GREEN. Our strategy will be to write a **letters()** method that returns only the letters in the content string. In other words, the code

```
Phrase("Madam, I'm Adam.").letters()
```

should evaluate to this:

```
"MadamImAdam"
```

Getting to that state will allow us to use our current palindrome detector to determine whether the original phrase is a palindrome or not.

Having made this specification, we can now write a simple test for **letters()** by asserting that the result is as indicated:

```
assert Phrase("Madam, I'm Adam.").letters() == "MadamImAdam"
```

The new test appears with the others in Listing 8.27.

Listing 8.27: Adding a test for the **letters()** method. RED
test/test_phrase.py

```python
from pytest import skip

from palindrome_mhartl.phrase import Phrase


def test_non_palindrome():
    assert not Phrase("apple").ispalindrome()

def test_literal_palindrome():
    assert Phrase("racecar").ispalindrome()

def test_mixed_case_palindrome():
    assert Phrase("RaceCar").ispalindrome()
```

```
def test_palindrome_with_punctuation():
    assert Phrase("Madam, I'm Adam.").ispalindrome()

def test_letters():
    assert Phrase("Madam, I'm Adam.").letters() == "MadamImAdam"
```

Meanwhile, although we aren't yet ready to define a working **letters()** method, we can add a *stub*: a method that doesn't work, but at least exists. For simplicity, we'll simply return nothing (using the special **pass** keyword), as shown in Listing 8.28.

Listing 8.28: A stub for the **letters()** method. RED

src/palindrome/phrase.py

```
class Phrase:
    """A class to represent phrases."""

    def __init__(self, content):
        self.content = content

    def ispalindrome(self):
        """Return True for a palindrome, False otherwise."""
        return self.processed_content() == reverse(self.processed_content())

    def processed_content(self):
        """Return content for palindrome testing."""
        return self.content.lower()

    def letters(self):
        """Return the letters in the content."""
        pass

def reverse(string):
    """Reverse a string."""
    return "".join(reversed(string))
```

The new test for **letters()** is RED as expected (which also shows that the **pass** in Listing 8.28 just returns **None**):

Listing 8.29: RED

```
(venv) $ pytest
=========================== test session starts ===========================
collected 5 items

tests/test_phrase.py ...FF                                        [100%]

================================= FAILURES =================================
_____ test_palindrome_with_punctuation _____

    def test_palindrome_with_punctuation():
>       assert Phrase("Madam, I'm Adam.").ispalindrome()
E       assert False

tests/test_phrase.py:14: AssertionError
_____ test_letters _____

    def test_letters():
>       assert Phrase("Madam, I'm Adam.").letters() == "MadamImAdam"
E       assert None == 'MadamImAdam'
tests/test_phrase.py:17: AssertionError
========================== short test summary info ========================
FAILED tests/test_phrase.py::test_palindrome_with_punctuation - assert False
FAILED tests/test_phrase.py::test_letters - assert None == 'MadamImAdam'
========================= 2 failed, 3 passed in 0.01s =====================
```

With our two RED tests capturing the desired behavior, we're now ready to move on to the application code and try getting it to GREEN.

8.3.1 Exercise

1. Confirm that commenting out the **letters()** stub in Listing 8.28 yields a failing state rather than an error state. (This behavior is relatively unusual, with many other languages distinguishing between a non-working method and one that's missing altogether. In Python, though, the result is the same failing state in either case.)

8.4 Green

Now that we have RED tests to capture the enhanced behavior of our palindrome detector, it's time to make them GREEN. Part of the philosophy of TDD is to get them passing without worrying too much at first about the quality of the implementation. Once the test suite is GREEN, we can polish it up without introducing regressions (Box 8.1).

The main challenge is implementing **letters()**, which returns a string of the letters (but not any other characters) making up the **content** of the **Phrase**. In other words, we need to select the characters that match a certain pattern. This sounds like a job for regular expressions (Section 4.3).

At times like these, using an online regex matcher with a regex reference like the one shown in Figure 4.5 is an excellent idea. Indeed, sometimes they make things a little *too* easy, such as when the reference has the exact regex you need (Figure 8.8).

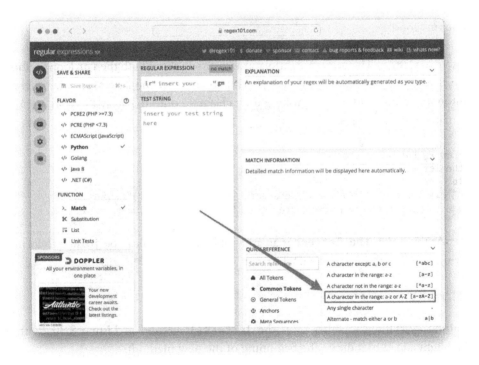

Figure 8.8: The exact regex we need.

Let's test it in the console to make sure it satisfies our criteria (using the
re.search() method introduced in Section 4.3):[7]

```
$ source venv/bin/activate
(venv) $ python3
>>> import re
>>> re.search(r"[a-zA-Z]", "M")
<re.Match object; span=(0, 1), match='M'>
>>> bool(re.search(r"[a-zA-Z]", "M"))
True
>>> bool(re.search(r"[a-zA-Z]", "d"))
True
>>> bool(re.search(r"[a-zA-Z]", ","))
False
```

Lookin' good!

We're now in a position to build up an array of characters that matches upper- or
lowercase letters. The most straightforward way to do this is with the **for** loop method
we first saw in Section 2.6. We'll start with an array for the letters, and then iterate
through the **content** string, pushing each character onto the array (Section 3.4.3) if
it matches the letter regex:

```
# Works but not Pythonic
the_letters = []
for character in self.content:
    if re.search(r"[a-zA-Z]", character):
        the_letters.append(character)
```

At this point, **the_letters** is an array of letters, which can be **join**ed to form a
string of the letters in the original string:

```
"".join(the_letters)
```

Putting everything together gives the **letters()** method in Listing 8.30 (with a
highlight added to indicate the beginning of the new method).

---

7. Note that this won't work for non–ASCII characters. If you need to match words containing such characters, the Google search python unicode letter regular expression might be helpful. Thanks to reader Paul
Gemperle for pointing out this issue.

Listing 8.30: A working `letters()` method (but with full suite still RED).
src/palindrome/phrase.py

```python
import re

class Phrase:
    """A class to represent phrases."""

    def __init__(self, content):
        self.content = content

    def ispalindrome(self):
        """Return True for a palindrome, False otherwise."""
        return self.processed_content() == reverse(self.processed_content())

    def processed_content(self):
        """Return content for palindrome testing."""
        return self.content.lower()

    def letters(self):
        """Return the letters in the content."""
        the_letters = []
        for character in self.content:
            if re.search(r"[a-zA-Z]", character):
                the_letters.append(character)
        return "".join(the_letters)

def reverse(string):
    """Reverse a string."""
    return "".join(reversed(string))
```

Although the full test suite is still RED, our `letters()` test should now be GREEN, as indicated by the number of failing tests changing from 2 to 1:

Listing 8.31: RED

```
(venv) $ pytest
============================ test session starts ============================
platform darwin -- Python 3.10.6, pytest-7.1.3, pluggy-1.0.0
rootdir: /Users/mhartl/repos/python_package_tutorial
collected 5 items

tests/test_phrase.py ...F.                                          [100%]

================================= FAILURES =================================
```

```
_____ test_palindrome_with_punctuation _____

    def test_palindrome_with_punctuation():
>       assert Phrase("Madam, I'm Adam.").ispalindrome()
E       assert False

tests/test_phrase.py:14: AssertionError
=========================== short test summary info ============================
FAILED tests/test_phrase.py::test_palindrome_with_punctuation - assert False
========================== 1 failed, 4 passed in 0.01s ========================
```

We can get the final RED test to pass by replacing **self.content** with **self. letters()** in the **processed_content()** method. The result appears in Listing 8.32.

Listing 8.32: A working **ispalindrome()** method. GREEN
src/palindrome/phrase.py

```python
import re


class Phrase:
    """A class to represent phrases."""

    def __init__(self, content):
        self.content = content

    def ispalindrome(self):
        """Return True for a palindrome, False otherwise."""
        return self.processed_content() == reverse(self.processed_content())

    def processed_content(self):
        """Return content for palindrome testing."""
        return self.letters().lower()

    def letters(self):
        """Return the letters in the content."""
        the_letters = []
        for character in self.content:
            if re.search(r"[a-zA-Z]", character):
                the_letters.append(character)
        return "".join(the_letters)

def reverse(string):
    """Reverse a string."""
    return "".join(reversed(string))
```

Figure 8.9: Our detector finally understands Adam's palindromic nature.

The result of Listing 8.32 is a GREEN test suite (Figure 8.9[8]):

Listing 8.33: GREEN

```
(venv) $ pytest
============================ test session starts =============================
collected 5 items

tests/test_phrase.py .....                                           [100%]

============================= 5 passed in 0.00s =============================
```

It may not be the prettiest code in the world, but this GREEN test suite means our code is working!

---

8. Image courtesy of Album/Alamy Stock Photo.

8.4.1 Exercise

1. Using the same code shown in Listing 8.16, import the **Phrase** class into the
   Python REPL and confirm directly that **ispalindrome()** can successfully detect
   palindromes of the form "Madam, I'm Adam."

8.5 Refactor

Although the code in Listing 8.32 is now working, as evidenced by our GREEN test
suite, it relies on a rather cumbersome **for** loop that appends to a list rather than
creating it all at once. In this section, we'll *refactor* our code, which is the process of
changing the form of code without changing its function.

By running our test suite after any significant changes, we'll catch any regressions
quickly, thereby giving us confidence that the final form of the refactored code is still
correct. Throughout this section, I suggest making changes incrementally and running
the test suite after each change to confirm that the suite is still GREEN.

Per Chapter 6, a more Pythonic way of creating a list of the sort in Listing 8.32
is to use a list comprehension. In particular, the loop in Listing 8.32 bears a strong
resemblance to the **imperative_singles()** function from Listing 6.4:

```
states = ["Kansas", "Nebraska", "North Dakota", "South Dakota"]
  .

  .

  .
# singles: Imperative version
def imperative_singles(states):
    singles = []
    for state in states:
        if len(state.split()) == 1:
            singles.append(state)
    return singles
```

As we saw in Listing 6.5, this can be replaced using a list comprehension with a
condition:

```
# singles: Functional version
def functional_singles(states):
    return [state for state in states if len(state.split()) == 1]
```

Let's drop into the REPL to see how to do the same thing in the present case:

```
>>> content = "Madam, I'm Adam."
>>> [c for c in content]
['M', 'a', 'd', 'a', 'm', ',', ' ', 'I', "'", 'm', ' ', 'A', 'd', 'a', 'm', '.']
>>> [c for c in content if re.search(r"[a-zA-Z]", c)]
['M', 'a', 'd', 'a', 'm', 'I', 'm', 'A', 'd', 'a', 'm']
>>> "".join([c for c in content if re.search(r"[a-zA-Z]", c)])
'MadamImAdam'
```

We see here how combining a list comprehension with a condition and a **join()** lets us replicate the current functionality of **letters()**. In fact, inside the argument to **join()** we can omit the square brackets and use a generator comprehension (Section 6.4) instead:

```
>>> "".join(c for c in content if re.search(r"[a-zA-Z]", c))
'MadamImAdam'
```

This leads to the updated method shown in Listing 8.34. As is so often the case with comprehension solutions, we have been able to condense the imperative solution down to a single line.

Listing 8.34: Refactoring **letters()** down to a single line. GREEN
src/palindrome/phrase.py

```python
import re


class Phrase:
    """A class to represent phrases."""

    def __init__(self, content):
        self.content = content

    def ispalindrome(self):
        """Return True for a palindrome, False otherwise."""
        return self.processed_content() == reverse(self.processed_content())

    def processed_content(self):
        """Return content for palindrome testing."""
        return self.letters().lower()

    def letters(self):
        """Return the letters in the content."""
```

```
    return "".join(c for c in self.content if re.search(r"[a-zA-Z]", c))

def reverse(string):
    """Reverse a string."""
    return "".join(reversed(string))
```

As noted in Chapter 6, functional programs are harder to build up incrementally, which is one reason why it's so nice to have a test suite to check that our changes had their intended effect (that is, no effect at all):

Listing 8.35: GREEN

```
(venv) $ pytest
============================ test session starts ============================
collected 5 items

tests/test_phrase.py .....                                           [100%]

============================ 5 passed in 0.01s =============================
```

Huzzah! Our test suite still passes, so our new one-line **letters()** method works.

This is a major improvement, but in fact there's one more refactoring that represents a great example of the power of Python. Recall from Section 4.3 that regular expressions have a **findall()** method that lets us select regex-matching characters directly from a string:

```
>>> re.findall(r"[a-zA-Z]", content)
['M', 'a', 'd', 'a', 'm', 'I', 'm', 'A', 'd', 'a', 'm']
>>> "".join(re.findall(r"[a-zA-Z]", content))
'MadamImAdam'
```

By using **findall()** with the same regex we've been using throughout this section and then joining on the empty string, we can simplify the application code even further by eliminating the list comprehension, as shown in Listing 8.36.

Listing 8.36: Using `re.findall`. GREEN

src/palindrome/phrase.py

```python
import re


class Phrase:
    """A class to represent phrases."""

    def __init__(self, content):
        self.content = content

    def ispalindrome(self):
        """Return True for a palindrome, False otherwise."""
        return self.processed_content() == reverse(self.processed_content())

    def processed_content(self):
        """Return content for palindrome testing."""
        return self.letters().lower()

    def letters(self):
        """Return the letters in the content."""
        return "".join(re.findall(r"[a-zA-Z]", self.content))

def reverse(string):
    """Reverse a string."""
    return "".join(reversed(string))
```

One more run of the test suite confirms that everything is still copacetic (Figure 8.10[9]):

Listing 8.37: GREEN

```
(venv) $ pytest
============================ test session starts ============================
collected 5 items

tests/test_phrase.py .....                                          [100%]

============================= 5 passed in 0.01s =============================
```

---

9. Image courtesy of Album/Alamy Stock Photo.

Figure 8.10: Still a palindrome after all our work.

8.5.1 Publishing the Python Package

As a final step, and in line with our philosophy of shipping (Box 1.5), in this final section we'll publish our **palindrome** package to the Python Package Index, also known as PyPI.

Unusually among programming languages, Python actually has a dedicated test package index called TestPyPI, which means we can publish (and use) our test package without uploading to a real package index. Before proceeding, you'll need to register an account at TestPyPI and verify your email address.

Once you've set up your account, you'll be ready to build and publish your package. To do this, we'll be using the **build** and **twine** packages, which you should install at this time:

```
(venv) $ pip install build==0.8.0
(venv) $ pip install twine==4.0.1
```

The first step is to build the package as follows:

```
(venv) $ python3 -m build
```

This uses the information in **pyproject.toml** (Listing 8.3) to create a **dist** ("distribution") directory with files based on the name and version number of your package. For example, on my system the **dist** directory looks like this:

```
(venv) $ ls dist
palindrome\_mhartl-0.0.1.tar.gz
palindrome_mhartl-0.0.1-py3-none-any.whl
```

These are a tarball and wheel file, respectively, but the truth is that you don't need to know anything about these files specifically; all you need to know is that the **build** step is necessary to publish a package to TestPyPI. (Being comfortable with ignoring these sorts of details is a good sign of technical sophistication.)

Actually publishing the package involves using the **twine** command, which looks like this (and is just copied from the TestPyPI documentation):[10]

```
(venv) $ twine upload --repository testpypi dist/*
```

(For future uploads, you may need to remove older versions of your package using **rm** because TestPyPI doesn't let you reuse filenames.)

At this point, your package is published and you can test it by installing it on your local system. Because we already have an editable and testable version of the package in our main venv (Listing 8.18), it's a good idea to spin up a new venv in a temp directory:

```
$ cd
$ mkdir -p tmp/test_palindrome
$ cd tmp/test_palindrome
$ python3 -m venv venv
$ source venv/bin/activate
(venv) $
```

---

10. At this point, you will be prompted either for a username and password or for an API key. For the latter, see the TestPyPI page on tokens for more information.

Now you can install your package by using the **--index-url** option to tell **pip** to use the test index instead of the real one:

```
(venv) $ pip install <package> --index-url https://test.pypi.org/simple/
```

For example, I can install my version of the test package, which is called **palindrome_mhartl**, as follows:[11]

```
(venv) $ pip install palindrome_mhartl --index-url https://test.pypi.org/simple/
```

To test the installation, you can load the package in the REPL:

```
(venv) $ python3
>>> from palindrome_mhartl.phrase import Phrase
>>> Phrase("Madam, I'm Adam.").ispalindrome()
True
```

It works! (If it doesn't work for you—which is a real possibility since so many things can go wrong—the only recourse is to use your technical sophistication to resolve the discrepancy.)

For a general Python package, you can continue adding features and making new releases. All you need to do is increment the version number in **pyproject.toml** to reflect the changes you've made. For more guidance on how to increment the versions, I suggest learning a bit about the rules of so-called *semantic versioning*, or *semver* (Box 8.2).

Box 8.2: Semver

You might have noticed in this section that we've used the version number 0.1.0 for our new package. The leading zero indicates that our package is at an early stage, often called "beta" (or even "alpha" for very early-stage projects).

---

11. The _mhartl part comes from the **name** setting in **pyproject.toml**, which for me is **palindrome_-mhartl**. If you install my version of the package, you may notice that the version number is higher than 0.0.1, which is due to the aforementioned issue regarding package-name reuse. Because I've made quite a few changes in the course of developing this tutorial, I've incremented the version number (**version** in **pyproject.toml**) several times.

We can indicate updates by incrementing the middle number in the version, e.g., from 0.1.0 to 0.2.0, 0.3.0, etc. Bugfixes are represented by incrementing the rightmost number, as in 0.2.1, 0.2.2, etc., and a mature version (suitable for use by others, and which may not be backward-compatible with prior versions) is indicated by version 1.0.0.

After reaching version 1.0.0, further changes follow this same general pattern: 1.0.1 would represent minor changes (a "patch release"), 1.1.0 would represent new (but backward-compatible) features (a "minor release"), and 2.0.0 would represent major or backward-incompatible changes (a "major release").

These numbering conventions are known as *semantic versioning*, or *semver* for short. For more information, see semver.org.

Finally, if you ever go on to develop a package that isn't just a test like the one in this chapter, you can publish it to the real Python Package Index (PyPI). Although there is ample PyPI documentation, there is little doubt in such a case that you will also have ample opportunity to apply your technical sophistication.

8.5.2 Exercises

1. Let's generalize our palindrome detector by adding the capability to detect integer palindromes like **12321**. By filling in **FILL_IN** in Listing 8.38, write tests for integer non-palindromes and palindromes. Get both tests to GREEN using the code in Listing 8.39, which adds a call to **str** to ensure the content is a string and includes **\d** in the regex to match digits as well as letters. (Note that we have updated the name of the **letters()** method accordingly.)

2. Bump the version number in **pyproject.toml**, commit and push your changes, build your package with **build**, and upload it with **twine**. In your temp directory, upgrade your package using the command in Listing 8.40 and confirm in the REPL that integer-palindrome detection is working. *Note*: The backslash \ in Listing 8.40 is a *continuation character* and should be typed literally, but the right angle bracket **>** should be added by your shell program automatically and should not be typed.

Listing 8.38: Testing integer palindromes. RED
tests/test_phrase.py

```python
from pytest import skip

from palindrome_mhartl.phrase import Phrase


def test_non_palindrome():
    assert not Phrase("apple").ispalindrome()

def test_literal_palindrome():
    assert Phrase("racecar").ispalindrome()

def test_mixed_case_palindrome():
    assert Phrase("RaceCar").ispalindrome()

def test_palindrome_with_punctuation():
    assert Phrase("Madam, I'm Adam.").ispalindrome()

def test_letters_and_digits():
    assert Phrase("Madam, I'm Adam.").letters_and_digits() == "MadamImAdam"

def test_integer_non_palindrome():
    FILL_IN Phrase(12345).ispalindrome()

def test_integer_palindrome():
    FILL_IN Phrase(12321).ispalindrome()
```

Listing 8.39: Adding detection of integer palindromes. GREEN
src/palindrome/phrase.py

```python
import re


class Phrase:
    """A class to represent phrases."""

    def __init__(self, content):
        self.content = str(content)

    def ispalindrome(self):
        """Return True for a palindrome, False otherwise."""
        return self.processed_content() == reverse(self.processed_content())
```

```
    def processed_content(self):
        """Return content for palindrome testing."""
        return self.letters_and_digits().lower()

    def letters_and_digits(self):
        """Return the letters and digits in the content."""
        return "".join(re.findall(r"[a-zA-Z]", self.content))

def reverse(string):
    """Reverse a string."""
    return "".join(reversed(string))
```

Listing 8.40: Upgrading the test package.

```
(venv) $ pip install --upgrade your-package \
> --index-url https://test.pypi.org/simple/
```

CHAPTER 9
Shell Scripts

In this chapter, we'll build on the foundation laid in Section 1.4 and write three *shell scripts* of increasing sophistication. In the first two programs (Section 9.1 and Section 9.2), we'll take the Python package developed in Chapter 8 and put it to work detecting palindromes drawn from two different sources: a file, and the Web. In the process, we'll learn how to read and write from files with Python, and also how to read from a live Web URL. Finally, in Section 9.3, we'll write a real-life utility program adapted from one I once wrote for myself. It includes an introduction to manipulation of the Document Object Model (or *DOM*) in a context outside a web browser.[1]

9.1 Reading from Files

Our first task is to read and process the contents of a file. The example is simple by design, but it demonstrates the necessary principles, and gives you the background needed to read more advanced documentation.

We'll start by using **curl** to download a file of simple phrases (note that this should be in the **python_tutorial** directory we used prior to Chapter 8, not the palindrome package directory):

```
$ cd ~/repos/python_tutorial/
$ curl -OL https://cdn.learnenough.com/phrases.txt
```

---

1. The Document Object Model was introduced (https://www.learnenough.com/css-and-layout-tutorial/introduction#sec-start_stylin) in *Learn Enough CSS & Layout to Be Dangerous* (https://www.learnenough.com/css-and-layout) and is explored (https://www.learnenough.com/javascript-tutorial/dom_manipulation#cha-dom_manipulation) in more depth in *Learn Enough JavaScript to Be Dangerous* (https://www.learnenough.com/javascript).

As you can confirm by running **less phrases.txt** at the command line, this file contains a large number of phrases—some of which (surprise!) happen to be palindromes.

Our specific task is to write a palindrome detector that iterates through each line in this file and prints out any phrases that are palindromes (while ignoring others). To do this, we'll need to open the file and read its contents. We'll then use the package developed in Chapter 8 to determine which phrases are palindromes.

Python handles file operations natively through the **open()** function, which we can use to create an open file, read the file contents with **read()**, and then close it with **close()**, as shown in Listing 9.1.[2]

Listing 9.1: Opening a file in the REPL.

```
$ source venv/bin/activate
(venv) $ python3
>>> file = open("phrases.txt")     # Not fully Pythonic
>>> text = file.read()
>>> file.close()
```

This reads the contents of **phrases.txt** and puts it in the **text** variable.

We can confirm that the assignment worked using the **splitlines()** method introduced in Section 3.1 (Listing 3.2):

```
>>> len(text)
1373
>>> text.splitlines()[0]     # Split on newlines and extract the 1st phrase.
'A butt tuba'
```

The second command here splits the text on the newline character **\n** and selects the zeroth element, revealing the enigmatic first line of the file, "A butt tuba".

As noted in Listing 9.1, opening a file as shown isn't fully Pythonic. The reason is that we have to remember to close the file every time we open one, which can cause unpredictable behavior if we forget. We can avoid such issues by using the special **with** keyword, together with **as** and the desired filename:

---

2. See the article "Reading and Writing Files in Python" (https://realpython.com/read-write-files-python/) for more on this useful subject.

```
>>> with open("phrases.txt") as file:      # Pythonic
...     text = file.read()
...
>>> len(text)
1373
```

This code arranges to close the file automatically at the end of the **with** statement, and the result is the same as before.

Let's take the ideas from the Python interpreter and put them in a script to detect the palindromes in **phrases.txt**:

```
(venv) $ touch palindrome_file
(venv) $ chmod +x palindrome_file
```

We'll then put in the necessary shebang line (Section 1.4) and require the palindrome package, as shown in Listing 9.2. You should use your package if possible, but you can use **palindrome-mhartl** if you didn't publish your own in Section 8.5.1:

```
(venv) $ pip install palindrome_mhartl --index-url https://test.pypi.org/simple/
```

Listing 9.2: Including the shebang line and package.
palindrome_file

```
#!/usr/bin/env python3
from palindrome_mhartl.phrase import Phrase


print("hello, world!")
```

The final line in Listing 9.2 is a habit I have of always making sure a script is in a working state before writing any more code:

```
(venv) $ ./palindrome_file
hello, world!
```

In earlier versions of this tutorial, this command actually failed, which led me toward changes that got it to work straightaway. This is the great thing about "hello, world!"—the code is so simple that, if it fails, you know something else must have gone wrong.

The script to read and detect palindromes from **phrases.txt** is fairly straight-forward: We open the file, split the contents on newlines, and iterate through the resulting array, printing any line that's a palindrome. The result, which at this stage you should aspire to read fairly easily, appears in Listing 9.3.

Listing 9.3: Reading and processing the contents of a file.
palindrome_file

```python
#!/usr/bin/env python3
from palindrome_mhartl.phrase import Phrase


with open("phrases.txt") as file:
    text = file.read()
    for line in text.splitlines():     # Arguably not Pythonic
        if Phrase(line).ispalindrome():
            print(f"palindrome detected: {line}")
```

Running the script at the command line confirms that there are quite a few palindromes in the file:

```
(venv) $ ./palindrome_file
.
.
.
palindrome detected: Dennis sinned.
palindrome detected: Dennis and Edna sinned.
palindrome detected: Dennis, Nell, Edna, Leon, Nedra, Anita, Rolf, Nora,
Alice, Carol, Leo, Jane, Reed, Dena, Dale, Basil, Rae, Penny, Lana, Dave,
Denny, Lena, Ida, Bernadette, Ben, Ray, Lila, Nina, Jo, Ira, Mara, Sara,
Mario, Jan, Ina, Lily, Arne, Bette, Dan, Reba, Diane, Lynn, Ed, Eva, Dana,
Lynne, Pearl, Isabel, Ada, Ned, Dee, Rena, Joel, Lora, Cecil, Aaron, Flora,
Tina, Arden, Noel, and Ellen sinned.
palindrome detected: Go hang a salami, I'm a lasagna hog.
palindrome detected: level
palindrome detected: Madam, I'm Adam.
palindrome detected: No "x" in "Nixon"
palindrome detected: No devil lived on
palindrome detected: Race fast, safe car
palindrome detected: racecar
palindrome detected: radar
palindrome detected: Was it a bar or a bat I saw?
palindrome detected: Was it a car or a cat I saw?
```

Figure 9.1: Dennis, Nell, Edna, Leon, Nedra, and many others sinned.

```
palindrome detected: Was it a cat I saw?
palindrome detected: Yo, banana boy!
palindrome detected:
```

Among others, we see a rather elaborate expansion on the simple palindrome "Dennis sinned" (Figure 9.1[3])!

This is a great start, but in fact files have a **readlines()** method that reads all the lines by default, without needing the call to **splitlines()**. Applying this to Listing 9.3 gives Listing 9.4.

Listing 9.4: Switching to **readlines()**.
palindrome_file

```
#!/usr/bin/env python3
from palindrome_mhartl.phrase import Phrase
```

---

3. Image courtesy of Historical Images Archive/Alamy Stock Photo.

```
with open("phrases.txt") as file:
    for line in file.readlines():    # Pythonic
        if Phrase(line).ispalindrome():
            print(f"palindrome detected: {line}")
```

You should confirm at the command line that the result is almost the same:

```
(venv) $ ./palindrome_file
.
.
.
palindrome detected: Was it a bar or a bat I saw?

palindrome detected: Was it a car or a cat I saw?

palindrome detected: Was it a cat I saw?

palindrome detected: Yo, banana boy!
```

There are now extra newlines between the palindrome lines, which is due to each element in **open(...).readlines()** actually *including* the newline.

In order to replicate the output from Listing 9.3, we can apply the common and useful technique of *stripping* each string, which simply removes any whitespace at the beginning or end, as we can see in the interpreter:

```
>>> greeting = "    hello, world!    \n"
>>> greeting.strip()
'hello, world!'
```

Applying this technique to the code in Listing 9.4 yields Listing 9.5.[4] (The version with **readlines()** is probably the most Pythonic solution, but it comes at the cost of a call to **strip()**, so the **splitlines()** version in Listing 9.3 is defensible as well.)

Listing 9.5: Removing a newline with **strip()**.
palindrome_file

```
#!/usr/bin/env python3
from palindrome_mhartl.phrase import Phrase
```

---

4. Using the **end=""** argument to **print()** (Section 2.3) would work as well.

```
with open("phrases.txt") as file:
    for line in file.readlines():
        if Phrase(line).ispalindrome():
            print(f"palindrome detected: {line.strip()}")
```

At this point, the output of **palindrome_file** should be just the palindrome lines, with no extra newlines and no blank palindrome at the end:

```
(venv) $ ./palindrome_file
.

.

.
palindrome detected: Was it a bar or a bat I saw?
palindrome detected: Was it a car or a cat I saw?
palindrome detected: Was it a cat I saw?
palindrome detected: Yo, banana boy!
```

Finally, let's look at how to *write* files in Python. It could hardly be simpler; the template looks like this:

```
file.write(content_string)
```

We can build up a content string consisting of palindromes by capturing the output of **readlines()** in a separate variable (called **lines**) and then using a list comprehension with a condition (Section 6.2):

```
with open("phrases.txt") as file:
    lines = file.readlines()
    for line in lines:
        if Phrase(line).ispalindrome():
            print(f"palindrome detected: {line.strip()}")

palindromes = [line for line in lines if Phrase(line).ispalindrome()]
```

Joining the **palindromes** list on the empty string and writing the resulting string to a **palindromes_file.txt** file is then just two lines total, as seen in Listing 9.6.

Listing 9.6: Writing out the palindromes.
palindrome_file

```
#!/usr/bin/env python3
from palindrome_mhartl.phrase import Phrase
```

```python
with open("phrases.txt") as file:
    lines = file.readlines()
    for line in lines:
        if Phrase(line).ispalindrome():
            print(f"palindrome detected: {line.strip()}")

palindromes = [line for line in lines if Phrase(line).ispalindrome()]
with open("palindromes_file.txt", "w") as file:
    file.write("".join(palindromes))
```

Running the script then writes out the file as a side effect:

```
(venv) $ ./palindrome_file
.
.
.
palindrome detected: Madam, I'm Adam.
palindrome detected: No "x" in "Nixon"
palindrome detected: No devil lived on
palindrome detected: Race fast, safe car
palindrome detected: racecar
palindrome detected: radar
palindrome detected: Was it a bar or a bat I saw?
palindrome detected: Was it a car or a cat I saw?
palindrome detected: Was it a cat I saw?
palindrome detected: Yo, banana boy!
(venv) $ tail palindromes_file.txt
Madam, I'm Adam.
No "x" in "Nixon"
No devil lived on
Race fast, safe car
racecar
radar
Was it a bar or a bat I saw?
Was it a car or a cat I saw?
Was it a cat I saw?
Yo, banana boy!
```

9.1.1 Exercises

1. You may have noticed some duplication in Listing 9.6: We first detect all palindromes, writing them out one at a time, and then find a list of all palindromes
   again (using a list comprehension). Show that we can eliminate this duplication

by replacing the whole file with the more compact code shown in Listing 9.7. (Because the palindrome content itself already ends with a newline, Listing 9.7 calls **print()** with the **end=""** option mentioned in Section 2.3 to prevent a duplicate newline.)

2. One common pattern in Python shell scripts is to put the main steps in a separate function (often called **main()**) and then call the function only when the file itself is called as a shell script. (See this video (https://www.youtube.com/watch?v=g_wlZ9IhbTs) for more.) Using the special syntax introduced in Section 7.1, show that the shell script in Listing 9.7 can be converted to Listing 9.8. Does it give the same result when executed at the command line?

3. Some Python programmers even prefer to put the content of the script in a different function and then have **main()** call that function, as seen in Listing 9.9. Show that this code still produces the same output as before.

Listing 9.7: Writing out palindromes the unduplicated way.
palindrome_file

```
#!/usr/bin/env python3
from palindrome_mhartl.phrase import Phrase


with open("phrases.txt") as file:
    palindromes = [line for line in file.readlines()
                   if Phrase(line).ispalindrome()]

palindrome_content = "".join(palindromes)
print(palindrome_content, end="")

with open("palindromes_file.txt", "w") as file:
    file.write(palindrome_content)
```

Listing 9.8: Calling **main()** only at the command line.
palindrome_file

```
#!/usr/bin/env python3
from palindrome_mhartl.phrase import Phrase


def main():
```

```
    with open("phrases.txt") as file:
        palindromes = [line for line in file.readlines()
                           if Phrase(line).ispalindrome()]

    palindrome_content = "".join(palindromes)
    print(palindrome_content, end="")

    with open("palindromes_file.txt", "w") as file:
        file.write(palindrome_content)

if __name__ == "__main__":
    main()
```

Listing 9.9: Adding another layer between the script and **main()**.

palindrome_file

```
#!/usr/bin/env python3
from palindrome_mhartl.phrase import Phrase


def main():
    detect_palindromes()

def detect_palindromes():
    with open("phrases.txt") as file:
        palindromes = [line for line in file.readlines()
                           if Phrase(line).ispalindrome()]

    palindrome_content = "".join(palindromes)
    print(palindrome_content, end="")

    with open("palindromes_file.txt", "w") as file:
        file.write(palindrome_content)

if __name__ == "__main__":
    main()
```

9.2 Reading from URLs

In this section, we'll write a script whose effect is identical to the one in Section 9.1, except that it reads the **phrases.txt** file directly from its public URL. By itself, the program doesn't do anything fancy, but realize what a miracle this is: The ideas aren't specific to the URL we're hitting, which means that after this section you'll have the power to write programs to access and process practically any site on the Web. (This practice, sometimes called "web scraping", should be done with due consideration and caution.)

The main trick is to use the Requests package, which we can install using **pip**:[5]

```
(venv) $ pip install requests==2.28.1
```

As noted in the documentation, Requests includes a **get()** method that can just, well, *get* a URI (also called a URL; the difference rarely matters):

```
>>> import requests
>>> url = "https://cdn.learnenough.com/phrases.txt"
>>> response = requests.get(url)
>>> response.text
'A butt tuba\nA bad penny always turns up.\n...Yo, banana boy!\n'
```

We see here that the **response** object has an attribute called **text** that includes the text returned by **requests.get()**, which we can combine with the **splitlines()** method from Listing 9.3 to extract the lines.[6]

We can create our script as in Section 9.1:

```
$ touch palindrome_url
$ chmod +x palindrome_url
```

The implementation then broadly parallels the code in Listing 9.3, just without the call to **with**, as shown in Listing 9.10.

---

5. Older Python code often uses the **urllib.request** module from the **urllib** package, but this isn't as user-friendly as Requests, and indeed the **urllib.request** documentation itself explicitly recommends Requests ("The Requests package is recommended for a higher-level HTTP client interface.").

6. There is also an **iter_lines()** method that returns an iterator that iterates over the lines, which at first glance effectively replicates the **readlines()** solution in Listing 9.5. As it turns out, though, the resulting elements are returned as raw bytes and have to be decoded before they can be used. As a result, the **splitlines()** solution is actually a little simpler in this case.

Listing 9.10: Reading from a URL.
palindrome_url

```
#!/usr/bin/env python3
import requests

from palindrome_mhartl.phrase import Phrase

URL = "https://cdn.learnenough.com/phrases.txt"


for line in requests.get(URL).text.splitlines():
    if Phrase(line).ispalindrome():
        print(f"palindrome detected: {line}")
```

At this point, we're ready to try the script out at the command line:

```
$ ./palindrome_url
.
.
palindrome detected: Madam, I'm Adam.
palindrome detected: No "x" in "Nixon"
palindrome detected: No devil lived on
palindrome detected: Race fast, safe car
palindrome detected: racecar
palindrome detected: radar
palindrome detected: Was it a bar or a bat I saw?
palindrome detected: Was it a car or a cat I saw?
palindrome detected: Was it a cat I saw?
palindrome detected: Yo, banana boy!
```

Amazing! The result is almost exactly as we saw in Section 9.1, but this time, we got the data right off the live Web.

There's actually one little detail left, which is that the em dash in "A man, a plan, a canal—Panama!" didn't quite come out right (Figure 9.2). This is a hint of a character encoding issue, and a little investigation shows that **requests.get()** can also download using a **content** attribute that can be *decoded* to include characters like the em dash we need. Specifically, we can indicate that the character encoding is UTF-8 using the **decode()** method, as shown in Listing 9.11. (We'll meet UTF-8 again in Chapter 10, where we'll include it as a standard element on the HTML web page; it is also covered in *Learn Enough HTML to Be Dangerous* (https://www.learnenough.com/html).)

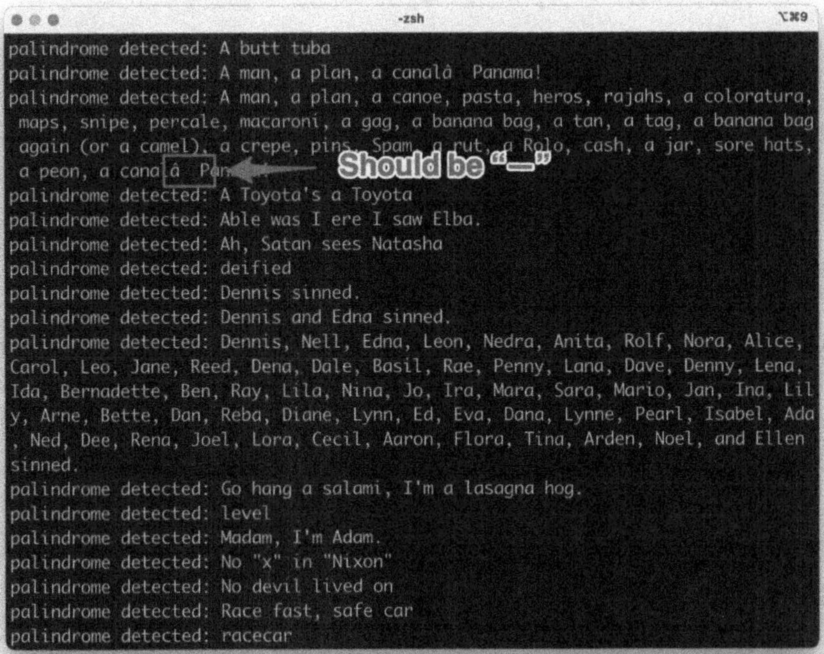

Figure 9.2: The wrong character.

Listing 9.11: Decoding the **content**.
palindrome_url

```
#!/usr/bin/env python3
import requests

from palindrome_mhartl.phrase import Phrase

URL = "https://cdn.learnenough.com/phrases.txt"

for line in requests.get(URL).content.decode("utf-8").splitlines():
    if Phrase(line).ispalindrome():
        print(f"palindrome detected: {line}")
```

The result is the em dash we are looking for:

```
$ ./palindrome_url
.
.
.
palindrome detected: A man, a plan, a canal--Panama!
.
.
.
```

By the way, if you actually visit the URL cdn.learnenough.com/phrases.txt, you'll find that in fact it *forwards* (using a 301 redirect) to a page on Amazon's Simple Storage Service (S3), as seen in Figure 9.3. Luckily, the **requests.get()** method we used in Listing 9.10 automatically follows such redirects, so the script worked as written, but

Figure 9.3: Visiting the phrase URL.

this behavior is not universal among URL libraries. Depending on the exact library you use, you might have to manually configure the web requester to follow redirects.

9.2.1 Exercises

1. In analogy with Listing 9.6, add code to Listing 9.10 that writes out a file called **palindromes_url.txt**. Confirm using the **diff** utility (https://www.learnenough.com/command-line-tutorial/manipulating_files#sec-redirecting_and_appending) that the output is identical to the **palindromes_file.txt** file from Section 9.1.

2. Modify Listing 9.10 to use the more compact programming style seen in Listing 9.7 (including the step to write out the file).

9.3 DOM Manipulation at the Command Line

In this final section, we're going to put the URL-reading tricks we learned in Section 9.2 to good use by writing a version of an actual utility script I once wrote for myself. To begin, I'll explain the context in which the script arose, and the problem it solves.

In recent years, there has been an explosion in the resources available for learning foreign languages, including things like Duolingo, Google Translate, and native OS support for multilingual text-to-speech (TTS). A few years ago, I decided to take advantage of this opportunity to brush up on my high-school/college Spanish.

One of the resources I found myself turning to was Wikipedia, with its huge number of articles in languages other than English. In particular, I discovered how useful it was to copy text from Spanish-language Wikipedia (Figure 9.4) and drop it into Google Translate (Figure 9.5). At that point, I could use the text-to-speech from either Google Translate (the red square in Figure 9.5) or macOS to hear the words spoken in Spanish, while following along with either the native language or the translation. Es muy útil.

After a while, I noticed two consistent sources of friction:

1. Copying a large number of paragraphs by hand was cumbersome.

2. Hand-copying text often selected things that I didn't want, particularly *reference numbers*, which the TTS system duly pronounced, resulting in random numbers

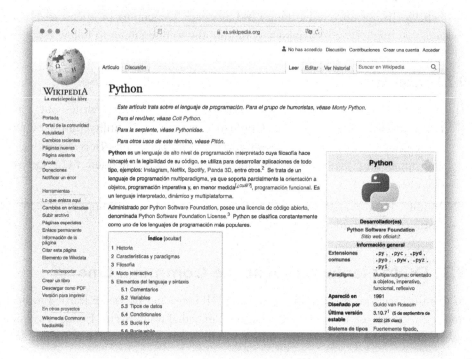

Figure 9.4: Un artículo sobre Python.

being spoken (e.g., "entre otros.2[dos] Se trata de un lenguaje" = "among others.2 It is treated as a language". ¿Qué pasó?).

Friction like this has inspired many a utility script, and thus was born **wikp** ("Wikipedia paragraphs"), a program to download a Wikipedia article's HTML source, extract its paragraphs, and eliminate its reference numbers, dumping all the results to the screen.

The original **wikp** program was written in Ruby; what appears here is a slightly simplified version. Let's think about how it will work.

We already know from Listing 9.10 how to download the source of a URL. The remaining tasks are then to:

1. Take an arbitrary URL argument at the command line.
2. Manipulate the downloaded HTML using the DOM (Figure 9.6).

Figure 9.5: An article about Python dropped into Google Translate.

3. Remove the references.

4. Collect and print the paragraphs.

Let's get started by creating the initial script:

```
$ touch wikp
$ chmod +x wikp
```

Now we're ready to get going on the main program. For each task above, I'll include the kind of Google search you might use to figure out how to do it.

There are several options for processing HTML in Python; one of the most powerful and highly regarded ones goes by the rather whimsical name Beautiful Soup (a reference to a song from Chapter 9 of *Alice's Adventures in Wonderland*)[7] that can

_____

7. What this song has to do with HTML processing is anybody's guess.

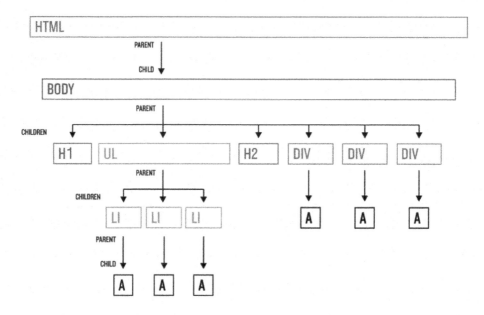

Figure 9.6: The Document Object Model (DOM).

manipulate the DOM (python dom manipulation). We'll use version 4, which is compatible with Python 3:

```
(venv) $ pip install beautifulsoup4==4.11.1
```

The Beautiful Soup package itself is available via the abbreviated name **bs4**.

Our principal task is sometimes known as "HTML parsing", and Beautiful Soup comes equipped with a powerful HTML parser. The official Beautiful Soup website has a bunch of useful tutorials; for our purposes, the most important method looks like Listing 9.12.

Listing 9.12: Parsing some HTML.

```
>>> from bs4 import BeautifulSoup
>>> html = '<p>lorem<sup class="reference">1</sup></p><p>ipsum</p>'
>>> doc = BeautifulSoup(html)
```

The resulting **doc** variable is a Beautiful Soup document, in this case with two paragraphs, one of which contains a **sup** (superscript) tag with CSS class **reference**.

Beautiful Soup documents can be manipulated in any number of ways. My favorite method for selecting elements is **find_all**, which lets us pull out HTML tags (beautiful soup select html tag) using an intuitive syntax. For example:

```
>>> doc.find_all("p")
[<p>lorem<sup class="reference">1</sup></p>, <p>ipsum</p>]
```

This operation is so common that it's the default when we pass an argument directly to a document object:

```
>>> doc("p")
[<p>lorem<sup class="reference">1</sup></p>, <p>ipsum</p>]
>>> len(doc("p"))
2
>>> doc("p")[0].text
'lorem1'
```

We see from the final line that we can get the text of a particular result using the **text** property, which in this case includes the reference number **1**. Meanwhile, we can grab the elements (in this case, only one) with a **"reference"** class using the **class_** option:[8]

```
>>> doc("sup", class_="reference")
[<sup class="reference">1</sup>]
>>> len(doc("sup", class_="reference"))
1
```

Perhaps you can see where we're going with this. We're now in a position to parse an HTML document and select all the paragraphs and all the references (assuming, of course, they have class **reference**). All we need now is a way to *remove* the references from the document. As it happens, this is not hard at all using the **decompose()** method (beautiful soup remove element), as seen in Listing 9.13.

---

8. The extra underscore in **class_** is included because **class** (no underscore) is reserved for creating Python classes (Chapter 7). By the way, **doc.select(".reference")** selects *all* the elements (not just **sup** tags) with class **"reference"** using much the same "dot" notation used by CSS itself.

Listing 9.13: Removing DOM elements.

```
>>> for reference in doc("sup", class_="reference"):
...        reference.decompose()
...
>>> doc
<html><body><p>lorem</p><p>ipsum</p></body></html>
```

Then, we can collect all the paragraph content using **doc("p")** and print each paragraph (Listing 9.14).

Listing 9.14: Printing paragraph content.

```
>>> for paragraph_tag in doc("p"):
...        print(paragraph_tag.text)
...
lorem
ipsum
```

We're now ready to put together the script itself. We'll start by taking in the URL as a command-line argument using the **sys** (system) library (python script command line argument), as seen in Listing 9.15. Note that we've included a **print** line as a temporary way to make sure the argument is being accepted properly. We've also used a lowercase name (**url**) since, unlike in Section 9.2, it is now a variable and not a constant. (Either **URL** or **url** would work; the choice of case is just a convention.)

Listing 9.15: Accepting a command-line argument.
wikp

```
#!/usr/bin/env python3
import sys

import requests
from bs4 import BeautifulSoup


# Return the paragraphs from a Wikipedia link, stripped of reference numbers.
# Especially useful for text-to-speech (both native and foreign).

# Get URL from the command line.
url = sys.argv[1]
print(url)
```

We can confirm that Listing 9.15 works as advertised:

```
$ ./wikp https://es.wikipedia.org/wiki/Python
https://es.wikipedia.org/wiki/Python
```

Next, we need to open the URL and read its contents, which we learned in Section 9.2 (Listing 9.11) can be done using the following code:

```
requests.get(url).content.decode("utf-8")
```

Feeding the result of this into **BeautifulSoup()** then gives Listing 9.16. Note that we've explicitly specified the parser to be for HTML, which is the default but can give rise to warning messages if omitted.

Listing 9.16: Parsing the live URL with Beautiful Soup.
wikp

```
#!/usr/bin/env python3
import sys

import requests
from bs4 import BeautifulSoup


# Return the paragraphs from a Wikipedia link, stripped of reference numbers.
# Especially useful for text-to-speech (both native and foreign).

# Get URL from the command line.
url = sys.argv[1]
# Create Beautiful Soup document from live URL.
content = requests.get(url).content.decode("utf-8")
doc = BeautifulSoup(content, features="html.parser")
```

Now all we need to do is apply the reference removal and paragraph collection code from Listing 9.13 and Listing 9.14. As hinted above, Wikipedia identifies its references with the **.reference** class, which we can confirm using a web inspector (https://www.learnenough.com/css-and-layout-tutorial/templates_and_frontmatter#sec-pages-folders) (Figure 9.7). This suggests the reference removal code shown in Listing 9.17.

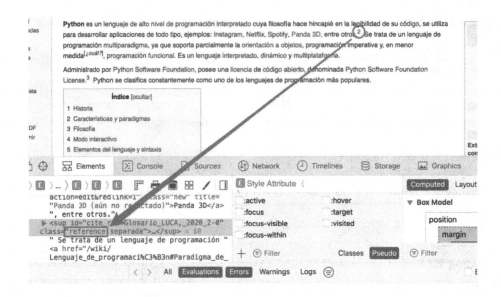

Figure 9.7: Viewing a reference in the web inspector.

Listing 9.17: Removing the references.

wikp

```
#!/usr/bin/env python3
import sys

import requests
from bs4 import BeautifulSoup


# Return the paragraphs from a Wikipedia link, stripped of reference numbers.
# Especially useful for text-to-speech (both native and foreign).

# Get URL from the command line.
url = sys.argv[1]
# Create Beautiful Soup document from live URL.
content = requests.get(url).content.decode("utf-8")
doc = BeautifulSoup(content, features="html.parser")
# Remove references.
for reference in doc("sup", class_="reference"):
    reference.decompose()
```

Now all that's left is to extract the paragraph content and print it out (Listing 9.18).

Listing 9.18: Printing the content.
wikp

```
#!/usr/bin/env python3
import sys

import requests
from bs4 import BeautifulSoup


# Return the paragraphs from a Wikipedia link, stripped of reference numbers.
# Especially useful for text-to-speech (both native and foreign).

# Get URL from the command line.
url = sys.argv[1]
# Create Beautiful Soup document from live URL.
content = requests.get(url).content.decode("utf-8")
doc = BeautifulSoup(content, features="html.parser")
# Remove references.
for reference in doc("sup", class_="reference"):
    reference.decompose()
# Print paragraphs.
for paragraph_tag in doc("p"):
    print(paragraph_tag.text)
```

Let's see how things went:

```
$ ./wikp https://es.wikipedia.org/wiki/Python
Python es un lenguaje de alto nivel de programación interpretado cuya
filosofía hace hincapié en la legibilidad de su código, se utiliza para
desarrollar aplicaciones de todo tipo, ejemplos: Instagram, Netflix, Spotify,
Panda 3D, entre otros. Se trata de un lenguaje de programación multiparadigma,
ya que soporta parcialmente la orientación a objetos, programación imperativa
y, en menor medida[?`cuál?], programación funcional. Es un lenguaje
interpretado, dinámico y multiplataforma.
.
.
.
Existen diversas implementaciones del lenguaje:

A lo largo de su historia, Python ha presentado una serie de incidencias, de
las cuales las más importantes han sido las siguientes:
```

Success! By scrolling up in our terminal, we can now select all the text and drop it into Google Translate or a text editor of our choice. On macOS, we can do even better by piping (https://www.learnenough.com/command-line-tutorial/inspecting_files

#sec-wordcount_and_pipes) the results to **pbcopy**, which automatically copies the results to the macOS **p**aste**b**oard (also called the "clipboard"):

```
$ ./wikp https://es.wikipedia.org/wiki/Python | pbcopy
```

At this point, pasting into Google Translate (or anywhere else) will paste the full text.

Consider how remarkable an accomplishment this is. The script in Listing 9.18 is a little tricky—and to get such a thing working completely on your own might involve quite a bit of Googling and more than a few **print** statements as you go along—but it's really only six lines of code: not exactly rocket science. And yet, it's genuinely useful, something that (if you're active in foreign-language learning) you might well use all the time. Moreover, the basic skills involved—including not just the programming, but also the technical sophistication (<cough>Googling</cough>)—unlock a huge number of potential applications.

9.3.1 Exercises

1. By moving the file or changing your system's configuration, add the **wikp** script to your environment's PATH. (You may find the steps (https://www.learnenough. com/text-editor-tutorial/advanced_text_editing#sec-writing_an_executable_ script) in *Learn Enough Text Editor to Be Dangerous* (https://www.learnenough. com/text-editor) helpful.) Confirm that you can run **wikp** without prepending **./** to the command name. *Note*: If you have a conflicting **wikp** program from following *Learn Enough JavaScript to Be Dangerous* or *Learn Enough Ruby to Be Dangerous* (https://www.learnenough.com/ruby), I suggest replacing it—thus demonstrating the principle that the file's name is the user interface, and the implementation can change language without affecting users.

2. What happens if you run **wikp** with no argument? Add code to your script to detect the absence of a command-line argument and output an appropriate usage statement. *Hint*: After printing out the usage statement, you will have to *exit*, which you can learn how to do with the search python how to exit script.

3. The "pipe to **pbcopy**" trick mentioned in the text works only on macOS, but any Unix-compatible system can redirect the output to a file. What's the command to redirect the output of **wikp** to a file called **article.txt**? (You could then open this file, select all, and copy the contents, which has the same basic result as piping to **pbcopy**.)

CHAPTER 10

A Live Web Application

This chapter develops a dynamic web application in Python using the same Flask framework introduced in Section 1.5 and applied further in Section 5.2. Although simple, Flask is not a toy—it's a production-ready web framework used by companies like Netflix, Lyft, and reddit. Flask also serves as excellent lightweight preparation for a more complex framework like Django. By the end of this chapter, you'll basically understand how web apps work, including layouts (Section 10.3), templates (Section 10.4), testing, and deployment.[1]

Our example web app will put the custom Python package developed in Chapter 8 to good use through the development of a web-based *palindrome detector*. Along the way, we'll learn how to create dynamic content using *Python templates*.

Detecting palindromes from the Web requires using a back-end web application to handle *form submission*, a task at which Flask excels. Our palindrome app will also feature two other pages—Home and About—which will give us an opportunity to learn how to use a Flask-based site layout. As part of this, we'll apply and extend the work in Chapter 8 to write automated tests for our app.

Finally, as in Section 1.5, we will also deploy our full palindrome app to the live Web. We'll end with pointers to further resources for Python, Flask, and other topics like JavaScript and Django.

---

1. The main additional subject to learn is how to store and retrieve information using a database, which represents a new technology but doesn't involve any fundamentally new principles. You can use databases both with Flask and with a fuller-featured framework like Django.

10.1 Setup

Our first step is to set up our app as a proof-of-concept and deploy it to production. We'll start by making a directory for it:

```
$ cd ~/repos              # cd ~/environments/repos on the cloud IDE
$ mkdir palindrome_app
$ cd palindrome_app/
```

Next, we'll configure our system for Flask development and make a subdirectory for the palindrome detector itself:

```
$ python3 -m venv venv
$ source venv/bin/activate
(venv) $ pip install --upgrade pip
(venv) $ pip install Flask==2.2.2
(venv) $ mkdir palindrome_detector
(venv) $ touch palindrome_detector/__init__.py
(venv) $ touch setup.py
(venv) $ touch MANIFEST.in
```

This directory structure broadly parallels the official Flask tutorial, and allows for more sophisticated design practices (such as templates and testing) than the "hello, world" app from Section 1.5 (which was just a single file in a directory used for other things as well).

As part of the app setup, we also need to fill a couple of setup files. Note in particular that, as of this writing, the Flask documentation includes **setup.py** and **MANIFEST.in** files (Listing 10.1 and Listing 10.2) rather than following the "best practice" of consolidating configuration settings in **pyproject.toml** (as we did in Chapter 8); practical experience shows that deviating from official documentation, especially when deploying applications, is most unwise, but beware that Flask's own convention may have changed since this writing. Also, don't worry if you don't understand it, because neither do I; as with reading the documentation, selective ignorance is definitely part of technical sophistication (Box 1.2).

Listing 10.1: A setup file.

setup.py

```
from setuptools import find_packages, setup

setup(
    name='palindrome_detector',
    version='1.0.0',
    packages=find_packages(),
 include_package_data=True,
    zip_safe=False,
 install_requires=[
        'flask',
    ],
)
```

Listing 10.2: A manifest file.

MANIFEST.in

```
graft palindrome_detector/static
graft palindrome_detector/templates
global-exclude *.pyc
```

To get started with the app itself, let's write "hello, world!", as shown in Listing 10.3.[2] Most of Listing 10.3 is Flask boilerplate code, again drawn largely from the official documentation, so don't worry about the details. Incidentally, the **@app.route("/")** syntax right before the function definition is called a *decorator*, which has many uses in Python in addition to defining Flask routes.

Listing 10.3: Writing "hello, world!" in Flask.

```
import os

from flask import Flask


def create_app(test_config=None):
```

---

2. The **os** package includes utilities for dealing with the underlying operating system (OS).

```
"""Create and configure the app."""
app = Flask(__name__, instance_relative_config=True)

if test_config is None:
    # Load the instance config, if it exists, when not testing.
    app.config.from_pyfile("config.py", silent=True)
else:
    # Load the test config if passed in.
    app.config.from_mapping(test_config)

# Ensure the instance folder exists.
try:
    os.makedirs(app.instance_path)
except OSError:
    pass

@app.route("/")
def index():
    return "hello, world!"

return app

app = create_app()
```

Then run the app using the **flask** command (Listing 10.4).

Listing 10.4: Running the Flask app.

```
(venv) $ flask --app palindrome_detector --debug run
 * Running on http://127.0.0.1:5000/
```

The result of visiting 127.0.0.1:5000/ appears in Figure 10.1.

Finally, following our practice to deploy early and often, we'll put our project under version control with Git in preparation for deploying to Fly.io. As in Section 1.5.1, we need a **.gitignore** file to tell Git which files and directories to ignore (Listing 10.5).

hello, world!

Figure 10.1: Our initial app.

Listing 10.5: Ignoring certain files and directories.
.gitignore

```
venv/

*.pyc
__pycache__/

instance/

.pytest_cache/
.coverage
htmlcov/

dist/
build/
*.egg-info/

.DS_Store
```

Next, we'll initialize the repository:

```
(venv) $ git init
(venv) $ git add -A
(venv) $ git commit -m "Initialize repository"
```

I suggest setting up a new repository at GitHub at this time as well.

Also as in Section 1.5.1, we'll install the Gunicorn server:

```
(venv) $ pip install gunicorn==20.1.0
```

Then we'll create **requirements.txt** for the sake of Fly.io (Listing 10.6).

Listing 10.6: Specifying the requirements for our app.
requirements.txt

```
click==8.1.3
Flask==2.2.2
gunicorn==20.1.0
itsdangerous==2.1.2
Jinja2==3.1.2
MarkupSafe==2.1.1
Werkzeug==2.2.2
```

Now log in (Listing 10.7) and "launch" the app to create the production configuration (Listing 10.8). Edit the generated **Procfile** to use the name of the palindrome app (Listing 10.9).

Listing 10.7: Signing in to Fly.io.

```
(venv) $ flyctl auth login --interactive
```

Listing 10.8: "Launching" the app (which is just local configuration).

```
(venv) $ flyctl launch
```

Listing 10.9: *Procfile*

```
web: gunicorn palindrome_detector:app
```

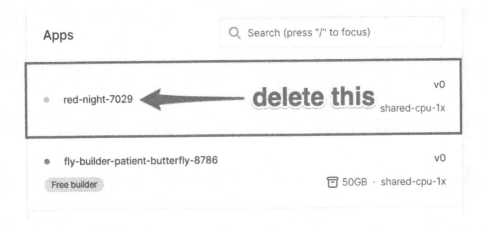

Figure 10.2: Deleting an app at Fly.io.

At this point, we're nearly ready to deploy to production. The only issue is that you're likely to have an app already defined from Section 1.5.1, and as of this writing Fly.io allows only one app when using its free tier. As a result, you will probably have to delete the old app, which you can find on your Fly.io dashboard (Figure 10.2): Click app name > Settings > Delete app. (You can reuse the builder, though, so there is no need to delete that as well.)

I recommend you commit the configuration changes to Git (and continue making commits and pushes throughout this chapter):

```
(venv) $ git add -A
(venv) $ git commit -m "Add configuration"
```

We're now ready for the actual deployment:

```
(venv) $ flyctl deploy
(venv) $ flyctl open     # won't work on the cloud IDE, so use displayed URL
```

The result is a working app in production, as seen in Figure 10.3. Although for brevity I'll omit further deployments until Section 10.5.1, I recommend deploying regularly as you work through the chapter to turn up any production issues as quickly as possible.

Figure 10.3: Our initial app in production.

10.1.1 Exercise

1. There's a nice trick for installing all of an app's requirements from a generated **requirements.txt** file using **pip -r**. Confirm that the sequence shown in Listing 10.10 results in a restored and working app.

Listing 10.10: Tearing down and rebuilding the app environment.

```
(venv) $ deactivate
$ rm -rf venv/
$ python3 -m venv venv
$ source venv/bin/activate
(venv) $ pip install -r requirements.txt
(venv) $ flask --app palindrome_detector --debug run
 * Running on http://127.0.0.1:5000/
```

10.2 Site Pages

Now that we've taken care of all the overhead involved in setting up and deploying the palindrome app, we're in a position to make rapid progress toward our final application. We'll start by making three pages for our site: Home, About, and Palindrome Detector. In contrast to our previous Flask apps, which have operated by simply returning strings in response to GET requests, for our full app we'll use a more powerful technique known as *templates*. Initially, these templates will consist of static HTML, but we'll add code to eliminate duplication in Section 10.3 and then add dynamic content starting in Section 10.4.

In preparation for filling in the site pages, let's create the (currently empty) template files at the command line, which should be located in a directory called **templates** inside the **palindrome_detector** app directory:

```
(venv) $ mkdir palindrome_detector/templates
(venv) $ cd palindrome_detector/templates
(venv) $ touch index.html about.html palindrome.html
(venv) $ cd -
```

(As noted (https://www.learnenough.com/command-line-tutorial/directories#sec-navigating_directories) in *Learn Enough Command Line to Be Dangerous* (https://www.learnenough.com/command-line), the **cd -** command changes to the previous directory, whichever it was; in this case, it's **palindrome_app**, i.e., the base directory for our web application.)

Initially, these templates will actually just be static HTML, but we'll see starting in Section 10.4 how to use them to generate HTML dynamically. The way to render a template inside a Flask app is with the **render_template** function. For example, to render the index page on the root URL /, we can write

```
@app.route("/")
def index():
    return render_template("index.html")
```

This code causes Flask to look for **index.html** in the **templates** directory.

Because the code to render all three templates is basically the same, we'll add them all at the same time, as shown in Listing 10.11. Note that we've added an extra statement to import **render_template** from the **flask** package in addition to the Flask class itself.

Listing 10.11: Rendering three templates.
palindrome_app/palindrome_detector/__init__.py

```python
import os

from flask import Flask, render_template

def create_app(test_config=None):
    """Create and configure the app."""
    app = Flask(__name__, instance_relative_config=True)
    .
    .
    .


    @app.route("/")
    def index():
        return render_template("index.html")

    @app.route("/about")
    def about():
        return render_template("about.html")

    @app.route("/palindrome")
    def palindrome():
        return render_template("palindrome.html")

    return app

app = create_app()
```

The file in Listing 10.11 is in effect a *controller*, which coordinates between different parts of the application, defines the URLs (or *routes*) supported by the app, responds to requests, etc. The templates, meanwhile, are sometimes called *views*, which determine the HTML that actually gets returned to the browser. Together, the views and controllers are two-thirds of the *Model-View-Controller* architecture (https://www.railstutorial.org/book/beginning#sec-mvc) for developing web applications, also known as *MVC*.

The next step is to fill the three template files with HTML; this is straightforward but tedious, so I suggest you copy and paste from Listing 10.12, Listing 10.13, and Listing 10.14. In case you're not reading this online, note that you can find the source for these and all other listings at the reference site mentioned briefly in Chapter 1: https://github.com/learnenough/learn_enough_python_code_listings. By the way, the indentation of the material inside the **body** tags is at the wrong depth, but we'll see in Section 10.3 why this is. Also note that we use two spaces for indentation, which is common in HTML markup, rather than the four spaces traditionally used in Python code.

It's worth noting that the hyperlink reference (**href**) URLs are hard-coded, like this:

```
<link rel="stylesheet" type="text/css" href="/static/stylesheets/main.css">
```

This is fine for small applications like the one in this chapter, but for a more powerful (but also more complex) approach, see the Flask documentation on **url_for** (https://flask.palletsprojects.com/en/2.2.x/api/#flask.Flask.url_for) and this helpful Stack Overflow comment (https://stackoverflow.com/questions/7478366/create-dynamic-urls-in-flask-with-url-for/35936261#35936261) on the subject.

Listing 10.12: The initial Home (index) view.
palindrome_detector/templates/index.html

```
<!DOCTYPE html>
<html>
  <head>
    <meta charset="utf-8">
    <title>Learn Enough Python Sample App</title>
    <link rel="stylesheet" type="text/css" href="/static/stylesheets/main.css">
    <link href="https://fonts.googleapis.com/css?family=Open+Sans:300,400"
          rel="stylesheet">
  </head>
  <body>
    <a href="/" class="header-logo">
      <img src="/static/images/logo_b.png" alt="Learn Enough logo">
    </a>
    <div class="container">
      <div class="content">

<h1>Sample Flask App</h1>

<p>
  This is the sample Flask app for
  <a href="https://www.learnenough.com/python-tutorial"><em>Learn Enough Python
  to Be Dangerous</em></a>. Learn more on the <a href="/about">About</a> page.
</p>

<p>
  Click the <a href="https://en.wikipedia.org/wiki/Sator_Square">Sator
  Square</a> below to run the custom <a href="/palindrome">Palindrome
  Detector</a>.
</p>
```

```
    <a class="sator-square" href="/palindrome">
      <img src="/static/images/sator_square.jpg" alt="Sator Square">
    </a>
        </div>
      </div>
    </body>
</html>
```

Listing 10.13: The initial About template.
palindrome_detector/templates/about.html

```
<!DOCTYPE html>
<html>
  <head>
    <meta charset="utf-8">
    <title>Learn Enough Python Sample App</title>
    <link rel="stylesheet" type="text/css" href="/static/stylesheets/main.css">
    <link href="https://fonts.googleapis.com/css?family=Open+Sans:300,400"
          rel="stylesheet">
  </head>
  <body>
    <a href="/" class="header-logo">
      <img src="/static/images/logo_b.png" alt="Learn Enough logo">
    </a>
    <div class="container">
      <div class="content">

  <h1>About</h1>

  <p>
    This site is the final application in
    <a href="https://www.learnenough.com/python-tutorial"><em>Learn Enough Python
    to Be Dangerous</em></a>
    by <a href="https://www.michaelhartl.com/">Michael Hartl</a>,
    a tutorial introduction to the
    <a href="https://www.python.org/">Python programming language</a> that
    is part of
    <a href="https://www.learnenough.com/">LearnEnough.com</a>.
  </p>
        </div>
      </div>
    </body>
</html>
```

Listing 10.14: The initial Palindrome Detector template.
palindrome_detector/templates/palindrome.html

```
<!DOCTYPE html>
<html>
  <head>
    <meta charset="utf-8">
    <title>Learn Enough Python Sample App</title>
    <link rel="stylesheet" type="text/css" href="/static/stylesheets/main.css">
    <link href="https://fonts.googleapis.com/css?family=Open+Sans:300,400"
          rel="stylesheet">
  </head>
  <body>
    <a href="/" class="header-logo">
      <img src="/static/images/logo_b.png" alt="Learn Enough logo">
    </a>
    <div class="container">
      <div class="content">

  <h1>Palindrome Detector</h1>

  <p>This will be the palindrome detector.</p>

      </div>
    </div>
  </body>
</html>
```

Visiting 127.0.0.1:5000 causes Flask to serve up the default (index) page, as shown in Figure 10.4. To get to the About page, we can type 127.0.0.1:5000/about into the browser address bar, as seen in Figure 10.5.

Figure 10.4 and Figure 10.5 show that the pages are basically working, but Listing 10.12 and subsequent listings include both images and a CSS file, which aren't currently present on the local system. We can change this situation by downloading the needed files from the Learn Enough CDN and putting them in the **static** directory, which is a standard choice for such static assets.

The way to do this is to use **curl** to fetch a *tarball*, which is similar to a ZIP file and is common on Unix-compatible systems:

```
(venv) $ curl -OL https://cdn.learnenough.com/le_python_palindrome_static.tar.gz
```

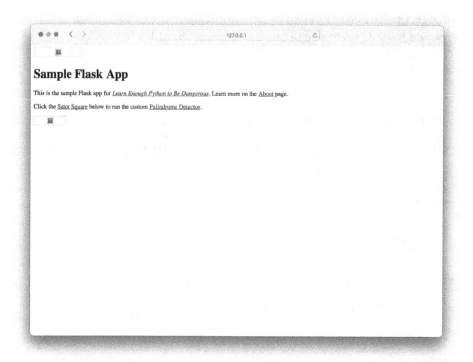

Figure 10.4: The initial Home page.

This kind of file is created by **tar**, or "tape archive", whose name is an old-school throwback to the time when external tapes were routinely used for large backups. Meanwhile, the **gz** extension refers to the important *gzip* method for compressing files.

The way to unzip the file is to use **tar zxvf**, which stands for "**t**ape **ar**chive **g**zip **ex**tract **v**erbose **f**ile" (as noted briefly in Section 8.5.2, the backslash \ is a *continuation character* and should be typed literally, but the right angle bracket > should be added by your shell program automatically and should not be typed):[3]

```
(venv) $ tar zxvf le_python_palindrome_static.tar.gz \
> --directory palindrome_detector/
```

---

3. I created this tarball using the command **tar zcf <filename>.tar.gz**, where **c** stands for **c**reate.

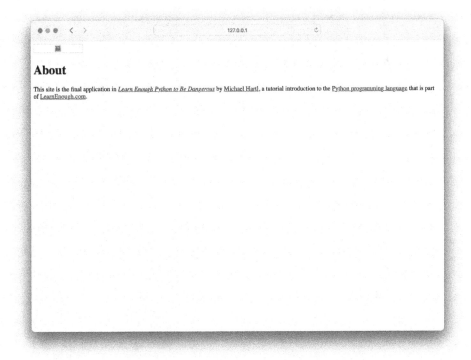

Figure 10.5: The initial About page.

```
x static/
x static/static/images/
x static/static/stylesheets/
x static/static/stylesheets/main.css
x static/static/images/sator_square.jpg
x static/static/images/logo_b.png
(venv) $ rm -f le_python_palindrome_static.tar.gz
```

With experience, you may prefer to omit the **v** flag, but I suggest using verbose output initially so that you can see what's going on during the extraction process. By the way, note that **tar** flags are just letters by themselves, with no preceding hyphens as in most other Unix commands. On many systems, you can in fact use hyphens, as in **tar -z -x -v -f <filename>**, but for reasons unknown to me the usual convention with **tar** is to omit them.

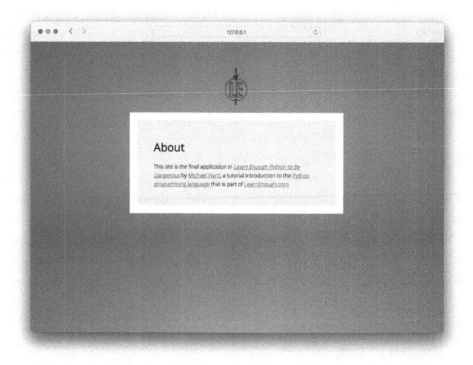

Figure 10.6: A nicer-looking About page.

As seen from the verbose output above, unzipping the file has created a **static** directory:

```
(venv) $ ls palindrome_detector/static
images      stylesheets
```

Refreshing the About page confirms that the logo image and CSS are now working (Figure 10.6). The improvement on the Home page is even more dramatic, as seen in Figure 10.7.

10.2.1 Exercises

1. Visit the /palindrome URL and confirm that the CSS and images are working.
2. Make a commit and deploy the changes.

Figure 10.7: A much-improved Home page.

10.3 Layouts

At this point, our app is looking pretty good, but there are two significant blemishes: The HTML code for the three pages is highly repetitive, and navigating by hand from page to page is rather cumbersome. We'll fix the first blemish in this section, and the second in Section 10.4. (And of course our app doesn't yet detect palindromes, which is the subject of Section 10.5.)

If you followed *Learn Enough CSS & Layout to Be Dangerous* (https://www. learnenough.com/css-and-layout), you'll know that the *Layout* in the title referred to page layout generally—using Cascading Style Sheets to move elements around on the page, align them properly, etc.—but we also saw (https://www.learnenough.com/css-and-layout-tutorial/struct-layout#cha-struct-layout) that doing this properly requires defining *layout templates* that capture common patterns and eliminate duplication.

In the present case, each of our site's pages has the same basic structure, as shown in Listing 10.15.

Listing 10.15: The HTML structure of our site's pages.

```
<!DOCTYPE html>
<html>
  <head>
    <meta charset="utf-8">
    <title>Learn Enough Python Sample App</title>
    <link rel="stylesheet" type="text/css" href="/static/stylesheets/main.css">
    <link href="https://fonts.googleapis.com/css?family=Open+Sans:300,400"
          rel="stylesheet">
  </head>
  <body>
    <a href="/" class="header-logo">
      <img src="/static/images/logo_b.png" alt="Learn Enough logo">
    </a>
    <div class="container">
      <div class="content">
        <!-- page-specific content -->
      </div>
    </div>
  </body>
</html>
```

Everything except the page-specific content (indicated by the highlighted HTML comment) is the same on each page. In *Learn Enough CSS & Layout to Be Dangerous*, we eliminated this duplication using Jekyll templates (https://www.learnenough. com/css-and-layout-tutorial/struct-layout#sec-jekyll-templates); in this tutorial, we'll use the *Jinja templating engine* instead, which is the default template system for Flask.

Right now, our site is currently working, in the sense that each page has the proper content at this stage of development. We're about to make a change that involves moving around and deleting a bunch of HTML, and we'd like to do this without breaking the site. Does that sound like something we've seen before?

It does indeed. This is exactly the kind of problem we faced in Chapter 8 when we developed and then refactored the palindrome package. In that case, we wrote automated tests to catch any regressions, and in this case we're going to do the same. (I started making websites long before automated testing of web applications was possible, much less the norm, and believe me, automated tests are a *huge* improvement over testing web apps by hand.)

To get started, we'll add **pytest** as we did in Section 8.1:

```
(venv) $ pip install pytest==7.1.3
```

(By design, our tests will be as simple as possible; for more sophisticated tests, see the pytest-flask project (https://pytest-flask.readthedocs.io/en/latest/index.html).)

In order to get our tests to work, we have to install our app locally as an editable Python package. Without the installation, you'll probably get an error that looks like this:

```
E   ModuleNotFoundError: No module named 'palindrome_detector'
```

To prevent this, run the same command as in Listing 8.18, shown again in Listing 10.16.

Listing 10.16: Installing the app as an editable package.

```
$ pip install -e .
```

We'll put the tests themselves in a **tests** directory, with one test file to start:

```
(venv) $ mkdir tests
(venv) $ touch tests/test_site_pages.py
```

We'll add a second test file in Section 10.5.1.

Our key tool in writing tests for our web app is the **client** object, which has a **get()** method that issues a GET request to a URL, thereby simulating visiting the corresponding page in a web browser. The result of such a request is a **response** object, which has a variety of useful attributes, including **status_code** (indicating the HTTP response code returned by the request) and **text** (which contains the text of the HTML returned by our application). We can define such a **client** object in the standard configuration file **conftest.py**:

```
(venv) $ touch tests/conftest.py
```

The code itself appears in Listing 10.17. (As with the rest of the configuration code in this chapter, Listing 10.17 is simply adapted from the Flask documentation.)

Listing 10.17: Creating the **client** object.
tests/conftest.py

```python
import pytest

from palindrome_detector import create_app


@pytest.fixture
def app():
    return create_app()

@pytest.fixture
def client(app):
    return app.test_client()
```

We'll start with super-basic tests making sure that the app serves up *something*, as indicated by the response code 200 (OK), which we can do like this:

```python
def test_index(client):
    response = client.get("/")
    assert response.status_code == 200
```

Here we use the **get()** method in the test to issue a GET request to the root URL /, verifying using the **assert** function introduced in Chapter 8 that the code is correct.

Applying the above discussion to the About and Palindrome Detector pages as well, we arrive at our initial test suite, shown in Listing 10.18.

Listing 10.18: Our initial test suite. GREEN
tests/test_site_pages.py

```python
def test_index(client):
    response = client.get("/")
    assert response.status_code == 200


def test_about(client):
    response = client.get("/about")
    assert response.status_code == 200


def test_palindrome(client):
    response = client.get("/palindrome")
    assert response.status_code == 200
```

Because the tests in Listing 10.18 are for code that's already working, the test suite should be GREEN:

Listing 10.19: GREEN

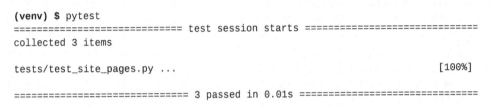

```
(venv) $ pytest
============================= test session starts ==============================
collected 3 items

tests/test_site_pages.py ...                                             [100%]

============================== 3 passed in 0.01s ===============================
```

The tests in Listing 10.18 are a fine start, but they really only check if the pages are there at all. It would be nice to have a slightly more stringent test of the HTML content, though not *too* stringent—we don't want our tests to make it hard to make changes in the future. As a middle ground, we'll check that each page in the site has a **title** tag and an **h1** tag somewhere in the document.

Although more sophisticated techniques are certainly possible,[4] we'll take the simplest approach that works and apply the **in** operator introduced in Section 2.5 to the **response.text** attribute. For example, to check for a **<title>** tag, we can use this:[5]

```
assert "<title>" in response.text
```

Adding such code for both **title** and **h1** tags to the test for each page in our site yields the updated test suite shown in Listing 10.20.

Listing 10.20: Adding assertions for the presence of some HTML tags. GREEN
tests/test_site_pages.py

```
def test_index(client):
    response = client.get("/")
    assert response.status_code == 200
```

---

4. For example, we could use the Beautiful Soup package from Section 9.3 to parse the HTML and make a **doc** object for use in the tests.

5. This assertion would still pass even if **<title>** appeared in a random spot on the page and not as a true title, but this is unlikely enough that the current technique is fine to demonstrate the main principles. As noted, a more sophisticated approach using a proper HTML parser is also possible and would be a good idea to use for more advanced applications.

```
    assert "<title>" in response.text
    assert "<h1>" in response.text

def test_about(client):
    response = client.get("/about")
    assert response.status_code == 200
    assert "<title>" in response.text
    assert "<h1>" in response.text

def test_palindrome(client):
    response = client.get("/palindrome")
    assert response.status_code == 200
    assert "<title>" in response.text
    assert "<h1>" in response.text
```

By the way, some programmers adopt the convention of only ever having one assertion per test, whereas in Listing 10.20 we have two. In my experience, the overhead associated with setting up the right state (e.g., duplicating the calls to **get()**) makes this convention inconvenient, and I've never run into any trouble from including multiple assertions in a test.

The tests in Listing 10.20 should now be GREEN as required:

Listing 10.21: GREEN

```
(venv) $ pytest
============================== test session starts ===============================
collected 3 items

tests/test_site_pages.py ...                                             [100%]

============================== 3 passed in 0.01s ================================
```

At this point, we're ready to use a Jinja template to eliminate duplication. Our first step is to define a layout template for the repeated code:

```
(venv) $ touch palindrome_detector/templates/layout.html
```

The contents of **layout.html** are the common HTML structure identified in Listing 10.15 combined with the special **block** function supplied by the Jinja template system. This involves replacing the HTML comment

```
<!-- page-specific content -->
```

in Listing 10.15 with the Jinja code

```
{% block content %}{% endblock %}
```

The **{% ... %}** syntax is used by Jinja to indicate code inside an HTML document.[6] This particular code inserts the text in a variable called **content** (which we'll define for each page in just a moment). The resulting template appears as in Listing 10.22.

Listing 10.22: A layout with shared HTML structure.
palindrome_detector/templates/layout.html

```
<!DOCTYPE html>
<html>
  <head>
    <meta charset="utf-8">
    <title>Learn Enough Python Sample App</title>
    <link rel="stylesheet" type="text/css" href="/static/stylesheets/main.css">
    <link href="https://fonts.googleapis.com/css?family=Open+Sans:300,400"
          rel="stylesheet">
  </head>
  <body>
    <a href="/" class="header-logo">
      <img src="/static/images/logo_b.png" alt="Learn Enough logo">
    </a>
    <div class="container">
      <div class="content">
        {% block content %}{% endblock %}
      </div>
    </div>
  </body>
</html>
```

At this point, we can remove the shared material from our pages, leaving only the core content, as shown in Listing 10.23, Listing 10.24, and Listing 10.25. (This is why the body content wasn't fully indented in Listing 10.12 and the other templates

---

6. This syntax is commonly used among template languages. For example, the same syntax is used by the Liquid template language used in *Learn Enough CSS & Layout to Be Dangerous* in combination with the Jekyll static site generator.

in Section 10.2.) Listing 10.23 and subsequent listings use the Jinja function **extends**
to tell the system to use the template **layout.html**, and then **{% block content
%}** defines the content to be inserted in Listing 10.22.

Listing 10.23: The core Home (index) view.
palindrome_detector/templates/index.html

```
{% extends "layout.html" %}

{% block content %}
  <h1>Sample Flask App</h1>

  <p>
    This is the sample Flask app for
    <a href="https://www.learnenough.com/python-tutorial"><em>Learn Enough Python
    to Be Dangerous</em></a>. Learn more on the <a href="/about">About</a> page.
  </p>

  <p>
    Click the <a href="https://en.wikipedia.org/wiki/Sator_Square">Sator
    Square</a> below to run the custom <a href="/palindrome">Palindrome
    Detector</a>.
  </p>

  <a class="sator-square" href="/palindrome">
    <img src="/static/images/sator_square.jpg" alt="Sator Square">
  </a>
{% endblock %}
```

Listing 10.24: The core About view.
palindrome_detector/templates/about.html

```
{% extends "layout.html" %}

{% block content %}
  <h1>About</h1>

  <p>
    This site is the final application in
    <a href="https://www.learnenough.com/python-tutorial"><em>Learn Enough Python
    to Be Dangerous</em></a>
    by <a href="https://www.michaelhartl.com/">Michael Hartl</a>,
    a tutorial introduction to the
    <a href="https://www.python.org/">Python programming language</a> that
```

```
  is part of
  <a href="https://www.learnenough.com/">LearnEnough.com</a>.
</p>
{% endblock %}
```

Listing 10.25: The core Palindrome Detector view.
palindrome_detector/templates/palindrome.html

```
{% extends "layout.html" %}

{% block content %}
  <h1>Palindrome Detector</h1>

  <p>This will be the palindrome detector.</p>
{% endblock %}
```

Assuming we did everything right in the steps above, our tests should still be GREEN:

Listing 10.26: GREEN

```
(venv) $ pytest
============================ test session starts ============================
collected 3 items

tests/test_site_pages.py ...                                        [100%]

============================ 3 passed in 0.01s ============================
```

A quick check in the browser confirms that things are working as expected (Figure 10.8).

But of course many things could have gone wrong in the refactoring we just did, and our test suite would have caught the problem immediately. Moreover, it would catch errors even on pages we didn't happen to check; for example, Figure 10.8 shows the index page, but how do we know the About page is working as well? The answer is that we don't, and the test suite saves us the trouble of checking every page in the site. As you might guess, this practice becomes increasingly valuable as the complexity of a site grows.

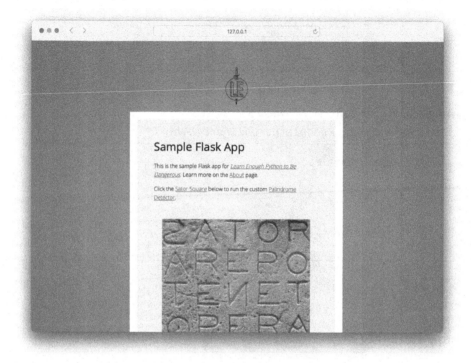

Figure 10.8: Our Home page, now created using a layout.

10.3.1 Exercises

1. As you can confirm by running the source of any page through an HTML valida-
   tor, the current pages are valid HTML, but there's a warning with a suggestion to
   add a **lang** (language) attribute to the **html** tag. Add the attribute **lang="en"** (for
   "English") to the **html** tag in Listing 10.22 and confirm using a web inspector
   that it appears correctly on all three pages.

2. Make a commit and deploy the changes.

10.4 Template Engine

Now that we've defined a proper layout, in this section we'll use the Jinja template
language (first seen in Listing 10.22) to add a couple of nice refinements to our site:
variable titles and *navigation*. Variable titles are HTML **title** tag contents that vary from

page to page, giving each page a nice polish of customization. Navigation, meanwhile, saves us the hassle of having to type each subpage in by hand—certainly not the kind of user experience we're trying to create.

10.4.1 Variable Titles

Our variable titles will combine a *base title*, which is the same on each page, with a piece that varies based on the page's name. In particular, for our Home, About, and Palindrome Detector pages, we want the titles to look something like this:

```
<title>Learn Enough Python Sample App | Home</title>
```

```
<title>Learn Enough Python Sample App | About</title>
```

```
<title>Learn Enough Python Sample App | Palindrome Detector</title>
```

Our strategy has three steps:

1. Write GREEN tests for the current page title.
2. Write RED tests for the variable titles.
3. Get to GREEN by adding the variable component of the title.

Note that Steps 2 & 3 constitute test-driven development. And indeed writing the tests for the variable title is easier than getting them to pass, which is one of the cases for TDD described in Box 8.1.

To get started with Step 1, we'll modify the **title** assertions defined in Listing 10.20 to include the current base title. For convenience in the next step, we'll define a **base_title** variable and use interpolation to form the title using

```
base_title = "Learn Enough Python Sample App"
title = f"<title>{base_title}</title>"
```

and then assert that the title appears in the response text. The result for all three site pages appears in Listing 10.27.

Listing 10.27: Adding assertions for the base title content. GREEN

tests/test_site_pages.py

```
def test_index(client):
    response = client.get("/")
    assert response.status_code == 200
    base_title = "Learn Enough Python Sample App"
    title = f"<title>{base_title}</title>"
    assert title in response.text
    assert "<h1>" in response.text

def test_about(client):
    response = client.get("/about")
    assert response.status_code == 200
    base_title = "Learn Enough Python Sample App"
    title = f"<title>{base_title}</title>"
    assert title in response.text
    assert "<h1>" in response.text

def test_palindrome(client):
    response = client.get("/palindrome")
    assert response.status_code == 200
    base_title = "Learn Enough Python Sample App"
    title = f"<title>{base_title}</title>"
    assert title in response.text
    assert "<h1>" in response.text
```

Note that there is a lot of repetition in Listing 10.27. Some of this repetition will disappear when we add the variable component to the titles; eliminating the rest of the repetition is left as an exercise (Section 10.4.3).

As required for tests of working code, the test suite is currently GREEN:

Listing 10.28: GREEN

```
(venv) $ pytest
============================== test session starts ==============================
collected 3 items

tests/test_site_pages.py ...                                             [100%]

=============================== 3 passed in 0.01s ===============================
```

Now we're ready for Step 2. All we need to do is add the vertical bar | and the page-specific titles, as shown in Listing 10.29.

Listing 10.29: Adding assertions for the variable title content. RED
tests/test_site_pages.py

```
def test_index(client):
    response = client.get("/")
    assert response.status_code == 200
    base_title = "Learn Enough Python Sample App"
    title = f"<title>{base_title} | Home</title>"
    assert title in response.text
    assert "<h1>" in response.text

def test_about(client):
    response = client.get("/about")
    assert response.status_code == 200
    base_title = "Learn Enough Python Sample App"
    title = f"<title>{base_title} | About</title>"
    assert title in response.text
    assert "<h1>" in response.text

def test_palindrome(client):
    response = client.get("/palindrome")
    assert response.status_code == 200
    base_title = "Learn Enough Python Sample App"
    title = f"<title>{base_title} | Palindrome Detector</title>"
    assert title in response.text
    assert "<h1>" in response.text
```

Because we haven't updated the application code, the tests are now RED:

Listing 10.30: RED

```
(venv) $ pytest
============================== test session starts ==============================
collected 3 items

tests/test_site_pages.py FFF                                            [100%]

==================================== FAILURES ===================================
_____ test_index _____
.
.
.
=========================== short test summary info ============================
FAILED tests/test_site_pages.py::test_index - assert '<title>Learn Enough Pyt...
FAILED tests/test_site_pages.py::test_about - assert '<title>Learn Enough Pyt...
FAILED tests/test_site_pages.py::test_palindrome - assert '<title>Learn Enoug...
============================== 3 failed in 0.03s ===============================
```

Now for Step 3. The trick is to pass a different **page_title** option from each of our app's functions and then render the result on the page layout. The way Jinja templates work is that we can pass a keyword argument (Section 5.1.2) to the template using

```
render_template("index.html", page_title="Home")
```

and automatically get access to a variable called **page_title** in the template (in this case, with the value **"Home"**). The result for our desired variable titles appears in Listing 10.31.

Listing 10.31: Adding **page_title** variables to each page. GREEN
palindrome_app/palindrome_detector/__init__.py

```python
import os

from flask import Flask, render_template


def create_app(test_config=None):
    """Create and configure the app."""
    app = Flask(__name__, instance_relative_config=True)

    if test_config is None:
        # Load the instance config, if it exists, when not testing.
        app.config.from_pyfile("config.py", silent=True)
    else:
        # Load the test config if passed in.
        app.config.from_mapping(test_config)

    # Ensure the instance folder exists.
    try:
        os.makedirs(app.instance_path)
    except OSError:
        pass

    @app.route("/")
    def index():
        return render_template("index.html", page_title="Home")

    @app.route("/about")
    def about():
        return render_template("about.html", page_title="About")
```

```
@app.route("/palindrome")
def palindrome():
    return render_template("palindrome.html",
                           page_title="Palindrome Detector")

    return app

app = create_app()
```

Once we have a variable inside a template using the code in Listing 10.31, we can insert it using the special syntax **{{ ... }}** used by Jinja templates:[7]

```
{{ page_title }}
```

This tells Jinja to insert the contents of **page_title** into the HTML template at that location. In particular, this means we can add the variable component of the title using the code shown in Listing 10.32.

Listing 10.32: Adding a variable component to the title. RED
palindrome_detector/templates/layout.html

```
<!DOCTYPE html>
<html>
  <head>
    <meta charset="utf-8">
    <title>Learn Enough Python Sample App | {{ page_title }}</title>
      .
      .
      .
```

When **page_title** is **"Home"**, the layout title will become

```
<title>Learn Enough Python Sample App | Home</title>
```

and so on for the other variable titles.

Because the variable title in Listing 10.31 matches the ones in the test from Listing 10.29, our test suite should be GREEN:

---

7. As with **{% ... %}**, the **{{ ... }}** syntax is commonly used in other templating systems as well, such as Liquid and Mustache.

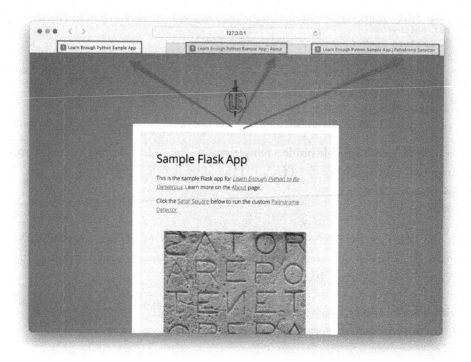

Figure 10.9: Confirming the correct variable titles in the browser.

Listing 10.33: GREEN

```
(venv) $ pytest
=============================== test session starts ===============================
collected 3 items

tests/test_site_pages.py ...                                            [100%]

============================== 3 passed in 0.01s ===============================
```

Success! We've managed to add variable titles to our application using TDD and we've confirmed that they're working without even touching a browser.

Of course, it's probably a good idea to double-check in the browser anyway, just to make sure (Figure 10.9).

10.4.2 Site Navigation

Now that we have a proper layout file, adding navigation to every page is easy. The nav code appears in Listing 10.34, with the result shown in Figure 10.10.

Listing 10.34: Adding site navigation.
palindrome_detector/templates/layout.html

```
<!DOCTYPE html>
<html>
  <head>
    <meta charset="utf-8">
    <title>Learn Enough Python Sample App | {{ page_title }}</title>
    <link rel="stylesheet" type="text/css" href="/static/stylesheets/main.css">
    <link href="https://fonts.googleapis.com/css?family=Open+Sans:300,400"
          rel="stylesheet">
  </head>
  <body>
    <a href="/" class="header-logo">
      <img src="/static/images/logo_b.png" alt="Learn Enough logo">
    </a>
    <div class="container">
      <header class="header">
        <nav>
          <ul class="header-nav">
            <li><a href="/">Home</a></li>
            <li><a href="/palindrome">Is It a Palindrome?</a></li>
            <li><a href="/about">About</a></li>
          </ul>
        </nav>
      </header>
      <div class="content">
        {% block content %}{% endblock %}
      </div>
    </div>
  </body>
</html>
```

As a final flourish, we'll factor the navigation from Listing 10.34 into a separate template, sometimes called a *partial template* (or *partial* for short) because it represents only a partial page. This will lead to a nicely clean and tidy layout page.

Because this involves refactoring the site, we'll add a simple test (per Box 8.1) to catch any regressions. Because the navigation appears on the site layout, we can use

Figure 10.10: The site navigation.

any page to test for its presence, and for convenience we'll use the index page. As
shown in Listing 10.35, all we need to do is assert the existence of a **nav** tag.

Listing 10.35: Testing the navigation. GREEN
tests/test_site_pages.py

```python
def test_index(client):
    response = client.get("/")
    assert response.status_code == 200
    base_title = "Learn Enough Python Sample App"
    title = f"<title>{base_title} | Home</title>"
    assert title in response.text
    assert "<h1>" in response.text
    assert "<nav>" in response.text

def test_about(client):
    response = client.get("/about")
```

```
    assert response.status_code == 200
    base_title = "Learn Enough Python Sample App"
    title = f"<title>{base_title} | About</title>"
    assert title in response.text
    assert "<h1>" in response.text

def test_palindrome(client):
    response = client.get("/palindrome")
    assert response.status_code == 200
    base_title = "Learn Enough Python Sample App"
    title = f"<title>{base_title} | Palindrome Detector</title>"
    assert title in response.text
    assert "<h1>" in response.text
```

Because the nav was already added, the tests should be GREEN:

Listing 10.36: GREEN

```
(venv) $ pytest
============================ test session starts ============================
collected 3 items

tests/test_site_pages.py ...                                        [100%]

============================ 3 passed in 0.01s ============================
```

It's a good practice to watch the tests change to RED to make sure we're testing the right thing, so we'll start by cutting the navigation (Listing 10.37) and pasting it into a separate file, which we'll call **navigation.html** (Listing 10.38):

```
(venv) $ touch palindrome_detector/templates/navigation.html
```

Listing 10.37: Cutting the navigation. RED
palindrome_detector/templates/layout.html

```
<!DOCTYPE html>
<html>
  <head>
    <meta charset="utf-8">
    <title>Learn Enough Python Sample App | {{ page_title }}</title>
    <link rel="stylesheet" type="text/css" href="/static/stylesheets/main.css">
    <link href="https://fonts.googleapis.com/css?family=Open+Sans:300,400"
```

```
        rel="stylesheet">
  </head>
  <body>
    <a href="/" class="header-logo">
      <img src="/static/images/logo_b.png" alt="Learn Enough logo">
    </a>
    <div class="container">

      <div class="content">
        {% block content %}{% endblock %}
      </div>
    </div>
  </body>
</html>
```

Listing 10.38: Adding a navigation partial template. RED
palindrome_detector/templates/navigation.html

```
<header class="header">
  <nav>
    <ul class="header-nav">
      <li><a href="/">Home</a></li>
      <li><a href="/palindrome">Is It a Palindrome?</a></li>
      <li><a href="/about">About</a></li>
    </ul>
  </nav>
</header>
```

You should confirm that the tests are now RED:

Listing 10.39: RED

```
(venv) $ pytest
============================= test session starts =============================
collected 3 items

tests/test_site_pages.py F..                                          [100%]

=================================== FAILURES ===================================
_____ test_index _____
  .
  .
  .
=========================== short test summary info ===========================
```

```
FAILED tests/test_site_pages.py::test_index - assert '<nav>' in '<!DOCTYPE ht...
========================= 1 failed, 2 passed in 0.03s =========================
```

To restore the navigation, we can use Jinja's template language to **include** the navigation partial:

```
{% include "navigation.html" %}
```

This code automatically looks for a file called **navigation.html** in the **palindrome_detector/templates/** directory, evaluates the result, and inserts the return value where it was called.

Putting this code into the layout gives Listing 10.40.

Listing 10.40: Evaluating the nav partial in the layout. GREEN
palindrome_detector/templates/layout.html

```
<!DOCTYPE html>
<html>
  <head>
    <meta charset="utf-8">
    <title>Learn Enough Python Sample App | {{ page_title }}</title>
    <link rel="stylesheet" type="text/css" href="/static/stylesheets/main.css">
    <link href="https://fonts.googleapis.com/css?family=Open+Sans:300,400"
          rel="stylesheet">
  </head>
  <body>
    <a href="/" class="header-logo">
      <img src="/static/images/logo_b.png" alt="Learn Enough logo">
    </a>
    <div class="container">
      {% include "navigation.html" %}
      <div class="content">
        {% block content %}{% endblock %}
      </div>
    </div>
  </body>
</html>
```

With the code in Listing 10.40, our test suite is once again GREEN:

Listing 10.41: GREEN

```
(venv) $ pytest
============================ test session starts ============================
```

Figure 10.11: The navigation menu on the About page.

```
collected 3 items

tests/test_site_pages.py ...                                              [100%]

=============================== 3 passed in 0.01s ================================
```

A quick click over to the About page confirms that the navigation is working (Figure 10.11). Sweet!

10.4.3 Exercises

1. We can eliminate some duplication in Listing 10.29 by creating a function that returns the base title, as shown in Listing 10.42. Confirm that this code still gives a GREEN test suite.

2. Make a commit and deploy the changes.

Listing 10.42: Adding a `full_title` method to eliminate some duplication. GREEN
tests/test_site_pages.py

```python
def test_index(client):
    response = client.get("/")
    assert response.status_code == 200
    assert full_title("Home") in response.text
    assert "<h1>" in response.text
    assert "<nav>" in response.text

def test_about(client):
    response = client.get("/about")
    assert response.status_code == 200
    assert full_title("About") in response.text
    assert "<h1>" in response.text

def test_palindrome(client):
    response = client.get("/palindrome")
    assert response.status_code == 200
    assert full_title("Palindrome Detector") in response.text
    assert "<h1>" in response.text

def full_title(variable_title):
    """Return the full title."""
    base_title = "Learn Enough Python Sample App"
    return f"<title>{base_title} | {variable_title}</title>"
```

10.5 Palindrome Detector

In this section, we'll complete the sample Flask app by adding a working palindrome detector. This will involve putting the Python package developed in Chapter 8 to good use. And if you haven't followed *Learn Enough Ruby to Be Dangerous* (https://www.learnenough.com/ruby) yet, we'll also see the first truly working HTML *form* in the Learn Enough introductory sequence (https://www.learnenough.com/courses).

Our first step is to add a palindrome package so that we can detect palindromes. I recommend using the one you created and published in Chapter 8:

```
(venv) $ pip install palindrome_YOUR_USERNAME \
> --index-url https://test.pypi.org/simple/
```

If for any reason you didn't complete that step, you can use mine instead:

```
(venv)$ pip install palindrome_mhartl --index-url https://test.pypi.org/simple/
```

At this point, we can include the palindrome package in our app (Listing 10.43).

Listing 10.43: Adding **request** and **Phrase** to the app.
palindrome_app/palindrome_detector/__init__.py

```
import os

from flask import Flask, render_template, request

from palindrome_mhartl.phrase import Phrase



.
.
.
```

Note that we've added **request** from the **flask** package, which we'll be using in this section to handle form submissions.

Since we'll be deploying the app to production, we should also update the app requirements to include the palindrome detector. The result for one version of my particular detector is shown in Listing 1.15, though you are encouraged to use your own. Also note that Listing 10.44 includes an extra line so that Fly.io knows to look for packages at the Test Python Package Index as well as the regular index.

Listing 10.44: Adding a Test Python Package Index lookup URL.
requirements.txt

```
--extra-index-url https://testpypi.python.org/pypi
palindrome_mhartl==0.0.12
click==8.1.3
Flask==2.2.2
.
.
.
```

With that prep work done, we're now ready to add a form to our Palindrome Detector page, which is currently just a placeholder (Figure 10.12). The form consists

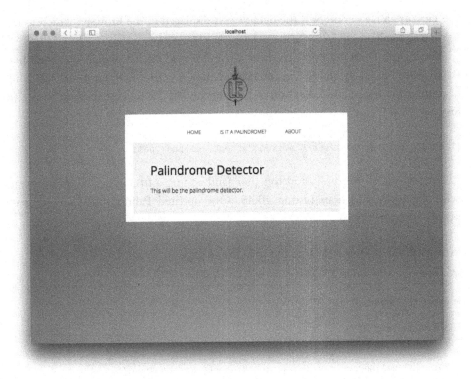

Figure 10.12: The current state of the palindrome page.

of three principal parts: a **form** tag to define the form, a **textarea** for entering a phrase, and a **button** for submitting the phrase to the server.

Let's work inside out. The **button** has two attributes—a CSS class for styling and a **type** indicating that it's designed to submit information:

```
<button class="form-submit" type="submit">Is it a palindrome?</button>
```

The **textarea** has three attributes—a **name** attribute, which as we'll see in a moment passes important information back to the server, along with **rows** and **cols** to define the size of the textarea box:

```
<textarea name="phrase" rows="10" cols="60"></textarea>
```

The **textarea** tag's content is the default text displayed in the browser, which in this case is just blank.

Finally, the **form** tag itself has three attributes—a CSS **id**, which isn't used here but is conventional to include; an **action**, which specifies the action to take when submitting the form; and a **method** indicating the HTTP request method to use (in this case, **POST**):

```
<form id="palindrome_tester" action="/check" method="post">
```

Putting the above discussion together (and adding a **br** tag to add a line break) yields the form shown in Listing 10.45. Our updated Palindrome Detector page appears in Figure 10.13.

Listing 10.45: Adding a form to the palindrome page.
palindrome_detector/templates/palindrome.html

```
{% extends "layout.html" %}

{% block content %}
  <h1>Palindrome Detector</h1>

  <form id="palindrome_tester" action="/check" method="post">
    <textarea name="phrase" rows="10" cols="60"></textarea>
    <br>
    <button class="form-submit" type="submit">Is it a palindrome?</button>
  </form>
{% endblock %}
```

The form in Listing 10.45 is, apart from cosmetic details, identical to the analogous form (https://www.learnenough.com/javascript-tutorial/dom_manipulation#code-form_tag) developed in *Learn Enough JavaScript to Be Dangerous* (https://www.learnenough.com/javascript):

```
<form id="palindromeTester">
  <textarea name="phrase" rows="10" cols="30"></textarea>
  <br>
  <button type="submit">Is it a palindrome?</button>
</form>
```

Figure 10.13: The new palindrome form.

In that case, though, we "cheated" by using a JavaScript event listener to inter-cept   (https://www.learnenough.com/javascript-tutorial/dom_manipulation#code-form_event_target) the submit request from the form, and no information ever got sent from the client (browser) to the server. (It's important to understand that, when developing web applications on a local computer, the client and server are the same physical machine, but in general they are different.)

This time, we won't cheat: The request will really go all the way to the server, which means we'll have to handle the **POST** request on the back-end. By default, a Flask function responds to **GET** requests, but we can arrange to respond to **POST** requests instead using the **method** keyword argument with value equal to a tuple of the methods to respond to. Because there's only one method in this case (namely, **POST**), we have to use the trailing-comma syntax mentioned in Section 3.6 for a tuple of one element:

```
@app.route("/check", methods=("POST",))
def check():
    # Do something to handle the submission
```

Here the name of the URL path, **/check**, matches the value of the **action** parameter in the form (Listing 10.45).

It turns out that the **request** include in Listing 10.43 has a **form** attribute that contains useful information, so let's **return** it as shown in Listing 10.46 and then submit the form to see what happens (Figure 10.14).

Listing 10.46: Investigating the effects of a form submission.
palindrome_app/palindrome_detector/__init__.py

```
import os

from flask import Flask, render_template, request

from palindrome_mhartl.phrase import Phrase


def create_app(test_config=None):
    .
    .
    .
    @app.route("/")
    def index():
        return render_template("index.html", page_title="Home")

    @app.route("/about")
    def about():
        return render_template("about.html", page_title="About")

    @app.route("/palindrome")
    def palindrome():
        return render_template("palindrome.html",
                               page_title="Palindrome Detector")

    @app.route("/check", methods=("POST",))
    def check():
        return request.form

    return app

app = create_app()
```

Figure 10.14: The result of submitting a form.

As seen in Figure 10.14, **request.form** is a dictionary (Section 4.4), with key **"phrase"** and value **"Madam, I'm Adam."**:

```
{
  "phrase": "Madam, I'm Adam."
}
```

This dictionary is created automatically by Flask according to the key–value pairs in the form (Listing 10.45). In this case, we have only one such pair, with key given by the **name** attribute of the **textarea** (**"phrase"**) and value given by the string entered by the user. This means that we can use the code

```
phrase = request.form["phrase"]
```

to extract the value of the phrase.

Now that we know about the existence and contents of **request.form**, we can use **ispalindrome()** to detect palindromes as in previous chapters. In plain Python, this would look something like Listing 10.47.

Listing 10.47: What our palindrome results might look like in plain Python.

```
if Phrase(phrase).ispalindrome():
    print(f'"{phrase}" is a palindrome!")
else:
    print(f'"{phrase}" isn\'t a palindrome.")
```

We can do the same basic thing in our web application using the Jinja template language, only using **{{ ... }}** instead of interpolation and surrounding any other code in **{% ... %}** tags, as shown schematically in Listing 10.48.

Listing 10.48: Schematic code for the palindrome result.

```
{% if Phrase(phrase).ispalindrome() %}
    "{{ phrase }}" is a palindrome!
{% else %}
    "{{ phrase }}" isn't a palindrome.
{% endif %}
```

Let's create a template file called **result.html** to display our results:

```
(venv) $ touch palindrome_detector/templates/result.html
```

The template code itself is an expanded version of Listing 10.48 with a few more HTML tags for a better appearance, as shown in Listing 10.49.

Listing 10.49: Displaying the palindrome result with Jinja.
palindrome_detector/templates/result.html

```
{% extends "layout.html" %}

{% block content %}
  <h1>Palindrome Result</h1>

  {% if Phrase(phrase).ispalindrome() %}
    <div class="result result-success">
```

```
      <p>"{{ phrase }}" is a palindrome!</p>
    </div>
  {% else %}
    <div class="result result-fail">
      <p>"{{ phrase }}" isn't a palindrome.</p>
    </div>
  {% endif %}
{% endblock %}
```

All that's left now is handling the submission, putting the value of **request.form** in **phrase**, and rendering the result. We can create a **phrase** variable in the template using the same keyword trick we used in Listing 10.31 to create **page_title**, and we can pass the **Phrase** class the same way as well. Using **render_template** as usual to render the template **result.html** gives the code shown in Listing 10.50.

Listing 10.50: Handling a palindrome form submission.
palindrome_app/palindrome_detector/__init__.py

```python
import os

from flask import Flask, render_template, request

from palindrome_mhartl.phrase import Phrase


def create_app(test_config=None):
    """Create and configure the app."""
    app = Flask(__name__, instance_relative_config=True)

    if test_config is None:
        # Load the instance config, if it exists, when not testing.
        app.config.from_pyfile("config.py", silent=True)
    else:
        # Load the test config if passed in.
        app.config.from_mapping(test_config)

    # Ensure the instance folder exists.
    try:
        os.makedirs(app.instance_path)
    except OSError:
        pass

    @app.route("/")
    def index():
        return render_template("index.html", page_title="Home")
```

```
@app.route("/about")
def about():
    return render_template("about.html", page_title="About")

@app.route("/palindrome")
def palindrome():
    return render_template("palindrome.html",
                           page_title="Palindrome Detector")
@app.route("/check", methods=("POST",))
def check():
    return render_template("result.html",
                           Phrase=Phrase,
                           phrase=request.form["phrase"])

    return app

app = create_app()
```

The code in Listing 10.49 is the most straightforward translation of the Python code from Listing 10.47, but it involves passing a full **Phrase** class to the template in Listing 10.50. Many developers prefer to pass only variables to templates, and we'll refactor the code to use this convention in Section 10.5.1.

At this point, our palindrome detector should be working! The result of submitting a non-palindrome is shown in Figure 10.15.

Now let's see if our detector can correctly identify one of the most ancient palindromes, the so-called Sator Square first found in the ruins of Pompeii (Figure 10.16[8]). (Authorities differ on the exact meaning of the Latin words in the square, but the likeliest translation is "The sower [farmer] Arepo holds the wheels with effort.")

Entering the text "SATOR AREPO TENET OPERA ROTAS" (Figure 10.17) and submitting it leads to the result shown in Figure 10.18. It works!

10.5.1 Form Tests

Our application is now working, but note that testing a *second* palindrome requires clicking on "IS IT A PALINDROME?" It would be more convenient if we included the same submission form on the result page as well.

---

8. Image courtesy of CPA Media Pte Ltd/Alamy Stock Photo.

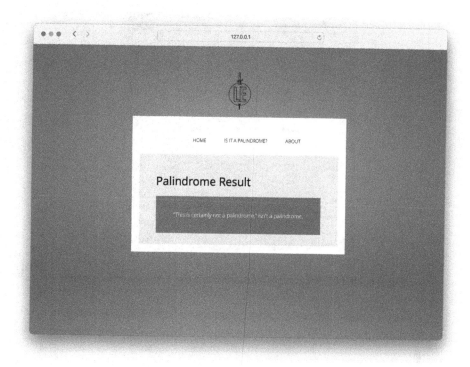

Figure 10.15: The result for a non-palindrome.

To do this, we'll first add a simple test for the presence of a **form** tag on the palindrome page. Because the tests we'll be adding are specific to that page, we'll create a new test file to contain them:

```
(venv) $ touch tests/test_palindrome.py
```

The test itself is closely analogous to the **h1** and **title** test in Listing 10.20, as shown in Listing 10.51. Note that we've defined a **form_tag()** helper function in anticipation of testing for the form on the result page as well (compare with the **full_title()** helper in Listing 10.42).

Figure 10.16: A Latin palindrome from the lost city of Pompeii.

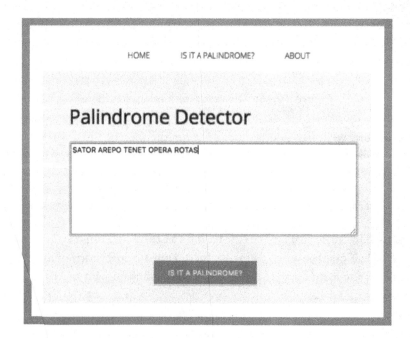

Figure 10.17: A Latin palindrome?

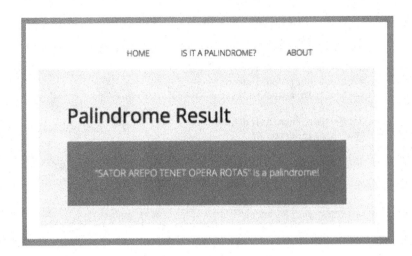

Figure 10.18: A Latin palindrome!

Listing 10.51: Testing for the presence of a form tag. GREEN
tests/test_palindrome.py

```
def test_palindrome_page(client):
    response = client.get("/palindrome")
    assert form_tag() in response.text

def form_tag():
    return '<form id="palindrome_tester" action="/check" method="post">'
```

Now we'll add tests for the existing form submission for both non-palindromes and palindromes. Just as **get()** in tests issues a GET request, **post()** in tests issues a POST request. The first argument of **post()** is the URL, and the second is the **data** hash (which gives rise to the contents of **response.form**):

```
client.post("/check", data={"phrase": "Not a palindrome"})
```

To test the response, we'll verify that the text in the page's paragraph tag includes the right result. Taking the ideas above and applying them to both non-palindromes and palindromes gives the tests shown in Listing 10.52.

Listing 10.52: Adding tests for form submission. GREEN

tests/test_palindrome.py

```python
def test_palindrome_page(client):
    response = client.get("/palindrome")
    assert form_tag() in response.text

def test_non_palindrome_submission(client):
    phrase = "Not a palindrome."
    response = client.post("/check", data={"phrase": phrase})
    assert f'<p>"{phrase}" isn\'t a palindrome.</p>' in response.text

def test_palindrome_submission(client):
    phrase = "Sator Arepo tenet opera rotas."
    response = client.post("/check", data={"phrase": phrase})
    assert f'<p>"{phrase}" is a palindrome!</p>' in response.text

def form_tag():
    return '<form id="palindrome_tester" action="/check" method="post">'
```

(Be careful when using sample phrases that contain non-alphanumeric characters like
quotes or apostrophes; by default, Jinja escapes these out in ways that make them
very difficult to test, which is why Listing 10.52 uses the Sator Square palindrome
instead of, say, **Madam, I'm Adam**. To see what the escaped HTML looks like in the
latter case, you can temporarily set **phrase** to **Madam, I'm Adam** and then include
print(response.text) in the test to output the result.)

Because we were testing existing functionality, the tests in Listing 10.52 should
already be GREEN:

Listing 10.53: GREEN

```
(venv) $ pytest
============================ test session starts ============================
collected 6 items

tests/test_palindrome.py ...                                        [ 50%]
tests/test_site_pages.py ...                                        [100%]

============================ 6 passed in 0.03s ============================
```

As a capstone to our development, we'll now add a form on the result page using
the RED, GREEN, refactor cycle that is a hallmark of TDD. Since there is only one

result template, it doesn't matter if we test the palindrome or non-palindrome page, so we'll choose the latter without loss of generality. All we need to do is add a **form** test identical to the one in Listing 10.51, as shown in Listing 10.54.

Listing 10.54: Adding a test for a form on the result page. RED

tests/test_palindrome.py

```python
def test_palindrome_page(client):
    response = client.get("/palindrome")
    assert form_tag() in response.text

def test_non_palindrome_submission(client):
    phrase = "Not a palindrome."
    response = client.post("/check", data={"phrase": phrase})
    assert f'<p>"{phrase}" isn\'t a palindrome.</p>' in response.text
    assert form_tag() in response.text

def test_palindrome_submission(client):
    phrase = "Sator Arepo tenet opera rotas."
    response = client.post("/check", data={"phrase": phrase})
    assert f'<p>"{phrase}" is a palindrome!</p>' in response.text

def form_tag():
    return '<form id="palindrome_tester" action="/check" method="post">'
```

As required, the test suite is now RED:

Listing 10.55: RED

```
(venv) $ pytest
============================ test session starts ============================
collected 6 items

tests/test_palindrome.py .FF                                        [ 50%]
tests/test_site_pages.py ...                                        [100%]

================================== FAILURES ==================================
_____ test_non_palindrome_submission _____
.
.
.
========================== short test summary info ==========================
FAILED tests/test_palindrome.py::test_non_palindrome_submission - assert '<fo...
FAILED tests/test_palindrome.py::test_palindrome_submission - assert '<form i...
========================= 2 failed, 4 passed in 0.04s =========================
```

We can get the tests to GREEN again by copying the form from **palindrome.html** and pasting it into **result.html**, as shown in Listing 10.56.

Listing 10.56: Adding a form to the result page. GREEN

palindrome_detector/templates/result.html

```
{% extends "layout.html" %}

{% block content %}
  <h1>Palindrome Result</h1>

  {% if Phrase(phrase).ispalindrome() %}
    <div class="result result-success">
      <p>"{{ phrase }}" is a palindrome!</p>
    </div>
  {% else %}
    <div class="result result-fail">
      <p>"{{ phrase }}" isn't a palindrome.</p>
    </div>
  {% endif %}

  <form id="palindrome_tester" action="/check" method="post">
    <textarea name="phrase" rows="10" cols="60"></textarea>
    <br>
    <button class="form-submit" type="submit">Is it a palindrome?</button>
  </form>
{% endblock %}
```

This gets our tests to GREEN:

Listing 10.57: GREEN

```
(venv) $ pytest
============================ test session starts ================================
collected 6 items

tests/test_palindrome.py ...                                          [ 50%]
tests/test_site_pages.py ...                                          [100%]

============================= 6 passed in 0.03s ================================
```

That copy-and-paste should have set your programmer Spidey-sense tingling, though: It's repetition! Pasting in content is a clear violation of the Don't Repeat

Yourself (DRY) principle. Happily, we saw how to eliminate such duplication in the case of the site navigation by refactoring the code to use a partial (Listing 10.40), which we can apply to this case as well. As with the nav, we'll first create a separate file for the form HTML:

```
(venv) $ touch palindrome_detector/templates/palindrome_form.html
```

Then we can fill it with the form (Listing 10.58), while replacing the form with a Jinja template **include** on the result page (Listing 10.59) and on the main palindrome page itself (Listing 10.60).

Listing 10.58: A partial for the palindrome form. GREEN
palindrome_detector/templates/palindrome_form.html

```
<form id="palindrome_tester" action="/check" method="post">
  <textarea name="phrase" rows="10" cols="60"></textarea>
  <br>
  <button class="form-submit" type="submit">Is it a palindrome?</button>
</form>
```

Listing 10.59: Rendering the form template on the result page. GREEN
palindrome_detector/templates/result.html

```
{% extends "layout.html" %}

{% block content %}
  <h1>Palindrome Result</h1>

  {% if Phrase(phrase).ispalindrome() %}
    <div class="result result-success">
      <p>"{{ phrase }}" is a palindrome!</p>
    </div>
  {% else %}
    <div class="result result-fail">
      <p>"{{ phrase }}" isn't a palindrome.</p>
    </div>
  {% endif %}

  <h2>Try another one!</h2>

  {% include "palindrome_form.html" %}
{% endblock %}
```

Listing 10.60: Rendering the form template on the main palindrome page. GREEN
palindrome_detector/templates/palindrome.html

```
{% extends "layout.html" %}

{% block content %}
  <h1>Palindrome Detector</h1>

  {% include "palindrome_form.html" %}
{% endblock %}
```

As a final refactoring, we'll adopt the convention of only passing variables (rather than, say, classes) to Jinja templates, as discussed immediately after Listing 10.50. To do this, we'll define an **is_palindrome** variable as follows:

```
phrase = request.form["phrase"]
is_palindrome = Phrase(phrase).ispalindrome()
```

We'll then pass these variables to the template, where we'll use this simplified **if** statement:

```
{% if is_palindrome %}
```

The results appear in Listing 10.61 and Listing 10.62.

Listing 10.61: Passing only a variable to the template. GREEN
palindrome_app/palindrome_detector/__init__.py

```
import os

from flask import Flask, render_template, request

from palindrome_mhartl.phrase import Phrase


def create_app(test_config=None):
    """Create and configure the app."""
    app = Flask(__name__, instance_relative_config=True)

    if test_config is None:
        # Load the instance config, if it exists, when not testing.
        app.config.from_pyfile("config.py", silent=True)
    else:
        # Load the test config if passed in.
```

```
        app.config.from_mapping(test_config)

    # Ensure the instance folder exists.
    try:
        os.makedirs(app.instance_path)
    except OSError:
        pass

    @app.route("/")
    def index():
        return render_template("index.html", page_title="Home")

    @app.route("/about")
    def about():
        return render_template("about.html", page_title="About")

    @app.route("/palindrome")
    def palindrome():
        return render_template("palindrome.html",
                               page_title="Palindrome Detector")

    @app.route("/check", methods=("POST",))
    def check():
        phrase = request.form["phrase"]
        is_palindrome = Phrase(phrase).ispalindrome()
        return render_template("result.html",
                               phrase=phrase,
                               is_palindrome=is_palindrome)

    return app

app = create_app()
```

Listing 10.62: Using a boolean variable in the template. GREEN
palindrome_detector/templates/result.html

```
{% extends "layout.html" %}

{% block content %}
  <h1>Palindrome Result</h1>

  {% if is_palindrome %}
    <div class="result result-success">
      <p>"{{ phrase }}" is a palindrome!</p>
    </div>
  {% else %}
    <div class="result result-fail">
      <p>"{{ phrase }}" isn't a palindrome.</p>
    </div>
```

```
{% endif %}

<h2>Try another one!</h2>

{% include "palindrome_form.html" %}
{% endblock %}
```

As required for a refactoring, the tests are still GREEN:

Listing 10.63: GREEN

```
(venv) $ pytest
=========================== test session starts ===========================
collected 6 items

tests/test_palindrome.py ...                                    [ 50%]
tests/test_site_pages.py ...                                    [100%]


=========================== 6 passed in 0.03s ===========================
```

Submitting the Sator Square palindrome shows that the form on the result page is rendering properly, as shown in Figure 10.19.

Filling the textarea with one of my favorite looooong palindromes (Figure 10.20) gives the result shown in Figure 10.21.[9]

And with that—"A man, a plan, a canoe, pasta, heros, rajahs, a coloratura, maps, snipe, percale, macaroni, a gag, a banana bag, a tan, a tag, a banana bag again (or a camel), a crepe, pins, Spam, a rut, a Rolo, cash, a jar, sore hats, a peon, a canal—Panama!"—we're done with our palindrome detector web application. Whew!

The only thing left is to commit and deploy:

```
(venv) $ git add -A
(venv) $ git commit -am "Finish working palindrome detector"
(venv) $ flyctl deploy
```

The result is a palindrome application working in production (Figure 10.22)![10]

---

9. The amazingly long palindrome in Figure 10.20 was created in 1983 by pioneering computer scientist Guy Steele with the aid of a custom program.

10. To learn how to host a Fly.io site using a custom domain, see the article on custom domains with Fly (https://fly.io/docs/app-guides/custom-domains-with-fly/).

Figure 10.19: The form on the result page.

10.5.2 Exercises

1. Confirm by submitting an empty textarea that the palindrome detector currently returns **True** for the empty string, which is a flaw in the palindrome package itself. What happens if you submit a bunch of spaces?

2. In the palindrome package, write tests asserting that the empty string and a string of spaces *aren't* palindromes (RED). Then write the application code necessary to get the tests to GREEN. (It's worth noting that the **processed_content()** method already filters out spaces, so in the application code you need only consider the case of the empty string, whose boolean value is **False** (Section 2.4.2).) Bump

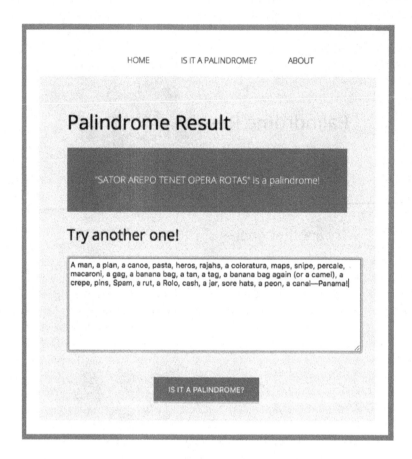

Figure 10.20: Entering a long string in the form's textarea field.

the version number and publish your package as in Section 8.5.1. (You can refer
to my version (https://github.com/mhartl/python_package_tutorial) if you'd like
some help.)

3. Upgrade the test package in your web app directory using Listing 10.64 as a template and confirm that it's working by submitting empty and blank phrases in the
browser. (Recall that you should type the continuation character \ in Listing 10.64
but not the right angle bracket > since the latter will be inserted automatically by
your shell program.)

4. Make a commit and deploy the changes. Confirm the correct behavior in the live
app.

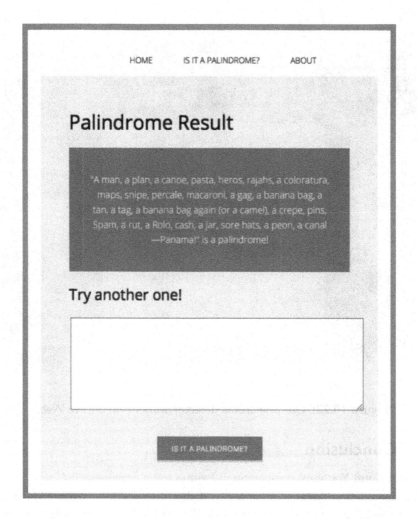

Figure 10.21: That long string is a palindrome!

Listing 10.64: Upgrading the test package.

```
(venv) $ pip install --upgrade palindrome_YOUR_USERNAME_HERE \
> --index-url https://test.pypi.org/simple/
```

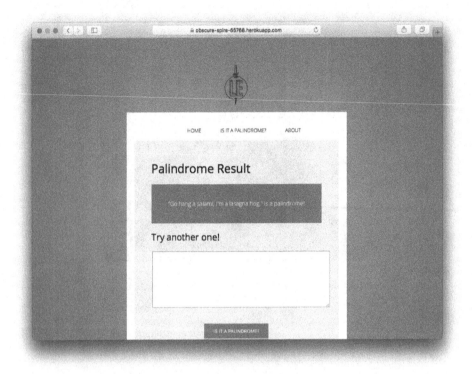

Figure 10.22: Our palindrome detector working on the live Web.

10.6 Conclusion

Congratulations! You now know enough Python to be *dangerous*.

There is one more challenge, should you choose to accept it: Chapter 11 on data science. This chapter is a bit specialized, and strictly speaking it can be considered optional. It introduces some valuable techniques, though, and reinforces other parts of the book, so I recommend giving it a try.

For more about Python (and programming generally), I recommend these fine resources:

- Replit's 100 days of code: This is a guided introduction to Python programming using Replit's amazing collaborative browser-based IDE.

- Practical Python Programming by Dave Beazley: I've long been a huge fan of Beazely's *Python Essential Reference* and highly recommend his (free) online course.

- *Learn Python the Hard Way* by Zed Shaw: This exercise- and syntax-heavy approach is an excellent complement to the breadth-first, narrative approach taken in this tutorial. *Fun fact*: Zed Shaw's "Learn Code the Hard Way" brand was a direct inspiration for "Learn Enough to Be Dangerous" (https://www.learnenough.com/).

- *Python Crash Course* and *Automate the Boring Stuff with Python* from No Starch Press: Both of these books are good follow-ons to *Learn Enough Python to Be Dangerous*; the former (by Eric Matthes) has more detailed coverage of Python syntax while the latter (by Al Sweigart) includes a great many applications of Python programming to everyday computer tasks.

- *Captain Code* by Ben Forta and Shmuel Forta: Although this book is principally aimed at children, many adult readers have reported enjoying it as well.

- Finally, for people who want the most solid foundation possible in technical sophistication, Learn Enough All Access (https://www.learnenough.com/all-access) is a subscription service that has special online versions of all the Learn Enough books and over 40 hours of streaming video tutorials, including *Learn Enough Python to Be Dangerous*, *Learn Enough Ruby to Be Dangerous*, and the full *Ruby on Rails Tutorial* (https://www.railstutorial.org/). We hope you'll check it out!

The material in this chapter is also excellent preparation for learning more about Flask, for which the Flask documentation is a good resource, and for learning web development with Django. If you'd like to go the Django route, the Django documentation is an excellent place to start. If you end up wanting to learn more about web development generally, I also recommend following *Learn Enough JavaScript to Be Dangerous* since JavaScript is the only language that can be executed inside web browsers. In addition, *Learn Enough Python to Be Dangerous* is excellent preparation for *Learn Enough Ruby to Be Dangerous*, which (like *Learn Enough JavaScript to Be Dangerous*) broadly follows the same outline as this tutorial, and is also great preparation for the *Ruby on Rails Tutorial*.

CHAPTER 11

Data Science

Data science is a rapidly developing field that combines tools from computation and statistics to create insights and draw conclusions from data. That description may sound a little vague, and indeed there is no universally accepted definition of the field; for example, some people think "data science" is just a fancy term for "statistics", while others hold that statistics is the *least* important part of data science.

Luckily, there *is* broad agreement that Python is an excellent tool for data science, whatever it is exactly.[1] There is also a general consensus about which specific Python tools are most useful for the subject. The purpose of this chapter is to introduce some of those tools and use them to investigate some aspects of data science for which Python is especially well-suited.

These subjects include Jupyter notebooks for interactive calculations (Section 11.1), NumPy for numerical computations (Section 11.2), Matplotlib for data visualization (Section 11.3), pandas for data analysis (Section 11.4, Section 11.5, and Section 11.6), and scikit-learn for machine learning (Section 11.7).[2] Almost all other Python data-science tools (such as PySpark, Databricks, and others) also build on the libraries in this chapter.

Data science is far too big to cover in so small a space, but this chapter will give you a great foundation for learning more about the subject. Section 11.8 includes

---

1. Python's main open-source rival in this space is R, which was originally developed by statisticians. Python has the advantage of being a general-purpose programming language as well, which is part of why many data scientists have come to prefer it. Nevertheless, R is undeniably powerful, and there are many resources for learning data science that actually cover both Python and R at the same time. I recommend using one of those resources if for any reason it is important for you to know R.

2. All of these resources are open-source software.

some suggestions and further resources if you decide you'd like to pursue data science further.

11.1 Data Science Setup

The first step is setting up our environment for doing data-science investigations. Here is an overview of some of the most important tools for Python data science:

- IPython and Jupyter: Packages that provide the computational environment in which many Python-using data scientists work.

- NumPy: A library that makes a variety of mathematical and statistical operations easier; it is also the basis for many features of the pandas library.

- Matplotlib: A visualization library that makes it quick and easy to generate graphs and charts from our data.

- pandas: A Python library created specifically to facilitate working with data. This is the bread and butter of a lot of Python data-science work.

- scikit-learn: Probably the most popular library for machine learning in Python.

Because the use of IPython and Jupyter is technically optional, we'll start by installing the packages that will be needed no matter what your environment looks like. For convenience, I suggest creating a new directory and setting up a fresh virtual environment, as shown in Listing 11.1.

Listing 11.1: Setting up a data-science environment.

```
$ cd ~/repos
$ mkdir python_data_science
$ cd python_data_science/
$ python3 -m venv venv
$ source venv/bin/activate
(venv) $
```

I also recommend putting your project under version control with Git and setting up a remote repository at GitHub or another repository host of your choice. If you go this route, you can use the **.gitignore** file shown in Listing 11.2, which includes an extra line for ignoring unneeded Jupyter changes.

Listing 11.2: A `.gitignore` file for Python data science.
.gitignore

```
venv/

*.pyc
__pycache__/

instance/

.pytest_cache/
.coverage
htmlcov/

dist/
build/
*.egg-info/

.ipynb_checkpoints

.DS_Store
```

At this point, we're ready to install the necessary packages. As with the rest of this tutorial, we'll install exact versions for maximum future compatibility, but feel free to try the latest versions by leaving off the **==\<version number>** part. Just be prepared for unpredictable results. The full set of necessary packages is shown in Listing 11.3.

Listing 11.3: Installing packages for Python data science.

```
(venv) $ pip install numpy==1.23.3
(venv) $ pip install matplotlib==3.6.1
(venv) $ pip install pandas==1.5.0
(venv) $ pip install scikit-learn==1.1.2
```

We saw as early as Section 1.3 that many Python developers prefer the Conda system for managing packages. If anything, this is even more the case among Python data scientists. But as also noted in Section 1.3, Conda makes more extensive changes to the environment and is (at least in my experience) harder to reverse or tear down if you need to reset the system. As you gain experience with using Python on your system, I suggest taking another look at Conda to see if it meets your needs.

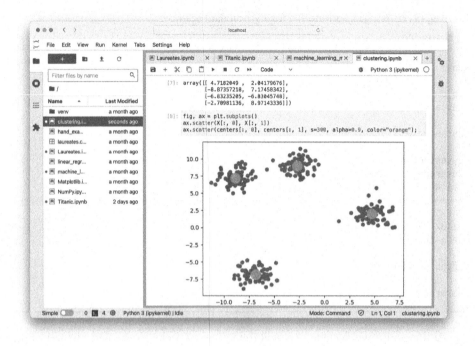

Figure 11.1: A working Jupyter notebook.

As noted in the introduction, I also highly recommend using Jupyter (pronounced "Jupiter", like the planet or Roman god),[3] which provides a *notebook interface* to a version of Python, typically a powerful variant known as *IPython* (Interactive Python). Notebooks consist of *cells* where you can type and execute code, seeing the results interactively (much like the REPL), which is especially convenient for visualizing plots. (Also like the REPL, Jupyter notebooks are often a good first step toward self-contained Python programs like the ones discussed in previous chapters.) After a while, your notebook might look something like Figure 11.1.

I suggest installing and using Jupyter via *JupyterLab*, which conveniently wraps multiple Jupyter notebooks and is also the interface recommended by the Jupyter project itself:

---

3. The name is a reference to the three main languages supported by the notebook interface: Julia, Python, and R.

```
(venv) $ pip install jupyterlab==3.4.8
```

JupyterLab can be started using the following command:[4]

```
(venv) $ jupyter-lab
```

The result of this is a Jupyter server running on the local system, typically at the address http://localhost:8889/lab (though details may differ). On my system, the **jupyter-lab** command automatically spawns a new browser window, with a directory tree and an interface for creating a new notebook (Figure 11.2).

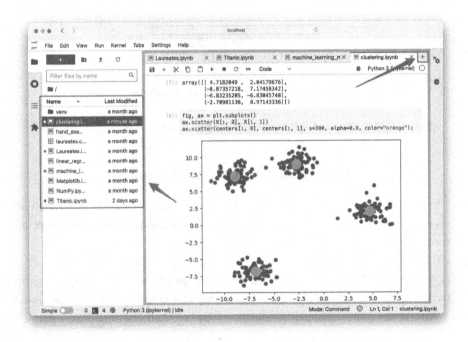

Figure 11.2: A directory tree and interface for creating a new notebook.

---

4. It is unclear why the library and package are JupyterLab and **jupyterlab** (no hyphen) while the command-line command is **jupyter-lab** (with a hyphen), but that's the way it is.

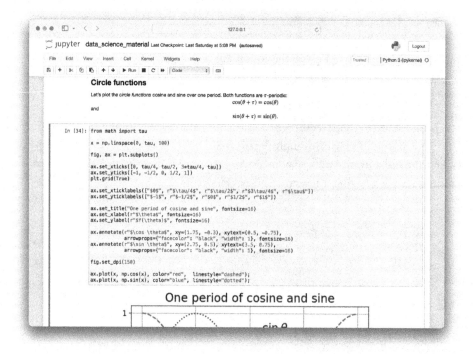

Figure 11.3: The "classic" Jupyter interface.

You may also sometimes encounter the "classic" Jupyter interface, which comes from installing the **jupyter** package by itself and running **jupyter notebook** at the command line (Figure 11.3).

Each Jupyter notebook runs inside an ordinary web browser and consists of cells of Python code that can be executed using the graphical user interface or (more conveniently) the keyboard shortcut Shift-Return.[5] On my system, Jupyter launches in whatever directory I happen to run the **jupyter-lab** command in, though this behavior may be system-dependent.

By the way, Jupyter doesn't autoreload modules by default, which can be annoying. The following code can be used to change this default behavior:

```
%load_ext autoreload
%autoreload 2
```

---

5. Users of *Mathematica*, from which Jupyter draws heavy inspiration, will find this notebook interface especially familiar.

Throughout the rest of this chapter, we'll mainly be using examples from the Python prompt because I don't want to assume you've installed Jupyter.[6] That being said, I strongly recommend installing and learning Jupyter at some point since it is a standard tool in Python data analysis and scientific computing. In particular, Jupyter can be used on the cloud IDE recommended in *Learn Enough Dev Environment to Be Dangerous* (https://www.learnenough.com/dev-environment) by following the steps in Box 11.1. Another option is CoCalc, a commercial service that supports Jupyter notebooks by default.

Box 11.1: Running Jupyter on the cloud IDE

Perhaps surprisingly, it's possible to get Jupyter notebooks to work on the cloud IDE recommended in *Learn Enough Dev Environment to Be Dangerous.* (At least, it was surprising to me.) The first step is to generate a configuration file as follows (be sure to run this and all commands in the `jupyter_data_science` directory created in Listing 11.1 and inside a virtual environment):

```
$ jupyter notebook --generate-config
```

This command generates a file in the `.jupyter` hidden directory under the home directory:

```
~/.jupyter/jupyter_notebook_config.py
```

Using a text editor such as `nano`, `vim`, or `c9` (the last one can be installed via `npm install --location=global c9`), include the following lines at the bottom of `jupyter_notebook_config.py`:

```
c.NotebookApp.allow_origin = "*"
c.NotebookApp.ip = "0.0.0.0"
c.NotebookApp.allow_remote_access = True
```

At this point, you should be ready to run

```
$ jupyter-lab --port $PORT --ip $IP --no-browser
```

at the command line.

---

6. Because the notebook interface is so instructive when used interactively, the videos that accompany this book *do* make use of Jupyter (or, more specifically, JupyterLab).

To view the notebook, use the menu item Preview > Preview Running Application. You might have to click the Pop Out Into New Window icon in the upper right of the window pane. You will probably be prompted for a token, which can be found in the output of the `jupyter-lab` command and should look something like this:

```
http://127.0.0.1:8080/?token=c33a7633b81ad52fc81
```

Copy and paste the unique token for your application (i.e., everything after `token=`) to get access to the page. The result should be a Jupyter notebook running on the cloud IDE (Figure 11.4).

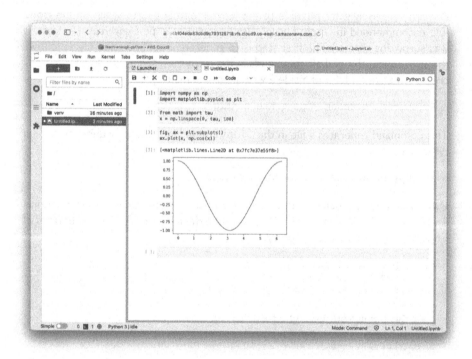

Figure 11.4: A Jupyter notebook on the cloud IDE.

11.2 Numerical Computations with NumPy

Although Python has a reputation for being a "slow language", in fact Python is written in C, one of the fastest languages in existence. The occasional slowness of Python is mostly a consequence of the things that also make it dynamic, which often involves layers of abstraction above the underlying C code. The NumPy library makes the underlying speed directly available to numerical computations by rewriting the most time-intensive parts directly in C.

NumPy (pronounced "NUM-pie", for "Numerical Python") was originally part of the large and powerful SciPy ("SIE-pie") library for scientific computing in Python but was factored out as a separate library because of its broad applicability. Indeed, data science is a great example: The core Python data-science library, pandas (Section 11.4), doesn't need SciPy but relies heavily on NumPy for numerical computations. As a result, although a complete mastery of NumPy isn't necessary for data science, it's important to at least know the basics.

Once NumPy has been installed (Listing 11.3), it can be included in a program, in the REPL, or in a Jupyter notebook as usual using **import**. The near-universal convention in data science and closely related communities is to import **numpy** as **np** for convenience:

```
>>> import numpy as np
```

(Most of the examples in this chapter include the REPL prompt **>>>**, but if you use Jupyter notebooks no prompt will be present, as seen in, e.g., Figure 11.1.)

11.2.1 Arrays

The combination SciPy + NumPy + Matplotlib (Section 11.3) represents an open-source alternative to the proprietary MATLAB system. Like MATLAB, NumPy is array-based, with the core data structure being an *ndarray* (short for "n-dimensional array"):

```
>>> np.array([1, 2, 3])
array([1, 2, 3])
```

NumPy ndarrays share many properties with regular Python lists (Chapter 3):

```
>>> a = np.array([1, 3, 2])
>>> len(a)
>>> a.sort()
>>> a
array([1, 2, 3])
```

In analogy with the list **range()** function (first seen in Listing 2.24), we can create array ranges using **arange()**:

```
>>> r = range(17)
>>> r
range(0, 17)
>>> list(r)
[0, 1, 2, 3, 4, 5, 6, 7, 8, 9, 10, 11, 12, 13, 14, 15, 16]
>>> a = np.arange(17)
>>> a
array([ 0,  1,  2,  3,  4,  5,  6,  7,  8,  9, 10, 11, 12, 13, 14, 15, 16])
```

These similarities raise the question of why we can't just use lists when doing data science with Python. The answer is that computations with arrays are much faster than the corresponding operations with lists. Because NumPy itself is array-based, such computations can also typically be expressed much more compactly, without the need for loops or even comprehensions.

In particular, NumPy arrays support *vectorized operations*, whereby we can (say) multiply every element in an array by a particular number all at once. For example, to create a list multiplying each element in a range by **3**, we could use a list comprehension (Section 6.1) as follows:

```
>>> [3 * i for i in r]
[0, 3, 6, 9, 12, 15, 18, 21, 24, 27, 30, 33, 36, 39, 42, 45, 48]
```

With a NumPy ndarray, we can just multiply by **3** directly:

```
>>> 3 * a
array([ 0,  3,  6,  9, 12, 15, 18, 21, 24, 27, 30, 33, 36, 39, 42, 45, 48])
```

Here NumPy automatically threads the multiplication over the array elements (essentially equivalent to "scalar multiplication" on vectors). We can also apply an operation like squaring in a similar manner:

```
>>> a**2
array([  0,   1,   4,   9,  16,  25,  36,  49,  64,  81, 100, 121, 144, 169,
       196, 225, 256])
```

Here each element of **a** has been squared without the need for a loop or comprehension.

As indicated above, this is not just for convenience, either; it's a lot faster as well. We can see this by using the **timeit** library to call the same code repeatedly and then time the result:

```
>>> import timeit
>>> t1 = timeit.timeit("[i**2 for i in range(50)]")
>>> t2 = timeit.timeit("import numpy as np; np.arange(50)**2")
>>> t1, t2, t1/t2
(9.171871625003405, 0.5006397919496521, 18.320300887960165)
```

Although exact results will vary, the result shown here indicates nearly a factor of 20 increase in speed for the vectorized version, which NumPy accomplishes by pushing the main loops into optimized C code. (*Note*: In a Jupyter notebook, we can use IPython to perform an even better comparison using the special **%%timeit** operation (Figure 11.5).)

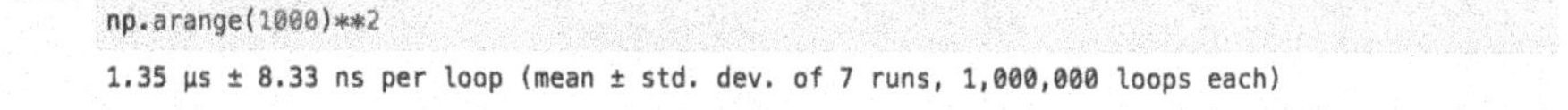

NumPy

```
[32]: import numpy as np

[31]: %%timeit
      [i**2 for i in range(1000)]

      176 µs ± 466 ns per loop (mean ± std. dev. of 7 runs, 10,000 loops each)

[33]: %%timeit
      np.arange(1000)**2

      1.35 µs ± 8.33 ns per loop (mean ± std. dev. of 7 runs, 1,000,000 loops each)
```

Figure 11.5: Using NumPy and **timeit** in a Jupyter notebook.

11.2.2 Multidimensional Arrays

NumPy also includes support for multidimensional arrays:

```
>>> a = np.array([[1, 2, 3], [4, 5, 6]])
>>> a
array([[1, 2, 3],
       [4, 5, 6]])
```

NumPy arrays have an attribute called **shape** that returns the number of rows and columns:

```
>>> a.shape
(2, 3)
```

Here **(2, 3)** corresponds to the 2 rows (**[1, 2, 3]** and **[4, 5, 6]**) and the 3 columns (**[1, 4]**, **[2, 5]**, and **[3, 6]**). You can think of this as a 2×3 matrix.

In analogy with list slicing (Section 3.3), NumPy supports array slicing for ndarrays of all dimensions. The colon notation introduced in Section 3.3 is especially useful for selecting full rows or columns by using a single colon by itself:

```
>>> a[0, :]        # first row
array([1, 2, 3])
>>> a[:, 0]        # first column
array([1, 4])
```

By combining colons with number ranges, we can slice out a subarray:

```
>>> A = a[0:2, 0:2]
>>> A
array([[1, 2],
       [4, 5]])
```

As with list slicing, you can omit the beginning or end of the range and get the same result:

```
>>> A = a[:2, :2]
>>> A
array([[1, 2],
       [4, 5]])
```

NumPy includes lots of support for common numerical operations such as linear algebra, in this case using super-optimized and battle-tested packages like BLAS and LAPACK. These routines are mostly written in C and Fortran, but we don't have to know those languages because they are wrapped by Python via the **linalg** library.[7]

Let's take a look at a quick example of NumPy's linear algebra support. The subarray **A** that we just defined is a square matrix (the same number of rows and columns), which means that we can try calculating its matrix inverse. The inverse of an invertible matrix, written as A^{-1} ("A inverse"), satisfies the relations $AA^{-1} = A^{-1}A = I$, where I is the $n \times n$ identity matrix (1s on the diagonal, 0s everywhere else). Matrix inversion is available in NumPy via **linalg.inv()**:

```
>>> Ainv = np.linalg.inv(A)          # inverse of a matrix
>>> Ainv
array([[-1.66666667,  0.66666667],
       [ 1.33333333, -0.33333333]])
```

We can try adding and multiplying the matrices using **+** and *****, respectively:

```
>>> A + Ainv
array([[-0.66666667,  2.66666667],
       [ 5.33333333,  4.66666667]])
>>> A * Ainv
array([[-1.66666667,  1.33333333],
       [ 5.33333333, -1.66666667]])
```

Although the array sum **A + Ainv** has no particular mathematical significance in this context, we see that the elements have been added in accordance with NumPy vectorized operations (Section 11.2.1). Similarly, the array product **A * Ainv** has also been calculated term by term. This is a possible source of confusion because in some systems (notably MATLAB) the ***** operator performs *matrix multiplication* in this context, yielding the expected result $AA^{-1} = I$. In NumPy, the most convenient way to perform matrix multiplication is with the **@** operator:[8]

```
>>> A @ Ainv
array([[1., 0.],
       [0., 1.]])
```

---

7. Although I did end up doing a lot of C programming in graduate school anyway, I was able to achieve my childhood dream of never having to learn Fortran.

8. The **matmul()** function works as well; with **numpy** imported as **np**, this would appear as **np.matmul(A, Ainv)** and is equivalent to **A @ Ainv**.

The result is the 2×2 identity matrix as expected. (Note that some elements may be close to but not exactly zero due to numerical roundoff error; see Section 11.2.3 for more information.)

One especially useful method for manipulating matrix objects is **reshape()**, which allows us to change (say) a one-dimensional array into a two-dimensional array. The argument to **reshape()** is a tuple (Section 3.6) with the target dimensions:

```
>>> a = np.arange(16)
>>> a.reshape((2, 8))
>>> a
array([[ 0,  1,  2,  3,  4,  5,  6,  7],
       [ 8,  9, 10, 11, 12, 13, 14, 15]])
>>> b = a.reshape((4, 4))
>>> b
array([[ 0,  1,  2,  3],
       [ 4,  5,  6,  7],
       [ 8,  9, 10, 11],
       [12, 13, 14, 15]])
```

Using **reshape()** is often much more convenient than building up the corresponding arrays by hand. Note that **reshape()** doesn't mutate the array, so we need to make an assignment if we want a name for the reshaped version.

The **reshape()** function supports using **-1** as one of the arguments, which has an effect described in the documentation:

> One shape dimension can be -1. In this case, the value is inferred from the length of the array and remaining dimensions.

For example, we can use the argument **(-1, 2)** with an array of 16 elements to get an 8×2 matrix, where the **8** comes from dividing **16** by **2**:

```
>>> a.reshape((-1, 2))
array([[ 0,  1],
       [ 2,  3],
       [ 4,  5],
       [ 6,  7],
       [ 8,  9],
       [10, 11],
       [12, 13],
       [14, 15]])
```

In effect, the **-1** is a placeholder that says "use the dimensionality needed to make the total number of elements correct."

Among other things, this **-1** technique can be used to convert a multidimensional array to an array of arrays of *one* element, which can be accomplished using the argument **(-1, 1)** (Listing 11.4). This format is common as an input to machine-learning algorithms (Section 11.7).

Listing 11.4: Creating an array of one-dimensional arrays.

```
>>> a.reshape((-1, 1))
array([[ 0],
       [ 1],
       [ 2],
       [ 3],
       [ 4],
       [ 5],
       [ 6],
       [ 7],
       [ 8],
       [ 9],
       [10],
       [11],
       [12],
       [13],
       [14],
       [15]])
```

11.2.3 Constants, Functions, and Linear Spacing

Like the **math** library discussed in Section 4.1, NumPy comes equipped with mathematical constants, such as Euler's number e:

```
>>> import math
>>> math.e
2.718281828459045
>>> np.e
2.718281828459045
>>> math.e == np.e
True
```

NumPy also defines **pi** but unfortunately doesn't have **tau** as of this writing:

```
>>> np.pi
3.141592653589793
>>> np.tau
Traceback (most recent call last):
    raise AttributeError("module {!r} has no attribute "
AttributeError: module 'numpy' has no attribute 'tau'
```

We can still use the one in **math**, though:

```
>>> math.tau
6.283185307179586
>>> math.tau == 2 * np.pi
True
```

Also like **math**, NumPy has operations like trigonometric functions and logarithms (see below for an explanation of the strange result of **np.sin(math.tau)**):

```
>>> np.cos(math.tau)
1.0
>>> np.sin(math.tau)
-2.4492935982947064e-16
>>> np.log(np.e)
1.0
>>> np.log10(np.e)
0.4342944819032518
```

Note that, again as with **math**, and like most programming languages, NumPy uses **log()** to denote the natural logarithm and **log10()** for base-ten logs.

At this point, you may wonder what the point is of including definitions in NumPy that duplicate those in **math**. For constants like e and π it's mainly for completeness, but with the functions there's actually a meaningful difference: Unlike **math** functions, NumPy's functions can be threaded over arrays using the same vectorized operations we first saw in Section 11.2.1.

Consider, for example, one period of $\cos x$, with angles ranging from 0 to τ (Listing 11.5).[9]

---

9. I prefer to use cosine instead of sine as the canonical example because it's more intuitive from the perspective of simple harmonic motion, which is one of the most important examples of sinusoidal functions. Because the cosine function starts at 1, it corresponds naturally to an oscillator moved some distance from equilibrium and released from rest. In contrast, using sine involves giving a kick or flick to such an oscillator so that it starts with a nonzero velocity at equilibrium, which is a much less common way of initiating such motion.

Listing 11.5: Angles corresponding to simple fractions of a period of $\cos x$.

```
>>> np.arange(5)
array([0, 1, 2, 3, 4])
>>> angles = math.tau * np.arange(5) / 4
>>> angles
array([0.        , 1.57079633, 3.14159265, 4.71238898, 6.28318531])
```

Note that the values of the **angles** array in Listing 11.5 are simply the numerical equivalents of 0, $\tau/4$, $\tau/2$, $3\tau/4$, and τ. Applying **cos()** to these angles doesn't work for the **math** version of cosine but does for the NumPy version (Listing 11.6).

Listing 11.6: Applying **cos()** to an array of angles.

```
>>> math.cos(angles)
Traceback (most recent call last):
  File "<stdin>", line 1, in <module>
TypeError: only size-1 arrays can be converted to Python scalars
>>> a = np.cos(angles)
>>> a
array([ 1.0000000e+00,  6.1232340e-17, -1.0000000e+00, -1.8369702e-16,
        1.0000000e+00])
```

Note that, due to floating-point roundoff errors, the zeros of $\cos x$ in Listing 11.6 appear as tiny numbers rather than as **0** (though such behavior is often system-dependent, so your exact results may differ). We can get rid of these using NumPy's **isclose()** function, which returns **True** if a number is "close" to the given number (essentially, within the margin of error of the system's floating-point arithmetic):

```
>>> np.isclose(0.01, 0)
False
>>> np.isclose(10**(-16), 0)
True
>>> np.isclose(a, 0)
array([False,  True, False,  True, False])
```

We can actually pass this array of boolean values to the original array itself and set the elements corresponding to **True** exactly to **0** (Listing 11.7).

Listing 11.7: Using `isclose()` to zero out values close to **0**.

```
>>> a[np.isclose(a, 0)]
array([ 6.1232340e-17, -1.8369702e-16])
>>> a[np.isclose(a, 0)] = 0
>>> a
array([ 1.,   0.,  -1.,   0.,   1.])
```

In Listing 11.5, we divided the **arange(5)** by 4 when generating the angles, but for technical reasons (related to numerical roundoff error) the preferred way to make such sequences is with **linspace()** ("linearly space(d)"). The most common arguments to the **linspace()** function are the beginning, end, and total number of points desired. For example, we can use **linspace()** to make an array of the four quarters of a period (with 5 total points since we're including **0**):

```
>>> angles = np.linspace(0, math.tau, 5)
>>> angles
array([0.        , 1.57079633, 3.14159265, 4.71238898, 6.28318531])
>>> a = np.cos(angles)
>>> a[np.isclose(a, 0)] = 0
>>> a
array([ 1.,   0.,  -1.,   0.,   1.])
```

The **linspace()** function is often used to create an array with much finer spacing using a larger number of points. For instance, we can get 100 points of cos x as follows:

```
>>> angles = np.linspace(0, math.tau, 100)
>>> angles
array([0.        , 0.06346652, 0.12693304, 0.19039955, 0.25386607,
       0.31733259, 0.38079911, 0.44426563, 0.50773215, 0.57119866,
       0.63466518, 0.6981317 , 0.76159822, 0.82506474, 0.88853126,
       0.95199777, 1.01546429, 1.07893081, 1.14239733, 1.20586385,
       1.26933037, 1.33279688, 1.3962634 , 1.45972992, 1.52319644,
       1.58666296, 1.65012947, 1.71359599, 1.77706251, 1.84052903,
       1.90399555, 1.96746207, 2.03092858, 2.0943951 , 2.15786162,
       2.22132814, 2.28479466, 2.34826118, 2.41172769, 2.47519421,
       2.53866073, 2.60212725, 2.66559377, 2.72906028, 2.7925268 ,
       2.85599332, 2.91945984, 2.98292636, 3.04639288, 3.10985939,
       3.17332591, 3.23679243, 3.30025895, 3.36372547, 3.42719199,
       3.4906585 , 3.55412502, 3.61759154, 3.68105806, 3.74452458,
       3.8079911 , 3.87145761, 3.93492413, 3.99839065, 4.06185717,
       4.12532369, 4.1887902 , 4.25225672, 4.31572324, 4.37918976,
       4.44265628, 4.5061228 , 4.56958931, 4.63305583, 4.69652235,
       4.75998887, 4.82345539, 4.88692191, 4.95038842, 5.01385494,
```

```
        5.07732146, 5.14078798, 5.2042545 , 5.26772102, 5.33118753,
        5.39465405, 5.45812057, 5.52158709, 5.58505361, 5.64852012,
        5.71198664, 5.77545316, 5.83891968, 5.9023862 , 5.96585272,
        6.02931923, 6.09278575, 6.15625227, 6.21971879, 6.28318531])
>>> np.cos(angles)
array([ 1.        ,  0.99798668,  0.99195481,  0.9819287 ,  0.9679487 ,
        0.95007112,  0.92836793,  0.90292654,  0.87384938,  0.84125353,
        0.80527026,  0.76604444,  0.72373404,  0.67850941,  0.63055267,
        0.58005691,  0.52722547,  0.47227107,  0.41541501,  0.35688622,
        0.29692038,  0.23575894,  0.17364818,  0.1108382 ,  0.04758192,
       -0.01586596, -0.07924996, -0.14231484, -0.20480667, -0.26647381,
       -0.32706796, -0.38634513, -0.44406661, -0.5       , -0.55392006,
       -0.60560969, -0.65486073, -0.70147489, -0.74526445, -0.78605309,
       -0.82367658, -0.85798341, -0.88883545, -0.91610846, -0.93969262,
       -0.95949297, -0.97542979, -0.98743889, -0.99547192, -0.99949654,
       -0.99949654, -0.99547192, -0.98743889, -0.97542979, -0.95949297,
       -0.93969262, -0.91610846, -0.88883545, -0.85798341, -0.82367658,
       -0.78605309, -0.74526445, -0.70147489, -0.65486073, -0.60560969,
       -0.55392006, -0.5       , -0.44406661, -0.38634513, -0.32706796,
       -0.26647381, -0.20480667, -0.14231484, -0.07924996, -0.01586596,
        0.04758192,  0.1108382 ,  0.17364818,  0.23575894,  0.29692038,
        0.35688622,  0.41541501,  0.47227107,  0.52722547,  0.58005691,
        0.63055267,  0.67850941,  0.72373404,  0.76604444,  0.80527026,
        0.84125353,  0.87384938,  0.90292654,  0.92836793,  0.95007112,
        0.9679487 ,  0.9819287 ,  0.99195481,  0.99798668,  1.        ])
```

It's rather hard to visualize this many raw values, but they are the perfect input to a plotting library like Matplotlib, which is the subject of Section 11.3.

11.2.4   Exercises

1. What happens if the dimensions in **reshape()** don't match the array size (e.g., **np.arange(16).reshape((4, 17))**)?

2. Confirm that **A = np.random.rand(5, 5)** lets you define a 5×5 random matrix.

3. Find the inverse **Ainv** of the 5×5 matrix in the previous exercise. (Calculating the inverse of a 2×2 matrix as in Section 11.2.2 is fairly simple by hand, but the task rapidly gets harder as the matrix size increases, in which case a computational system like NumPy is indispensable.)

4. What is the matrix product **I = A @ Ainv** of the matrices in the previous two exercises? Use the same **isclose()** trick from Listing 11.7 to zero out the elements of **I** close to zero and confirm that the resulting matrix is indeed the 5×5 identity matrix.

11.3 Data Visualization with Matplotlib

Matplotlib is a powerful visualization tool for Python that can do an absurdly large number of awesome things.[10] In this section, we'll start with a simple two-dimensional plot based on the work we did in Section 11.2 and incrementally include additional features, eventually reaching the figure shown in Figure 11.6. We'll then cover a couple of other important cases (scatter plots and histograms), which are important for data analysis with pandas (Section 11.4). The exact mechanics of displaying Matplotlib plots depends on the particular setup; refer to Box 11.2 to get the display of Matplotlib plots working on your system.

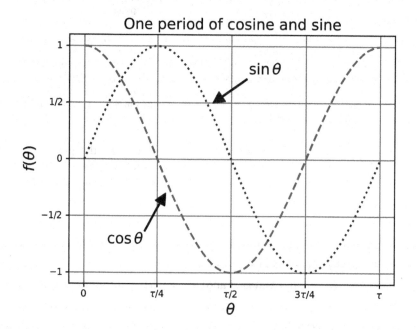

Figure 11.6: A fancy plot showing off features of Matplotlib.

---

10. It's worth noting that many Python data scientists also use seaborn, which is a data-visualization library built on Matplotlib. Although learning seaborn is certainly not necessary to be *dangerous*, it would make a natural follow-on to this section. The official seaborn tutorial would be a good place to start.

Box 11.2: **Matplotlib mechanics**

The exact mechanics of getting Matplotlib plots to display varies widely depending on the exact details of your setup. The most explicit way to show plots, which works on most systems from the REPL, is to use the show() method:

```
>>> import numpy as np
>>> import matplotlib.pyplot as plt
>>> x = np.linspace(-2, 2, 100)
>>> fig, ax = plt.subplots(1, 1)
>>> ax.plot(x, x*x)
>>> plt.show()
```

On many systems, this will spawn a window like Figure 11.7 with the result of the plot.

In Jupyter notebooks, the environment can be configured to show Matplotlib plots automatically ("inline", i.e., right in the notebook) by executing this command in a notebook cell:

```
%matplotlib inline
```

As far as I can tell, on some systems (including mine) this setting is on by default, with plots appearing automatically when the corresponding Jupyter cells are evaluated (Figure 11.8).

In an environment such as the cloud IDE, it's possible to switch to a non-graphical back-end, write out to a file, and then view the file in the browser. See this Stack Overflow thread (https://bit.ly/cloud-plot) if you'd like to go this route, but the recommended solution is to set up Jupyter on the cloud IDE as described in Box 11.1. In that case, you can set up inline plot display as described above (if in fact it's not available automatically).

11.3.1   Plotting

We'll start by reviewing the final example from Section 11.2, which defined a linearly spaced array with 100 points from 0 to τ:

```
(venv) $ python3
>>> import numpy as np
>>> import matplotlib.pyplot as plt
>>> from math import tau
>>> x = np.linspace(0, tau, 100)
```

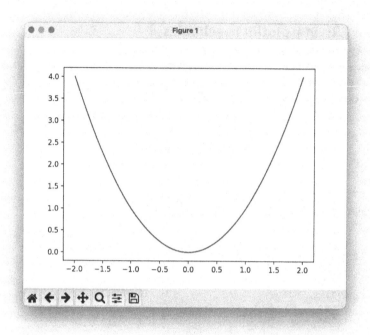

Figure 11.7: A window spawned by a call to `show()`.

Matplotlib has two key objects, **Figure** and **Axes**. Roughly speaking, **Figure** is a container for the elements that make up the image and **Axes** is the data representing the elements. Don't worry too much about exactly what this means, though; in practice, using Matplotlib often reduces to assigning figure and axes objects (conventionally called **fig** and **ax**) to the result of calling the **subplots()** function:

```
>>> fig, ax = plt.subplots()
```

This somewhat obscure syntax comes right from the Matplotlib documentation.[11]

---

11. In this chapter, we use the so-called "object-oriented" interface to Matplotlib, which is generally preferred by the Matplotlib project itself. There is a second interface, though, which is designed to behave like the plotting features in MATLAB. See the article "Pyplot vs Object Oriented Interface" (https://matplotlib.org/matplotblog/posts/pyplot-vs-object-oriented-interface/) for more information.

```
[4]: x = np.linspace(-1, 6, 100)

     plt.plot(x, wien(x));
     plt.plot(x, 0*x);
```

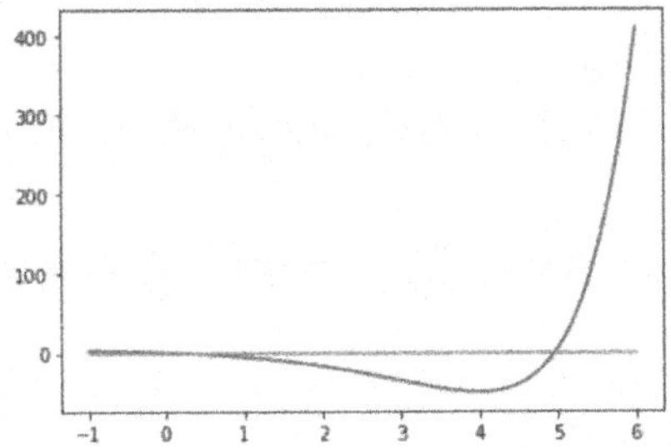

We'll find the root's numerical value by solving $\text{Wien}(x) = (x - 5)e^x + 5 = 0$ using several different methods:

- `find_root` from Sage
- `fsolve` from `scipy.optimize` to find all the roots given initial guesses
- `brentq` from `scipy.optimize` to find the single root closest to 5

```
[5]: var('x')
     find_root(wien(x) == 0, 1, 6)
```
```
[5]: 4.965114231744276
```

Figure 11.8: A plot appearing automatically in a Jupyter notebook.

To make a plot of the cosine function, we can then call the **ax** object's **plot()** method with x (horizontal) values equal to our 100 linearly spaced points and y (vertical) values given by calling **np.cos** on **x**:

```
>>> ax.plot(x, np.cos(x))
>>> plt.show()
```

As noted in Box 11.2, the step to view the plot will depend on your exact setup, so we'll use **plt.show()** as a shorthand for "whatever the corresponding command is on your system." (Note in particular that the **fig** object won't generally be needed unless you're saving the figure to disk; **ax** is where most of the action is.) The result in this case is the nice basic cosine plot shown in Figure 11.9.

For most of the remaining examples, I'll be leaving off the **>>>** prompt so that you can more easily copy and paste if you want. This is mainly because building up plots can be a bit cumbersome since you have to rerun all the commands every time. One

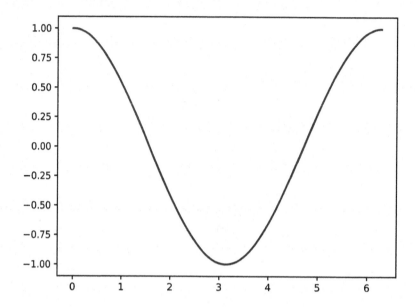

Figure 11.9: A nice basic plot of the cosine function.

big advantage of Jupyter notebooks is that you can avoid this by building up the plot incrementally in a single cell and then repeatedly execute the code using Shift-Return.

As a next step, let's include ticks for the x- and y-axes (using **set_xticks()** and **set_yticks()**) and add an overall grid (using **plt.grid()**):

```
fig, ax = plt.subplots()
ax.set_xticks([0, tau/4, tau/2, 3*tau/4, tau])
ax.set_yticks([-1, -1/2, 0, 1/2, 1])
plt.grid(True)
ax.plot(x, np.cos(x))
plt.show()
```

The resulting plot makes it easier to see the structure of cosine, with four congruent pieces corresponding to each of the four quarters of the full period (Figure 11.10).

The tick labels in Figure 11.10 are their default decimal values, but it would be more convenient to express them as fractions of the full period (i.e., τ) on the x-axis and as fractions of ±1 on the y-axis. One great thing about Matplotlib is that it supports the widely used LATEX syntax for mathematical typesetting, which typically

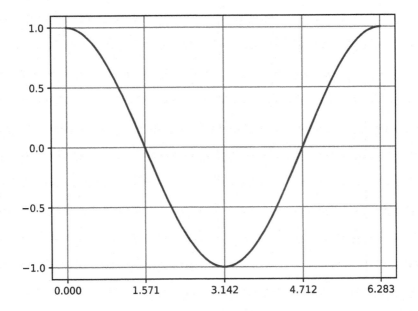

Figure 11.10: Adding ticks and a grid.

involves surrounding mathematical notation in dollar signs and indicating commands with backslashes.[12] For example, this paragraph contains the following LaTeX code:[13]

```
The tick labels in Figure~\ref{fig:cosine_ticks} are their default decimal
values, but it would be more convenient to express them as fractions of the
full period (i.e., $\tau$) on the $x$-axis and as fractions of $\pm 1$ on the
$y$-axis.
```

Because LaTeX commands generally contain pesky backslashes, which often have strange behavior when placed inside strings, we'll use raw strings (Section 2.2.2) so that we won't have to escape them out. The resulting tick labels, which use the **set_xticklabels()** and **set_yticklabels()** methods, appear as follows:

---

12. The pronunciation of LaTeX differs; my preferred pronunciation is *lay*-tech, with "tech" as in "technology". (I was gratified to discover that the text-to-speech program on macOS agrees.)

13. Using dollar signs (**$...$** for inline math, **$$...$$** for centered math) is properly associated with TeX, the system underlying LaTeX. Technically, the preferred LaTeX syntax is **\(...\)** for inline math and **\[...\]** for centered math. So far as I can tell, Jupyter notebooks support only the plain TeX syntax.

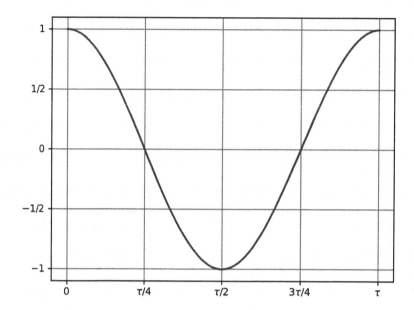

Figure 11.11: Adding nice LaTeX axis labels to the cosine plot.

```
fig, ax = plt.subplots()

ax.set_xticks([0, tau/4, tau/2, 3*tau/4, tau])
ax.set_yticks([-1, -1/2, 0, 1/2, 1])
plt.grid(True)

ax.set_xticklabels([r"$0$", r"$\tau/4$", r"$\tau/2$", r"$3\tau/4$", r"$\tau$"])
ax.set_yticklabels([r"$-1$", r"$-1/2$", r"$0$", r"$1/2$", r"$1$"])

ax.plot(x, np.cos(x))
plt.show()
```

The result appears in Figure 11.11.

Next, let's add sine as well, along with axis labels and a plot title:

```
fig, ax = plt.subplots()

ax.set_xticks([0, tau/4, tau/2, 3*tau/4, tau])
ax.set_yticks([-1, -1/2, 0, 1/2, 1])
plt.grid(True)
```

```
ax.set_xticklabels([r"$0$", r"$\tau/4$", r"$\tau/2$", r"$3\tau/4$", r"$\tau$"])
ax.set_yticklabels([r"$-1$", r"$-1/2$", r"$0$", r"$1/2$", r"$1$"])

ax.set_xlabel(r"$\theta$", fontsize=16)
ax.set_ylabel(r"$f(\theta)$", fontsize=16)
ax.set_title("One period of cosine and sine", fontsize=16)

ax.plot(x, np.cos(x))
ax.plot(x, np.sin(x))
plt.show()
```

Here we've used the Greek letter θ (theta) in the axis labels, which is a traditional letter for angles. The result appears in Figure 11.12.

Note from Figure 11.12 that Matplotlib automatically uses a new color for additional plots on the same **Axis** object to help us tell them apart. We can further distinguish cosine from sine by adding *annotations*, which can be accomplished with the **annotate()** method. See if you can figure out from context what the arguments **xy**, **xytext**, and **arrowprops** do:

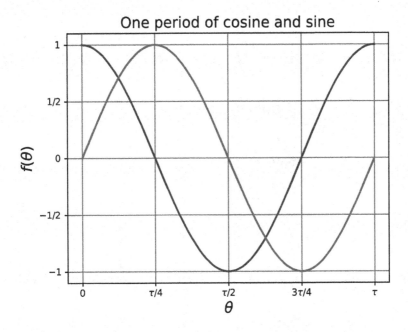

Figure 11.12: Adding sine and some additional labels.

```
fig, ax = plt.subplots()

ax.set_xticks([0, tau/4, tau/2, 3*tau/4, tau])
ax.set_yticks([-1, -1/2, 0, 1/2, 1])
plt.grid(True)

ax.set_xticklabels([r"$0$", r"$\tau/4$", r"$\tau/2$", r"$3\tau/4$", r"$\tau$"])
ax.set_yticklabels([r"$-1$", r"$-1/2$", r"$0$", r"$1/2$", r"$1$"])

ax.set_title("One period of cosine and sine", fontsize=16)
ax.set_xlabel(r"$\theta$", fontsize=16)
ax.set_ylabel(r"$f(\theta)$", fontsize=16)

ax.annotate(r"$\cos\theta$", xy=(1.75, -0.3), xytext=(0.5, -0.75),
            arrowprops="facecolor": "black", "width": 1, fontsize=16)
ax.annotate(r"$\sin\theta$", xy=(2.75, 0.5), xytext=(3.5, 0.75),
            arrowprops="facecolor": "black", "width": 1, fontsize=16)

ax.plot(x, np.cos(x))
ax.plot(x, np.sin(x))
plt.show()
```

We see from Figure 11.13 that **xy** indicates the point to be annotated, **xytext** indicates the location of the annotation text, and **arrowprops** determines the properties of the annotation arrow.

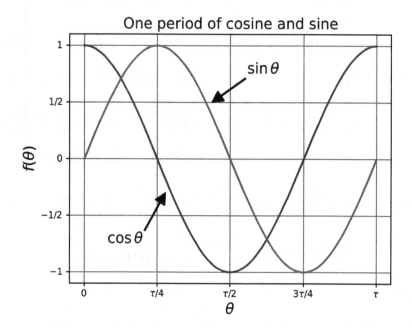

Figure 11.13: Adding annotations.

Finally, let's add custom colors and line styles, plus a higher resolution (in dots per inch, or **dpi**). For convenience, the resulting code, shown in Listing 11.8, includes all of the commands needed to create the full figure (Figure 11.14) from scratch.

Listing 11.8: The code for a fancy sinusoidal plot.

```
from math import tau

import numpy as np
import matplotlib.pyplot as plt


x = np.linspace(0, tau, 100)

fig, ax = plt.subplots()

ax.set_xticks([0, tau/4, tau/2, 3*tau/4, tau])
ax.set_yticks([-1, -1/2, 0, 1/2, 1])
plt.grid(True)

ax.set_xticklabels([r"$0$", r"$\tau/4$", r"$\tau/2$", r"$3\tau/4$", r"$\tau$"])
ax.set_yticklabels([r"$-1$", r"$-1/2$", r"$0$", r"$1/2$", r"$1$"])

ax.set_title("One period of cosine and sine", fontsize=16)
ax.set_xlabel(r"$\theta$", fontsize=16)
ax.set_ylabel(r"$f(\theta)$", fontsize=16)

ax.annotate(r"$\cos\theta$", xy=(1.75, -0.3), xytext=(0.5, -0.75),
            arrowprops={"facecolor": "black", "width": 1}, fontsize=16)
ax.annotate(r"$\sin\theta$", xy=(2.75, 0.5), xytext=(3.5, 0.75),
            arrowprops={"facecolor": "black", "width": 1}, fontsize=16)

fig.set_dpi(150)

ax.plot(x, np.cos(x), color="red", linestyle="dashed")
ax.plot(x, np.sin(x), color="blue", linestyle="dotted")
plt.show()
```

11.3.2 Scatter Plots

The plot in Section 11.3.1 introduced some of the key ideas of Matplotlib, and from this point there are a million possible ways to go. In this section and the next, we'll focus on two kinds of visualizations especially important in data science: *scatter*

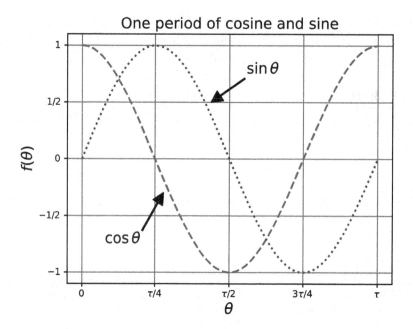

Figure 11.14: The final fancy plot of cosine and sine.

plots and *histograms*. Don't worry if everything doesn't sink in right away; we'll have ample opportunity to see further examples of both scatter plots and histograms in Section 11.5, Section 11.6, and Section 11.7.

A scatter plot just plots a bunch of discrete function values against the corresponding points, which is a great way to get an overall sense of what relationships the function values might satisfy. Let's take a look at a concrete example to see what this means.

We'll begin by generating some random points chosen from the *standard normal distribution*,[14] which is a normal distribution (or "bell curve") with an average value (mean) of 0 and a spread (standard deviation) of 1.[15] We can obtain these values using

---

14. There's nothing "abnormal" about other distributions; use of the word "normal" is in large part an idiosyncrasy of history.

15. The functional form of the standard normal distribution is given by the probability density $P(x) = \frac{1}{\sqrt{\tau}} e^{-\frac{1}{2}x^2}$, where $1/\sqrt{\tau} = 1/\sqrt{2\pi}$ is a normalization factor to ensure that the total probability

NumPy's **random** library, which includes a default random number generator called **default_rng()** (Listing 11.9).

Listing 11.9: Generating random values using the standard normal distribution.

```
>>> from numpy.random import default_rng
>>> rng = default_rng()
>>> n_pts = 50
>>> x = rng.standard_normal(n_pts)
>>> x
array([ 0.41256003,  0.67594205,  1.264653  ,  1.16351491, -0.41594407,
       -0.60157015,  0.84889823, -0.59984223,  0.24374326,  0.06055498,
       -0.48512829,  1.02253594, -1.10982933, -0.40609179,  0.55076245,
        0.13046238,  0.86712869,  0.06139358, -2.26538163,  1.45785923,
       -0.56220574, -1.38775239, -2.39643977, -0.77498392,  1.16794796,
       -0.6588802 ,  1.66343434,  1.57475219, -0.03374501, -0.62757059,
       -0.99378175,  0.69259747, -1.04555996,  0.62653116, -0.9042063 ,
       -0.32565268, -0.99762804, -0.4270288 ,  0.69940045, -0.46574267,
        1.82225132,  0.23925201, -1.0443741 , -0.54779683,  1.17466477,
       -2.54906663, -0.31495622,  0.25224765, -1.20869217, -1.02737145])
```

(You may see code like **random.standard_normal(50)** in tutorial examples online, but this variant is now deprecated, and the technique shown in Listing 11.9 is the current preferred method for generating random values with NumPy.)

With those *x* values in hand, let's create a set of *y* values by adding a constant multiple (the slope) of 5 times *x* plus another random factor:

```
>>> y = 5*x + rng.standard_normal(n_pts)
```

This broadly follows the pattern of the equation for a line, $y = mx + b$, only with random values for *x* and *b*. Because the functional form of *y* is essentially linear, a plot of *y* vs. *x* should look roughly like a line, which we can confirm with a scatter plot as follows:

$\int_{-\infty}^{\infty} P(x)\,dx$ is equal to 1. The density function for a general normal distribution with mean μ and standard deviation σ is $P(x; \mu, \sigma) = \frac{1}{\sigma\sqrt{\tau}}\,e^{-\frac{1}{2}\left(\frac{x-\mu}{\sigma}\right)^2}$; setting $\mu = 0$ and $\sigma = 1$ then yields the standard normal.

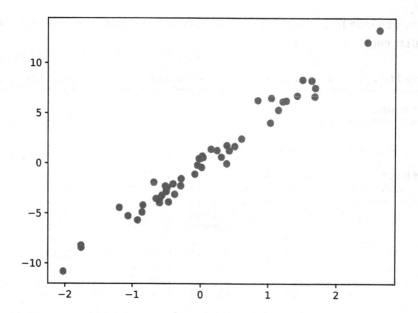

Figure 11.15: A Matplotlib scatter plot.

```
>>> fig, ax = plt.subplots()
>>> ax.scatter(x, y)
>>> plt.show()
```

As seen in Figure 11.15, our guess was correct. (Because we didn't fix a particular seed value for the random number generator, your exact results will differ.)

11.3.3 Histograms

Finally, let's apply some of the same ideas from Section 11.3.2 to visualize the distribution of 1000 random values drawn from the standard normal distribution:

```
>>> values = rng.standard_normal(1000)
```

A common way to get a sense of what these values look like is to make a fixed number of "bins" and plot how many values fit into each bin. The resulting plot is known as a *histogram*, and can be generated automatically using Matplotlib's **hist()** method:

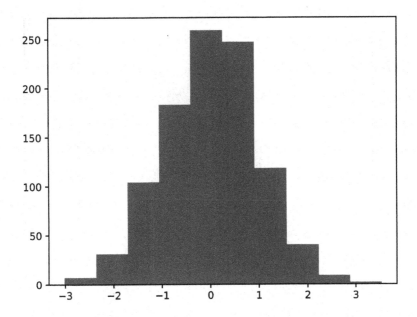

Figure 11.16: A histogram of normally distributed random values.

```
>>> fig, ax = plt.subplots()
>>> ax.hist(values)
>>> plt.show()
```

The result is a good approximation of a "bell curve", as seen in Figure 11.16.

The default number of bins is **10**, but we can investigate the result of different bin sizes by passing a **bins** argument to **hist()**, say **bins=20**:

```
>>> fig, ax = plt.subplots()
>>> ax.hist(values, bins=20)
>>> plt.show()
```

In this case, the result is a finer-grained version of the distribution (Figure 11.17).

Because Matplotlib is a general system for plotting and data visualization, there's practically no end to the things you can do with it. Although we've now covered the basics of what we'll need for the rest of this tutorial, I encourage you to explore further, and the Matplotlib documentation is a good place to start.

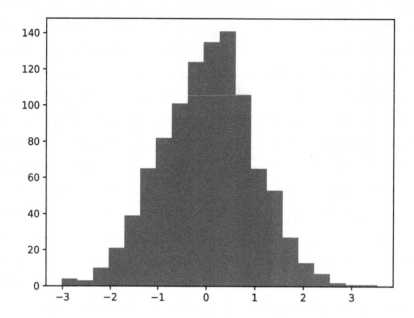

Figure 11.17: A rebinned version of Figure 11.16.

11.3.4 Exercises

1. Add a title and axis labels to the plot shown in Figure 11.15.

2. Add titles to the histograms in Section 11.3.3.

3. One common plotting task is including multiple subplots in the same figure. Show that the code in Listing 11.10 creates vertically stacked subplots, as shown in Figure 11.18. (Here the **suptitle()** method produces a "supertitle" that sits above both plots. See the Matplotlib documentation on subplots for other ways to create multiple subplots.)

4. Add a plot of the function $\cos(x - \tau/8)$ to the plot in Figure 11.14 with color **"orange"** and linestyle **"dashdot"**. *Extra credit*: Add an annotation as well. (The extra-credit step is *much* easier in an interactive Jupyter notebook, especially when finding the right coordinates for the annotation label and arrow.)

Listing 11.10: Stacking subplots.

```
>>> x = np.linspace(0, tau, 100)
>>> fig, (ax1, ax2) = plt.subplots(2)
>>> fig.suptitle(r"Vertically stacked plots of $\cos\theta$ and $\sin\theta$.")
>>> ax1.plot(x, np.cos(x))
>>> ax2.plot(x, np.sin(x))
```

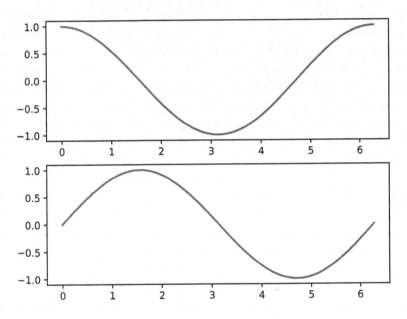

Figure 11.18: Vertically stacked plots.

11.4 Introduction to Data Analysis with pandas

One of the most heavily used tools in Python data science is *pandas*, a powerful library for analyzing data. In essence, pandas (from "**pan**el **da**ta") lets us perform many of the same tasks as a spreadsheet or Structured Query Language (SQL), only with the

Figure 11.19: Pandas are famous for their love of bamboo and their remarkable aptitude for data science.

power and flexibility of a full-strength, general-purpose programming language under the hood (Figure 11.19[16]).

The pandas interface can take some getting used to, and there's no substitute for seeing lots of examples. Thus, this chapter covers three cases of increasing sophistication, starting with simplified handcrafted examples (Section 11.4.1) and then showing more complex analysis techniques using two real-world datasets: Nobel Prizes (Section 11.5) and survival rates from *Titanic* (Section 11.6). (The second of these datasets will also serve as our main source of examples on machine learning in Section 11.7.)

In addition, there's *really* no substitute for asking and answering questions for yourself. In my experience, following tutorials such as this one can give you a great start, and often yields easy-looking results like Figure 11.20. But the minute you deviate even a millimeter from carefully chosen examples and try to answer something for yourself, you end up with things that look like Figure 11.21.

---

16. Image courtesy of San Hoyano/Shutterstock.

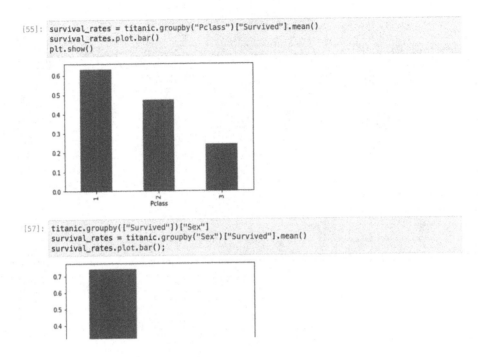

Figure 11.20: Making pandas look easy.

My best suggestion is to follow along at first to get your pandas bearings and then launch into the investigations of your own questions. But if you feel inspired at any point to venture out on your own, don't let me stop you—just know what to expect if you do.

11.4.1 Handcrafted Examples

The first steps to getting started are nearly always to import NumPy as **np** and pandas as **pd**, along with **matplotlib.pyplot** as **plt**:

```
>>> import numpy as np
>>> import pandas as pd
>>> import matplotlib.pyplot as plt
```

The core data structures of pandas are **Series** and **DataFrame**. The latter is more important, but it's built up from the former, so that's where we'll start.

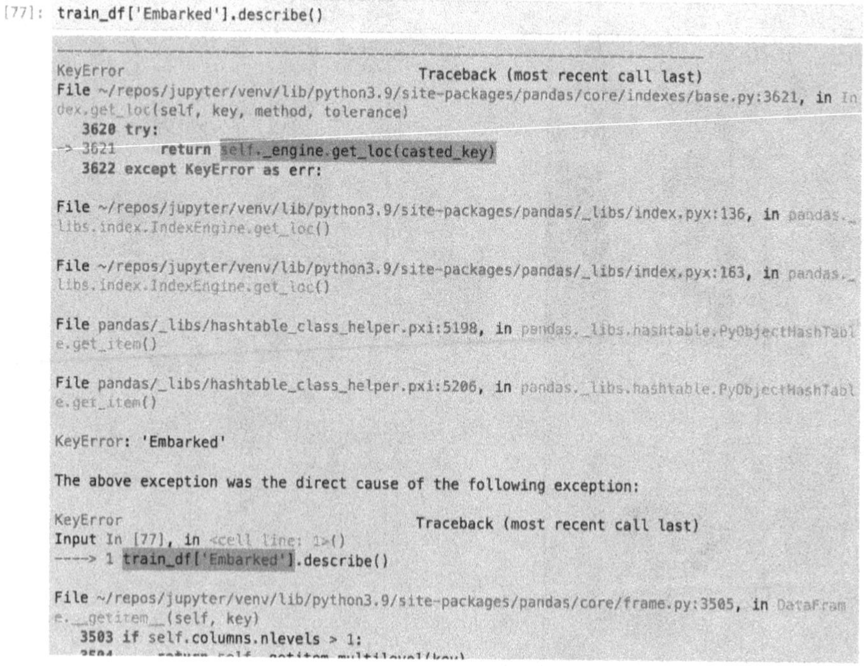

```
[77]:  train_df['Embarked'].describe()
```

```
KeyError                                    Traceback (most recent call last)
File ~/repos/jupyter/venv/lib/python3.9/site-packages/pandas/core/indexes/base.py:3621, in In
dex.get_loc(self, key, method, tolerance)
   3620 try:
-> 3621     return self._engine.get_loc(casted_key)
   3622 except KeyError as err:

File ~/repos/jupyter/venv/lib/python3.9/site-packages/pandas/_libs/index.pyx:136, in pandas._
libs.index.IndexEngine.get_loc()

File ~/repos/jupyter/venv/lib/python3.9/site-packages/pandas/_libs/index.pyx:163, in pandas._
libs.index.IndexEngine.get_loc()

File pandas/_libs/hashtable_class_helper.pxi:5198, in pandas._libs.hashtable.PyObjectHashTabl
e.get_item()

File pandas/_libs/hashtable_class_helper.pxi:5206, in pandas._libs.hashtable.PyObjectHashTabl
e.get_item()

KeyError: 'Embarked'

The above exception was the direct cause of the following exception:

KeyError                                    Traceback (most recent call last)
Input In [77], in <cell line: 1>()
----> 1 train_df['Embarked'].describe()

File ~/repos/jupyter/venv/lib/python3.9/site-packages/pandas/core/frame.py:3505, in DataFram
e.__getitem__(self, key)
   3503 if self.columns.nlevels > 1:
   3504     return self._getitem_multilevel(key)
```

Figure 11.21: The often hard reality.

Series

A Series is essentially a fancy array with elements of arbitrary types (much like a list), each of which is called an *axis*. For example, the following command defines a Series of numbers and strings, plus a special (and commonly encountered) value known as *NaN* ("Not a Number"):

```
>>> pd.Series([1, 2, 3, "foo", np.nan, "bar"])
0      1
1      2
2      3
3    foo
4    NaN
5    bar
dtype: object
>>> pd.Series([1, 2, 3, "foo", np.nan, "bar"]).dropna()
0      1
```

```
1       2
2       3
3     foo
5     bar
dtype: object
```

The second command here shows how to clean the data a bit using the **dropna()** method, which drops any "Not Available" values, such as **None**, **NaN**, or **NaT** ("Not a Time").

By default, Series axis labels are numbered just like array indices (in this case, **0–5**). The set of axes is known as the *index* of the Series:

```
>>> pd.Series([1, 2, 3, "foo", np.nan, "bar"]).index
RangeIndex(start=0, stop=6, step=1)
```

It's also possible to define our own axis labels, which must have the same number of elements as the Series:

```
>>> from numpy.random import default_rng
>>> rng = default_rng()
>>> s = pd.Series(rng.standard_normal(5), index=["a", "b", "c", "d", "e"])
>>> s
a    0.770407
b   -0.698040
c    1.977234
d   -1.559065
e   -0.713496
dtype: float64
```

Series act both like NumPy ndarrays and like regular Python dictionaries:

```
>>> s[0]                 # Acting like an ndarray
0.7704065892197263
>>> s[1:3]               # Supports slicing
b   -0.698040
c    1.977234
dtype: float64
>>> s["c"]               # Access by axis label
1.977233512910388
>>> s.keys()             # Keys are just the Series index.
Index(['a', 'b', 'c', 'd', 'e'], dtype='object')
>>> s.index
Index(['a', 'b', 'c', 'd', 'e'], dtype='object')
```

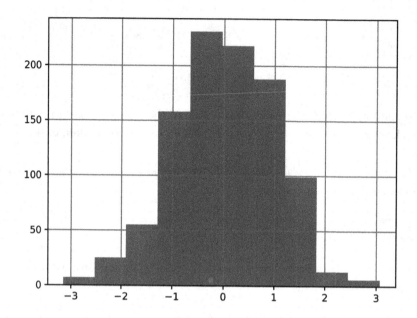

Figure 11.22: A Series histogram.

Series come equipped with a wealth of methods, including plotting methods that use Matplotlib (Section 11.3) under the hood. For example, here's a histogram for a Series with 1000 values generated with the standard normal distribution:

```
>>> s = pd.Series(rng.standard_normal(1000))
>>> s.hist()
>>> plt.show()
```

Apart from minor formatting differences, the result (Figure 11.22) is essentially the same as the histogram we created directly in Section 11.3.3 (Figure 11.16).

DataFrame

The other main pandas object type, known as a **DataFrame** object, is the heart of Python data analysis. A DataFrame can be thought of as a two-dimensional grid of cells containing arbitrary data types—roughly equivalent to an Excel worksheet. In this section, we'll create a few simple DataFrames by hand just to get a sense of how they work, but it's worth bearing in mind that most real-world DataFrame objects are created by importing data from files (or even from live URLs), a technique we'll cover starting in Section 11.5.

There are a large number of ways to initialize or build DataFrames appropriate to a correspondingly large number of circumstances. For example, one option is to initialize it with a Python dictionary, as shown in Listing 11.11.

Listing 11.11: Initializing a DataFrame with a dictionary.

```
>>> from math import tau
>>> from numpy.random import default_rng
>>> rng = default_rng()
>>> df = pd.DataFrame(
...     {
...         "Number": 1.0,
...         "String": "foo",
...         "Angles": np.linspace(0, tau, 5),
...         "Random": pd.Series(rng.standard_normal(5)),
...         "Timestamp": pd.Timestamp("20221020"),
...         "Size": pd.Categorical(["tiny", "small", "mid", "big", "huge"])
...     })
>>> df
   Number String    Angles    Random  Timestamp   Size
0     1.0    foo  0.000000 -1.954002 2022-10-20   tiny
1     1.0    foo  1.570796  0.967171 2022-10-20  small
2     1.0    foo  3.141593 -1.149739 2022-10-20    mid
3     1.0    foo  4.712389 -0.084962 2022-10-20    big
4     1.0    foo  6.283185  0.310634 2022-10-20   huge
```

Here we've applied the **linspace()** method from Section 11.2.3 and two new pandas methods, **TimeStamp** (just what it sounds like) and **Categorical** (which contains values of a *categorical variable*). The result is a set of labeled rows and columns with a heterogeneous set of data.

We can access a DataFrame column using the column name as a key:

```
>>> df["Size"]
0     tiny
1    small
2      mid
3      big
4     huge
```

We can also calculate statistics, such as the mean value of the **Random** column:

```
>>> df["Random"].mean()
-0.3821796291792846
```

One useful pandas function for getting a general overview of numeric data is **describe()**:

```
>>> df.describe()
          Number     Angles     Random
count       5.0   5.000000   5.000000
mean        1.0   3.141593  -0.382180
std         0.0   2.483647   1.167138
min         1.0   0.000000  -1.954002
25%         1.0   1.570796  -1.149739
50%         1.0   3.141593  -0.084962
75%         1.0   4.712389   0.310634
max         1.0   6.283185   0.96717
```

This automatically displays the total count, mean, standard deviation, minimum, and maximum values, and the middle three quartiles (25%, 50%, and 75%) of each numeric column. These values won't always be meaningful—the standard deviation of the linearly spaced angles, for example, doesn't really tell us anything useful—but **describe()** is often helpful as a first step in an analysis. We'll see examples of two other useful summary methods, **head()** and **info()**, starting in Section 11.5.

Another useful method is **map()**, which we can use to map categorical values to numbers. Suppose, for example, that **"Size"** corresponds to drink sizes in ounces, which we can represent as a **sizes** dictionary. Using **map()** on the **"Size"** column then gives the desired result (Listing 11.12).

Listing 11.12: Using **map()** to modify values.

```
>>> sizes = {"tiny": 4, "small": 8, "mid": 12, "big": 16, "huge": 24}
>>> df["Size"].map(sizes)
0     4
1     8
2    12
3    16
4    24
```

This technique is especially valuable when applying machine-learning algorithms (Section 11.7), which can't typically handle categorical data but do just fine with integers or floats.

11.4.2 Exercise

1. The **info()** method provides an overview of a DataFrame that is complementary to **describe()**. What is the result of running **df.info()** on the DataFrame defined in Listing 11.11?

11.5 pandas Example: Nobel Laureates

In Section 11.4, we got a glimpse of how to use pandas and what good it does us, but doing anything interesting typically requires bigger datasets, which are cumbersome to create by hand. Instead, the most common practice is to load data from external files and then take the analysis from there. Accordingly, in this section and the next (Section 11.6), we'll read the initial data from what is probably the most common input format, CSV files (for "comma-separated values").

Our first step is to download a dataset on winners of the Nobel Prize, who are typically known as *laureates* (a reference to the ancient practice of using wreaths from a laurel tree to honor great accomplishments).[17] We can do this by using the **curl** command-line command in the same directory being used for the data analysis:[18]

```
(venv) $ curl -OL https://cdn.learnenough.com/laureates.csv
```

We can then read the data using pandas' **read_csv()** function:

```
>>> nobel = pd.read_csv("laureates.csv")
```

The statistics for the numeric columns aren't very meaningful, so **describe()** doesn't tell us much:

---

17. This section draws on the excellent pandas section from Python for Scientific Computing.

18. This data was originally downloaded directly from the official Nobel Prize website at http://api.nobelprize.org/v1/laureate.csv. It has been uploaded to the Learn Enough CDN for maximum compatibility in case the version at nobelprize.org changes or disappears.

```
>>> nobel.describe()
               id          year        share
count  975.000000    975.000000   975.000000
mean   496.221538   1972.471795     2.014359
std    290.594353     34.058064     0.943909
min      1.000000   1901.000000     1.000000
25%    244.500000   1948.500000     1.000000
50%    488.000000   1978.000000     2.000000
75%    746.500000   2001.000000     3.000000
max   1009.000000   2021.000000     4.000000
```

We can get something a little more useful with **head()** (Listing 11.13).

Listing 11.13: Looking at the **head()** of the Nobel Prize data.

```
>>> nobel.head()
   id         firstname  ...        city          country
0   1  Wilhelm Conrad    ...      Munich          Germany
1   2        Hendrik A.  ...      Leiden  the Netherlands
2   3            Pieter  ...   Amsterdam  the Netherlands
3   4             Henri  ...       Paris           France
4   5            Pierre  ...       Paris           France
[5 rows x 20 columns]
```

Here we've used the **head()** method to take a peek at the first few entries; in a Jupyter notebook, you can scroll to see all of the columns, but in the terminal we see only a few. We can get more useful info using **info()**:

```
>>> nobel.info()
<class 'pandas.core.frame.DataFrame'>
RangeIndex: 975 entries, 0 to 974
Data columns (total 20 columns):
 #   Column           Non-Null Count  Dtype
---  ------           --------------  -----
 0   id               975 non-null    int64
 1   firstname        975 non-null    object
 2   surname          945 non-null    object
 3   born             974 non-null    object
 4   died             975 non-null    object
 5   bornCountry      946 non-null    object
 6   bornCountryCode  946 non-null    object
 7   bornCity         943 non-null    object
 8   diedCountry      640 non-null    object
 9   diedCountryCode  640 non-null    object
```

```
10   diedCity              634 non-null      object
11   gender                975 non-null      object
12   year                  975 non-null      int64
13   category              975 non-null      object
14   overallMotivation     23 non-null       object
15   share                 975 non-null      int64
16   motivation            975 non-null      object
17   name                  717 non-null      object
18   city                  712 non-null      object
19   country               713 non-null      object
dtypes: int64(3), object(17)
memory usage: 152.5+ KB
```

Here we see a complete list of the column names, together with the number of non-null values for each one.

Locating Data

One of the most useful tasks in pandas is locating data that satisfies desired criteria. For example, we can locate a Nobel laureate with a particular surname. As a Caltech graduate, I am contractually obligated to use one of Caltech's most beloved figures, physicist Richard Feynman (pronounced "FINE-mən"). In addition to his groundbreaking work in theoretical physics (especially quantum electrodynamics and its associated Feynman diagrams), Feynman is known for *The Feynman Lectures on Physics*, which covers the elementary physics curriculum (mechanics, thermal physics, electrodynamics, etc.) in an unusually entertaining and insightful way.

Let's use square brackets and a boolean criterion on the **"surname"** column to find Feynman's record in the laureates data:[19]

```
>>> nobel[nobel["surname"] == "Feynman"]
    id   firstname  ...          city country
86  86   Richard P. ...  Pasadena CA      USA
```

This array-style notation returns the full record, which allows us to determine the year Feynman won his Nobel Prize. In a Jupyter notebook, you can probably just scroll to the side and read it off (Figure 11.23), but in the REPL we can look directly at the **year** attribute:

---

19. From here on out, unimportant output such as **[1 rows x 20 columns]** and **Name: year, dtype: int64** will generally be omitted for brevity.

```
[8]:  nobel[nobel["surname"] == "Feynman"]
```

[8]:	orn	died	bornCountry	bornCountryCode	bornCity	diedCountry	diedCountryCode	diedCity	gender	year	category	overallM
	18-i-11	1988-02-15	USA	US	New York NY	USA	US	Los Angeles CA	male	1965	physics	

Figure 11.23: Examining a pandas record in a Jupyter notebook.

```
>>> nobel[nobel["surname"] == "Feynman"].year
86    1965
```

This method also allows us to, e.g., assign it to a variable, which is potentially more useful than inspecting it by eye.

By the way, the syntax

```
>>> nobel[nobel["surname"] == "Feynman"]
```

can be a little confusing since it might not be clear why we have to refer to **nobel** twice. The answer is that the inner part of the syntax returns a Series (Section 11.4.1) consisting of boolean values for every laureate, with **True** if the surname is equal to **"Feynman"** and **False** otherwise:

```
>>> nobel["surname"] == "Feynman"
0       False
1       False
2       False
3       False
4       False
        ...
970     False
971     False
972     False
973     False
974     False
```

By using the correct index (i.e., **86**), we can confirm that the value in that case is **True**:

```
>>> (nobel["surname"] == "Feynman")[86]
True
```

In this way, we arrange for

```
>>> nobel[nobel["surname"] == "Feynman"]
```

to select only the values of **nobel** where **nobel["surname"] == "Feynman"** is **True**. This is similar to the **isclose()** trick shown in Listing 11.7, where we used an ndarray of booleans to select the elements in a matrix close to 0 (and set them to exactly 0).

Another method for getting the year is by specifying the column along with the boolean criterion, which we might try like this (only the most relevant line of output is shown):

```
>>> nobel[nobel["surname"] == "Feynman", "year"]
pandas.errors.InvalidIndexError
```

This doesn't work, but we can accomplish what we want using the **loc** ("location") attribute:[20]

```
>>> nobel.loc[nobel["surname"] == "Feynman", "year"]
86    1965
```

This returns just the overall id (in this case, **86**) and the column of interest. The **loc** attribute can be used in place of brackets in many places and is generally a more flexible way to pull out data items of interest.

After I finished my Ph.D., I was recruited to work on a *Feynman Lectures* project (https://www.michaelhartl.com/feynman-lectures/) by Kip Thorne, who was one of my mentors at Caltech (Figure 11.24[21]). Kip went on to win a Nobel Prize himself, so let's figure out which year.

We could search by surname as we did with Feynman, but Kip insists on being called "Kip", so let's search by first name instead:

```
>>> nobel.loc[nobel["firstname"] == "Kip"]
Empty DataFrame
```

Hmm, the result is empty. Looking back at the **head()** in Listing 11.13, we can guess why; for example, the entry for Hendrik Lorentz includes a middle initial, so perhaps

---

20. More specifically, **loc** is a *property*, which is a special kind of attribute created using a property decorator.

21. Image copyright © 2012 Michael Hartl.

Figure 11.24: The author with Nobel laureate Kip Thorne and Stephen Hawking.

the same is the case for Kip's entry in the DataFrame. Kip's middle initial is "S." (for Stephen), so let's include that in our comparison:

```
>>> nobel.loc[nobel["firstname"] == "Kip S."]
     id firstname surname  ...                          name city country
916 943    Kip S.  Thorne  ...  LIGO/VIRGO Collaboration NaN     NaN
```

Bingo. Now we can look for the year as with Feynman's entry:

```
>>> nobel.loc[nobel["firstname"] == "Kip S."].year
2017
```

But what if we didn't happen to know Kip's middle initial (and didn't think to check Wikipedia for it)? It would be nice to be able to search all the first names for the string **"Kip"**. We can do this using **Series.str**, which allows us to use string functions on a Series, together with **contains()** to search for a substring (Listing 11.14).

Listing 11.14: Finding a record by substring.

```
>>> nobel.loc[nobel["firstname"].str.contains("Kip")]
        id firstname surname  ...             name city country
916    943   Kip S.  Thorne  ...  LIGO/VIRGO Collaboration  NaN     NaN
```

Perhaps unsurprisingly, since it's a fairly uncommon name, there's only one "Kip" in the dataset. What about any other Feynmans? We can try again with **"surname"** in place of **"firstname"**:

```
>>> nobel.loc[nobel["surname"].str.contains("Feynman")]
ValueError: Cannot mask with non-boolean array containing NA / NaN values
```

Oops, we got an error. This is because of a large number of NaNs from organizations that have won the Nobel Prize for Peace:

```
>>> nobel.loc[nobel["surname"].isnull()]
        id                                   firstname ... city country
465    467              Institute of International Law ...  NaN     NaN
474    477         Permanent International Peace Bureau ...  NaN     NaN
479    482      International Committee of the Red Cross ...  NaN     NaN
480    482      International Committee of the Red Cross ...  NaN     NaN
 .
 .
 .
```

We can filter out NaNs and other Not Available values by passing the option **na=False** to **contains()**:

```
>>> nobel.loc[nobel["surname"].str.contains("Feynman", na=False)]
     id  firstname  ...        city country
86   86  Richard P. ...  Pasadena CA     USA
```

It looks like there's only one result, which we can confirm with **len()**:

```
>>> len(nobel.loc[nobel["surname"].str.contains("Feynman", na=False)])
1
```

Although there's only one Nobel laureate named "Feynman", there are famously several named "Curie", as seen in Listing 11.15.

Listing 11.15: Finding Curies in the `laureates.csv` dataset.

```
>>> curies = nobel.loc[nobel["surname"].str.contains("Curie", na=False)]
>>> curies
     id firstname  ...    city country
4     5    Pierre  ...   Paris  France
5     6     Marie  ...     NaN     NaN
6     6     Marie  ...   Paris  France
191 194     Irène  ...   Paris  France
```

Here we've assigned the result to the variable **curies** for convenience. For example, we can get the first name and surname for each Curie laureate as follows:

```
>>> curies[["firstname", "surname"]]
4      Pierre         Curie
5       Marie         Curie
6       Marie         Curie
191     Irène  Joliot-Curie
```

We see that Marie Curie (also known as Marie Skłodowska-Curie)[22] won two Nobel Prizes (Figure 11.25[23]). The other Curie laureates are Pierre Curie, Marie's husband, and Irène Joliot-Curie, one of their daughters. (In fact, there's even one more Nobel laureate in the absurdly accomplished Curie family; see Section 11.5.1 for more.)

Marie Skłodowska-Curie is the only person to win a Nobel Prize for two different sciences. Let's use pandas to see if there are any other multiple Nobel prizewinners. One way to investigate this question is to use **groupby()** to group the winners by name and then use the **size()** method to see how many there are:

---

22. Although typically known only as "Marie Curie" in English-language sources, Marie herself preferred to use the Polish part of her name as well, and many European sources (including Polish ones) follow this convention.

23. Image courtesy of Morphart Creation/Shutterstock.

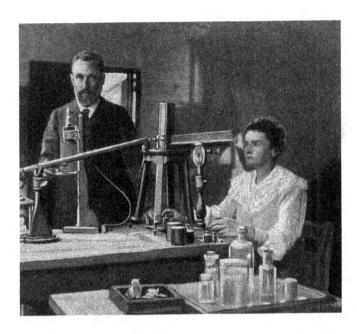

Figure 11.25: Marie Skłodowska-Curie with her husband and co-laureate Pierre Curie.

```
>>> nobel.groupby(["firstname", "surname"]).size()
firstname   surname
A. Michael  Spence          1
Aage N.     Bohr            1
Aaron       Ciechanover     1
            Klug            1
Abdulrazak  Gurnah          1
                           ..
Youyou      Tu              1
Yuan T.     Lee             1
Yves        Chauvin         1
Zhores      Alferov         1
Élie        Ducommun        1
```

All the displayed values here are **1**, but we can sort them using **sort_values()** to find any multiple laureates:

```
>>> nobel.groupby(["firstname", "surname"]).size().sort_values()
firstname      surname
A. Michael     Spence      1
Nicolay G.     Basov       1
Niels          Bohr        1
Niels K.       Jerne       1
Niels Ryberg   Finsen      1
                          ..
Élie           Ducommun    1
Linus          Pauling     2
John           Bardeen     2
Frederick      Sanger      2
Marie          Curie       2
```

This yields four multiple winners.

Although the **sort_values()** trick is nice, it would have failed if there had been too many multiple laureates. A more general way to select winners of more than one Prize is to use a boolean criterion directly. We can do this with the same grouping by size combined with the criterion **size > 1** (Listing 11.16). Note that we've added **"id"** to **groupby()** to take into account the (unlikely but possible) case of different people with the same name both winning Nobel Prizes.

Listing 11.16: Finding winners of multiple Nobel Prizes.

```
>>> laureates = nobel.groupby(["id", "firstname", "surname"])
>>> sizes = laureates.size()
>>> sizes[sizes > 1]
id    firstname   surname
6     Marie       Curie      2
66    John        Bardeen    2
217   Linus       Pauling    2
222   Frederick   Sanger     2
```

We see from Listing 11.16 that, at the time this dataset was assembled, only four people had ever won more than one Nobel Prize: Frederick Sanger (Chemistry), John Bardeen (Physics), Linus Pauling (Chemistry and Peace), and of course Marie Curie (Physics and Chemistry). (2022 saw the emergence of a fifth multiple-laureate when K. Barry Sharpless won his second Nobel Prize for Chemistry.)

Selecting Dates

One of pandas' greatest strengths is its ability to deal with times and *time series*, so let's start by taking a look at selecting dates. One way we can do this is by searching for laureates by exact birthday as a string:

```
>>> nobel.loc[nobel["born"] == "1879-03-14"]
    id firstname ...    city  country
25  26    Albert ...  Berlin  Germany
```

You might suspect that a Nobel Prize–winning "Albert" born in 1879 might be Albert Einstein, and you'd be right, as we can see by checking the **"surname"** field:[24]

```
>>> nobel.loc[nobel["born"] == "1879-03-14"]["surname"]
Einstein
```

Looking closely, we see that Einstein was born on March 14, which is sometimes known as Pi Day because of the resemblance between 03-14 (or 3/14 in the American calendar system) and the first three digits of $\pi \approx 3.14$. Fans of Pi Day are quick to point out how great this is.

As the founder of Tau Day (https://tauday.com/), I was naturally interested in finding some great Nobel laureate who was born on 06-28 (6/28) to match the first three digits of $\tau \approx 6.28$. We've seemingly already solved this problem of searching by substring (as in, e.g., Listing 11.14), so let's try it out with the **"born"** field:

```
>>> nobel.loc[nobel["born"].str.contains("06-08", na=False)]
      id   firstname  ...           city  country
79    79       Maria  ...  San Diego CA      USA
125  126       Klaus  ...     Stuttgart  Germany
281  283  F. Sherwood ...     Irvine CA      USA
304  306      Alexis  ...  New York NY      USA
598  607       Luigi  ...           NaN      NaN
790  809    Muhammad  ...           NaN      NaN
889  916  William C.  ...   Madison NJ      USA

[7 rows x 20 columns]
```

That's 7 rows. Let's narrow it down by restricting the results to Nobel laureates in Physics using the **&** operator to perform a logical *and* (note that this syntax differs from Python itself (Section 2.4.1)):

---

24. If you're using Jupyter, you can probably just read off the full name from the result of evaluating the cell.

```
>>> nobel.loc[(nobel["born"].astype('string').str.contains("06-28")) &
...           (nobel["category"] == "physics")]
     id firstname ...            city  country
79   79     Maria ...   San Diego CA      USA
125 126     Klaus ...      Stuttgart  Germany

[2 rows x 20 columns]
```

That's more like it. Let's take a look at the first record using **iloc** ("index location")
to find it by its index number, which is **79**:

```
>>> nobel.iloc[79]
id                               79
firstname                     Maria
surname              Goeppert Mayer
born                     1906-06-28
died                     1972-02-20
 .
 .
 .
```

That's Maria Goeppert Mayer (Figure 11.26[25]), who won a Nobel Prize in Physics
for her contributions to the nuclear shell model, and who is the official physicist of
Tau Day. (Take that, Al!)

Speaking of birthdates, the lifespans of Nobel laureates have been the subject of
some scientific research over the years.[26] Although we are not in a position to draw
any conclusions about the effect (if any) of winning a Nobel Prize on longevity, we
can make a histogram of the laureates' ages to get a sense of the distribution.

Let's begin by finding the record for Hans Bethe ("BAY-tuh"), one of the longest-
lived Nobel laureates:[27]

---

25. Image courtesy of Archive PL/Alamy Alamy Stock Photo.

26. See, for example, Matthew D. Rablen and Andrew J. Oswald, "Mortality and immortality: The Nobel
Prize as an experiment into the effect of status upon longevity". *Journal of Health Economics*, Volume 27, Issue
6. December 2008, pp. 1462–1471.

27. Bethe was already a famous physicist in the 1930s due to his groundbreaking series of papers on nuclear
theory. He later served as the head of the theoretical division at Los Alamos during the making of the atomic
bomb. And yet he lived so long that I had a chance to meet him in the early 2000s when he came to give
an astrophysics talk at Caltech.

Figure 11.26: Maria Goeppert Mayer, Nobel laureate and official physicist of Tau Day.

```
>>> bethe = nobel.loc[nobel["surname"] == "Bethe"]
>>> bethe["born"]
88    1906-07-02
>>> bethe["died"]
88    2005-03-06
```

By subtracting in our heads, we can see that Bethe lived to be 98, but doing this one by one for all the laureates would be most impractical.

Let's see if we can calculate Bethe's age by pure subtraction:

```
>>> bethe["died"] - bethe["born"]
TypeError: unsupported operand type(s) for -: 'str' and 'str'
```

OK, the dates are being stored as strings, so it's not surprising that simple subtraction didn't work. Let's try converting to **datetime** objects:

```
>>> diff = pd.to_datetime(bethe["died"]) - pd.to_datetime(bethe["born"])
>>> diff
88   36042 days
dtype: timedelta64[ns]
```

That's much more promising, but it's a Series of **timedelta64** objects, though, rather than floats. We can fix this by using **dt** to gain access to the datetime directly and **days** to find the number of days:

```
>>> diff.dt.days
88      36042
dtype: int64
```

At this point, we could then divide by 365 (or 365.25) to get the approximate number of years, which is probably good enough for a histogram, but it isn't quite right because of leap years, the number of which will vary based on the exact date range. Luckily, NumPy comes with a method called **timedelta64** that handles this automatically:

```
>>> diff/np.timedelta64(1, "Y")
88     98.679644
dtype: float64
```

Here **1, "Y"** refers to a time delta (change) of "1 Year".

Now let's apply the same idea to the full list of Nobel laureates:

```
>>> nobel["born"] = pd.to_datetime(nobel["born"])
dateutil.parser._parser.ParserError: month must be in 1..12: 1873-00-00
```

Here there's an error because at least one of the **"born"** dates has **00-00** for the month and year. Why?

```
>>> nobel.loc[nobel["born"] == "1873-00-00"]
      id                      firstname surname  ... name city country
465  467  Institute of International Law    NaN  ... NaN  NaN    NaN

[1 rows x 20 columns]
>>> nobel.iloc[465].born
>>> nobel.iloc[465].category
465    peace
Name: category, dtype: object
>>> nobel.iloc[465].year
465    1904
Name: year, dtype: int64
```

Ah, so an organization called the Institute of International Law won the Nobel Prize for Peace in 1904. As you might guess from the **"born"** date, it was founded in 1873, but because it's not a person the Nobel data declines to specify an exact "birth" date.

This complicates matters somewhat because we can't just drop Not Available values like **NaN** and **NaT**. Luckily, pandas has an option to force, or **coerce**, such values when making the conversion. We can convert in place (thereby overwriting the old data) like this:

```
>>> nobel["born"] = pd.to_datetime(nobel["born"], errors="coerce")
>>> nobel["died"] = pd.to_datetime(nobel["died"], errors="coerce")
```

Now we can double-check the value for the Institute of International Law:

```
>>> nobel.iloc[465].born
NaT
```

So the coercion converted the invalid date to Not a Time, which is perfect for our purposes because such values are ignored automatically when plotting histograms.

At this point, we're ready to calculate the laureates' lifespans by subtracting datetimes and dividing by NumPy's magic time delta:

```
>>> nobel["lifespan"] = (nobel["died"] - nobel["born"])/np.timedelta64(1, "Y")
```

Note that this dynamically creates a new **"lifespan"** column in our **nobel** DataFrame. We can do a reality check by making sure we've replicated the calculation we did for Bethe:

```
>>> bethe = nobel.loc[nobel["surname"] == "Bethe"]
>>> bethe["lifespan"]
88    98.679644
```

So Hans Bethe's lifespan checks out from our previous calculation.

We're now finally ready to make the histogram. With all the work we've done, it's as simple as calling **hist()** with the **"lifespan"** column (Listing 11.17).

Listing 11.17: The code to make a lifespan histogram.

```
>>> nobel.hist(column="lifespan")
array([[<AxesSubplot:title={'center':'lifespan'}>]], dtype=object)
>>> plt.show()
```

The result appears in Figure 11.27. As expected from the research on the subject, the lifespans of the Nobel laureates are skewed toward the upper end of the usual range.

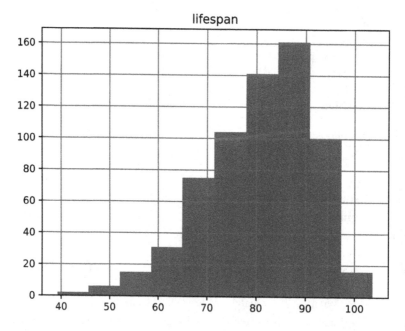

Figure 11.27: A histogram of Nobel laureates' lifespans.

11.5.1 Exercises

1. Confirm that Frédéric Joliot-Curie, who shared the 1935 Nobel Prize for Chemistry with his wife Irène, appears in the **laureates.csv** dataset. Why did we miss him when we searched for Curies in Listing 11.15? *Hint*: Search for an entry with **"firstname"** equal to **"Frédéric"** (making sure to include the proper accents).

2. Verify that the Nobel Prize categories cited after Listing 11.16 are correct (e.g., that Frederick Sanger's Nobel Prizes really were for Chemistry, etc.).

3. In Listing 11.17, what happens if you just call **nobel.hist()**, with no column specified?

11.6 pandas Example: *Titanic*

Our second major pandas example uses survival data from the tragic sinking of RMS *Titanic* in 1912 (Figure 11.28[28]). This is a standard dataset used by the pandas documentation itself,[29] and as such has been extensively analyzed, making the "Google for it" algorithm unusually effective.

As usual, our first step is to download the data, which we can do directly from the Web, as shown in Listing 11.18. (We saw in Section 9.2 that **request.get()** automatically follows redirects, but as far as I can tell **read_csv()** does not. I have been unable to figure out how to get it to do so (if it's even possible), so Listing 11.18 uses the raw Amazon S3 URL instead.)

Let's take a look at the **head()**:

```
>>> titanic.head()
   PassengerId  Survived  Pclass  ...      Fare Cabin  Embarked
0            1         0       3  ...    7.2500   NaN         S
1            2         1       1  ...   71.2833   C85         C
2            3         1       3  ...    7.9250   NaN         S
3            4         1       1  ...   53.1000  C123         S
4            5         0       3  ...    8.0500   NaN
```

28. Image courtesy of Shawshots/Alamy.

29. It's available at https://github.com/pandas-dev/pandas/blob/main/doc/data/titanic.csv, but as with the Nobel laureate data we'll use the version at the Learn Enough CDN for maximum compatibility in case the pandas version changes or disappears.

Figure 11.28: The ill-fated RMS *Titanic*.

Listing 11.18: Reading data right from a (raw S3) URL.

```
>>> URL = "https://learnenough.s3.amazonaws.com/titanic.csv"
>>> titanic = pd.read_csv(URL)
```

We see that the data is indexed by **PassengerId**, but that's not very meaningful, and we can give it a more personal touch by rereading the data and indexing on **Name** instead. The way to do this is by specifying an index column using **index_col** (Listing 11.19).

Listing 11.19: Setting a custom index column.

```
>>> titanic = pd.read_csv(URL, index_col="Name")
>>> titanic.head()
                                            PassengerId  ...  Embarked
                                                         ...
Name
Braund, Mr. Owen Harris                               1  ...         S
Cumings, Mrs. John Bradley (Florence Briggs Tha...    2  ...         C
Heikkinen, Miss. Laina                                3  ...         S
Futrelle, Mrs. Jacques Heath (Lily May Peel)          4  ...         S
Allen, Mr. William Henry                              5  ...         S
```

We can look at the value of the **"Survived"** column for each passenger whether they survived or not:

```
>>> titanic.iloc[0]["Survived"]
0
>>> titanic.iloc[1]["Survived"]
1
```

Here **1** is for "Survived" and **0** is for "Didn't Survive", which follows the standard practice for a category where each entry takes only one of two values (variously called a "binary predictor", an "indicator variable", or a "dummy variable").

Because of the choice of encoding, the mean value of the **"Survived"** attribute is the total survival rate:

$$\text{survival rate} = \sum_{i=1}^{N} \frac{\text{total number of survivors}}{\text{total number of passengers}} = \frac{\text{sum of 1s in "Survived"}}{N}.$$

As a result, we can get the overall survival rate by calling **mean()** on the **"Survived"** column:

```
>>> titanic["Survived"].mean()
0.3838383838383838
```

So the *Titanic* disaster survival rate was approximately 38%.

Let's take a look at how survival rate was affected by some of the variables applicable to the passengers. We'll start by getting some **info()**:

```
>>> titanic.info()
<class 'pandas.core.frame.DataFrame'>
Index: 891 entries, Braund, Mr. Owen Harris to Dooley, Mr. Patrick
Data columns (total 11 columns):
 #   Column       Non-Null Count   Dtype
---  ------       --------------   -----
 0   PassengerId  891 non-null     int64
 1   Survived     891 non-null     int64
 2   Pclass       891 non-null     int64
 3   Sex          891 non-null     object
 4   Age          714 non-null     float64
 5   SibSp        891 non-null     int64
 6   Parch        891 non-null     int64
 7   Ticket       891 non-null     object
 8   Fare         891 non-null     float64
 9   Cabin        204 non-null     object
 10  Embarked     889 non-null     object
dtypes: float64(2), int64(5), object(4)
```

The most interesting columns from the perspective of survival rate are probably passenger class (**"Pclass"**), sex (**"Sex"**), and age (**"Age"**).

We can use pandas to discover that passenger class consists of three categories:

```
>>> titanic["Pclass"].unique()
array([3, 1, 2])
```

These represent first-, second-, and third-class tickets, which correspond to accommodation quality from the highest to the lowest.

If we **groupby()** class we can see how survival rates vary:

```
>>> titanic.groupby("Pclass")["Survived"].mean()
Pclass
1    0.629630
2    0.472826
3    0.242363
```

So we see that the survival rate varies strongly by class, with first-class passengers surviving at a rate of 62.9% and third-class passengers surviving at only 24.2%.

We can visualize this result by plotting a bar chart of survival rate. Each pandas Series object has a **plot** attribute that lets us call **bar()** to make a bar chart, which includes the bar labels automatically. Heights are given by the height of each categorical variable, in this case the survival rates we just calculated:

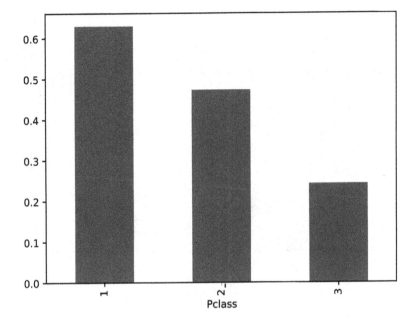

Figure 11.29: *Titanic* survival rates by passenger class.

```
>>> survival_rates = titanic.groupby("Pclass")["Survived"].mean()
>>> survival_rates.plot.bar()
>>> plt.show()
```

The result appears in Figure 11.29.

We can apply similar techniques to the categorical variable **"Sex"**:

```
>>> titanic["Sex"].unique()
array(['male', 'female'], dtype=object)
```

The code to make the bar chart is essentially the same but with grouping by **"Sex"** instead of **"Pclass"**:

```
>>> survival_rates = titanic.groupby("Sex")["Survived"].mean()
>>> survival_rates.plot.bar()
>>> plt.subplots_adjust(bottom=0.20)
>>> plt.show()
```

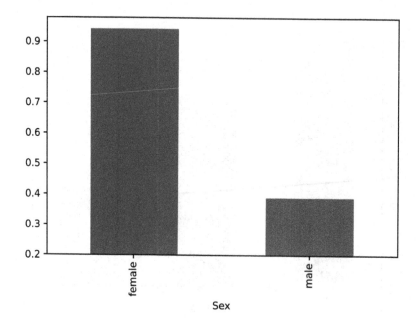

Figure 11.30: *Titanic* survival rates by sex.

The **subplots_adjust()** line here may be necessary to create enough room for the labels on the *x*-axis to display properly on some systems (it was on mine). The result should appear as in Figure 11.30. We see that the survival rate for female passengers was significantly higher than that for male passengers.

We come now to the third major variable of likely interest, age. The class and sex variables are categorical, which made creating a bar chart easy, but the **"Age"** variable is numeric, so we have to bin the data, similar to making a histogram (Section 11.3.3).

The ages of *Titanic* passengers ranged from infants to 80:

```
>>> titanic["Age"].min()
0.42
>>> titanic["Age"].max()
80.0
```

At this point, we have to decide how many bins to use. Using **7** gives an age of approximately 11 for the top of the first bin:

```
>>> (titanic["Age"].max() - titanic["Age"].min())/7
11.368571428571428
```

This is a reasonable cutoff for a "child".

The next step is to bin the data, which we can do with a pandas method called **cut()**. First, we need to select only passengers with valid ages, which we can accomplish with the **notna()** method to ensure that age is *not* Not Available (Listing 11.20).

Listing 11.20: Selecting only values that are *not* Not Available.

```
>>> titanic["Age"].notna()
Name
Braund, Mr. Owen Harris                                     True
Cumings, Mrs. John Bradley (Florence Briggs Thayer)         True
Heikkinen, Miss. Laina                                      True
Futrelle, Mrs. Jacques Heath (Lily May Peel)                True
Allen, Mr. William Henry                                    True
                                                            ...
Montvila, Rev. Juozas                                       True
Graham, Miss. Margaret Edith                                True
Johnston, Miss. Catherine Helen "Carrie"                    False
Behr, Mr. Karl Howell                                       True
Dooley, Mr. Patrick                                         True
Name: Age, Length: 891, dtype: bool
>>> valid_ages = titanic[titanic["Age"].notna()]
```

The values of **titanic["Age"].notna()** include booleans that are **True** if the age is valid, which we can then use as an index to the **titanic** object to select only the passengers with valid ages (the final line in Listing 11.20).

Next, we need to group the data by age and sort it to bring rows with similar ages next to each other before binning:

```
>>> sorted_by_age = valid_ages.sort_values(by="Age")
```

This is necessary because otherwise we would be binning ages based on passenger name, which doesn't make any sense since it would mix passengers of completely unrelated ages in the same bin.

At this point, we're ready to use **cut()** to put the data into the desired number of bins:

```
>>> sorted_by_age["Age range"] = pd.cut(sorted_by_age["Age"], 7)
```

Finally, we calculate the survival rate per bin by grouping by bins and finding the **mean()** of the **"Survived"** column (remember, this works because of the 1=Survived, 0=Didn't Survive encoding typically used for binary predictors):

```
>>> survival_rates = sorted_by_age.groupby("Age range")["Survived"].mean()
```

At this point, we can use the same bar chart technique used for **"Pclass"** and **"Sex"** (with a bottom adjustment to get the labels to fit):

```
>>> survival_rates.plot.bar()
>>> plt.subplots_adjust(bottom=0.33)
>>> plt.show()
```

The result appears as shown in Figure 11.31.

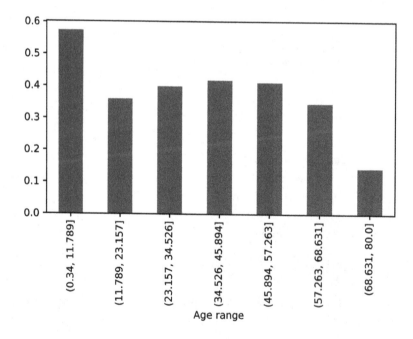

Figure 11.31: *Titanic* survival rates by age.

We see from Figure 11.31 that the survival rate was highest for the youngest passengers, was approximately constant for most adults, and then fell off sharply in the highest age range. But the male passengers were also older:

```
>>> titanic[titanic["Sex"] == "male"]["Age"].mean()
30.72664459161148
>>> titanic[titanic["Sex"] == "female"]["Age"].mean()
27.915708812260537
```

We know from Figure 11.30 that male passengers also had lower survival rates, so this could account for some of the age disparity. We'll see in Section 11.7 one way to examine the relative contribution of each variable separately.

11.6.1   Exercises

1. Confirm using the code in Listing 11.21 that the *Titanic* survival rate for female passengers in third class was 50%. How does this compare to the survival rate for *male* passengers in *first* class?

2. Make two versions of the bar chart for *Titanic* survival rates by age shown in Figure 11.31, one each for male passengers and female passengers. *Hint*: Define sex-specific variables as shown in Listing 11.22 and redo the analysis after Listing 11.20 separately for the **male_** and **female_** variables.

3. Widener Library at Harvard University was built by Eleanor Elkins Widener, who survived the *Titanic* sinking, to honor her son Harry (Figure 11.32[30]), who did not. Using a substring search similar to the one in Listing 11.14, show that Harry is in our *Titanic* dataset, but Eleanor is not. How old was Harry when he died? *Hint*: You can search for names containing the substring **"Widener"**, but because we set **"Name"** as the index column in Listing 11.19, you should use **titanic.index** instead of **titanic["Name"]** in the search.

Listing 11.21: Finding a survival rate using multiple boolean criteria.

```
titanic[(titanic["Sex"] == "female") &
        (titanic["Pclass"] == 3)]["Survived"].mean()
```

---

30. Image copyright © 2022 Michael Hartl.

Listing 11.22: Preparing to visualize *Titanic* survival rates by age separately by sex.

```
male_passengers = titanic[titanic["Sex"] == "male"]
female_passengers = titanic[titanic["Sex"] == "female"]
valid_male_ages = male_passengers[titanic["Age"].notna()]
valid_female_ages = female_passengers[titanic["Age"].notna()]
```

Figure 11.32: A portrait of Harry Elkins Widener inside Widener Library at Harvard University.

11.7 Machine Learning with scikit-learn

This section contains a brief introduction to *machine learning*, which is a field of computing involving programs that "learn" in response to data inputs. Although opinions differ over whether machine learning is part of "data science" per se, at the very least it's a closely related field, and is therefore suitable for inclusion in an introduction such as this one.

Machine learning is a giant subject, and in this section we can only scratch the surface. As with the other sections in this chapter, the main value is in developing a basic familiarity with a relevant Python package, which in this case is known as scikit-learn.

Building on the *Titanic* analysis in Section 11.6, we'll first look at an example of *linear regression* (Section 11.7.1), and we'll then consider more sophisticated machine-learning models (Section 11.7.2). We'll end with an example of a *clustering algorithm* as just one example of the many additional subjects at which scikit-learn excels.

11.7.1 Linear Regression

In this section, we'll use scikit-learn to perform a *linear regression*, which finds the best fit to a set of data (for a suitable definition of "best").[31] Referring to linear regression as "machine learning" is sometimes considered a sort of inside joke because the technique is relatively simple and has been in use for many years. Nevertheless, it's a great place to start.

As with Section 11.6, we'll use the survival data from *Titanic*. We'll start by importing the necessary libraries and creating a **titanic** DataFrame:

```
>>> import numpy as np
>>> import pandas as pd
>>> import matplotlib.pyplot as plt
>>> URL = "https://learnenough.s3.amazonaws.com/titanic.csv"
>>> titanic = pd.read_csv(URL)
```

Our goal is to consider the effect of age on survival rate. We'll start by making a scatter plot (Section 11.3.2) of survival rate vs. age and then find the best linear fit to the data using scikit-learn.

We'll first select just the **"Age"** and **"Survived"** columns, since those are the columns of interest. Then, as a basic matter of data cleaning, we'll consider only passengers with known age, so we'll use **dropna()** (Section 11.4.1) to drop the NaN values:

---

31. This section was inspired in part by the article "Linear Regression in Python" by Mirko Stojiljković.

```
>>> passenger_age = titanic[["Age" , "Survived"]].dropna()
>>> passenger_age.head()
    Age  Survived
0  22.0         0
1  38.0         1
2  26.0         1
3  35.0         1
4  35.0         0
```

For the *x*-axis of our plot, we'll use the ages of the survivors, which we can obtain by calculating the unique values of **passenger_age["Age"]** and then sorting them to put them in ascending order:

```
>>> passenger_ages = passenger_age["Age"].unique()
>>> passenger_ages.sort()
>>> passenger_ages
array([ 0.42,  0.67,  0.75,  0.83,  0.92,  1.  ,  2.  ,  3.  ,  4.  ,
        5.  ,  6.  ,  7.  ,  8.  ,  9.  , 10.  , 11.  , 12.  , 13.  ,
       14.  , 14.5 , 15.  , 16.  , 17.  , 18.  , 19.  , 20.  , 20.5 ,
       21.  , 22.  , 23.  , 23.5 , 24.  , 24.5 , 25.  , 26.  , 27.  ,
       28.  , 28.5 , 29.  , 30.  , 30.5 , 31.  , 32.  , 32.5 , 33.  ,
       34.  , 34.5 , 35.  , 36.  , 36.5 , 37.  , 38.  , 39.  , 40.  ,
       40.5 , 41.  , 42.  , 43.  , 44.  , 45.  , 45.5 , 46.  , 47.  ,
       48.  , 49.  , 50.  , 51.  , 52.  , 53.  , 54.  , 55.  , 55.5 ,
       56.  , 57.  , 58.  , 59.  , 60.  , 61.  , 62.  , 63.  , 64.  ,
       65.  , 66.  , 70.  , 70.5 , 71.  , 74.  , 80.  ])
```

At this point, we're ready to calculate the survival rate for each age:

```
>>> survival_rate = passenger_age.groupby("Age")["Survived"].mean()
```

Let's look at a slice from the middle as a reality check:

```
>>> survival_rate.loc[30:40]
Age
30.0    0.400000
30.5    0.000000
31.0    0.470588
32.0    0.500000
32.5    0.500000
33.0    0.400000
34.0    0.400000
34.5    0.000000
35.0    0.611111
```

```
36.0     0.500000
36.5     0.000000
37.0     0.166667
38.0     0.454545
39.0     0.357143
40.0     0.461538
Name: Survived, dtype: float64
```

So it looks like, say, 37-year-olds survived at a rate of $1/6 \approx 16.7\%$.

As noted in Section 11.3.2, a scatter plot is a great way to get a broad overview of the data:

```
>>> fig, ax = plt.subplots()
>>> ax.scatter(passenger_ages, survival_rate)
>>> plt.show()
```

The result is shown in Figure 11.33.

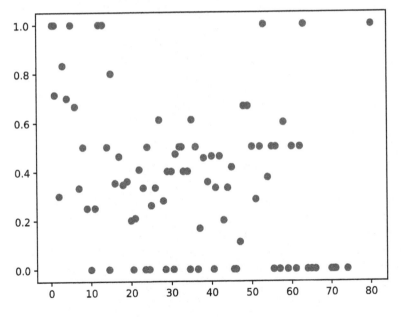

Figure 11.33: A scatter plot of *Titanic* survival rates by age.

It appears in Figure 11.33 that there is a general downward trend, in agreement with the bar chart in Figure 11.31. We can quantify this trend using the **LinearRegression** model from scikit-learn (Listing 11.23).[32]

Listing 11.23: Importing a linear regression model.

```
>>> from sklearn.linear_model import LinearRegression
```

We'll now define variables **X** and **Y** based on the ages and survival rates as inputs to the scikit-learn regression model.[33] The input format expected by scikit-learn models is an array of one-dimensional arrays for **X** and a regular NumPy ndarray for **Y**. The former is exactly the format created using the **reshape((-1, 1))** method in Section 11.2.2 (Listing 11.4):

```
>>> X = np.array(passenger_ages).reshape((-1, 1))
>>> X[:10]    # Look at the first 10 ages as a reality check.
array([[0.42],
       [0.67],
       [0.75],
       [0.83],
       [0.92],
       [1.  ],
       [2.  ],
       [3.  ],
       [4.  ],
       [5.  ]])
```

Defining **Y**, meanwhile, is much more straightforward:

```
>>> Y = np.array(survival_rate)
```

At this point, we're ready to use a linear regression to find the best fit of the model to the data:

---

32. SciPy also has a linear regression function (**scipy.stats.linregress**), but in this section we use the one in scikit-learn in order to unify the treatment with the more advanced models in Section 11.7.2.

33. Conventions for the capitalization of regression variables are rather complicated; see here (https://stats.stackexchange.com/questions/389395/why-uppercase-for-x-and-lowercase-for-y) for more.

```
>>> model = LinearRegression()
>>> model.fit(X, Y)
LinearRegression()
```

The results of this calculation include the coefficient of determination, also called R^2 (for technical reasons), which is the square of the Pearson correlation coefficient and can take any value between -1 and 1, with 1 being perfect correlation and -1 being perfect anti-correlation. R^2 is available as the **score()** of the model:

```
>>> model.score(X, Y)    # coefficient of determination R^2
0.13539675574075116
```

An R^2 value of 0.135 is small but not negligible, though it's important to bear in mind the difficulty of interpreting R^2.

We can get a visual indication of the fit by plotting the regression line itself. The slope and y-intercept of the line are available via the **coef_** and **intercept_** attributes of the model:

```
>>> m = model.coef_
>>> b = model.intercept_
```

Here the trailing underscores on the names are a scikit-learn convention for attributes that are available only after the model has been applied using **model.score()**.

We've named the slope and intercept using the standard names **m** and **b** for describing a line in the xy-plane:

$$y = mx + b \qquad \text{equation of a line.}$$

We can combine a plot of this line with the scatter plot from Figure 11.33 to visualize the fit (included here without the REPL prompt for ease of copying):

```
fig, ax = plt.subplots()
ax.scatter(passenger_ages, survival_rate)
ax.plot(passenger_ages, m * passenger_ages + b, color="orange")
ax.set_xlabel("Age")
ax.set_ylabel("Survival Rate")
ax.set_title("Titanic survival rates by age")
plt.show()
```

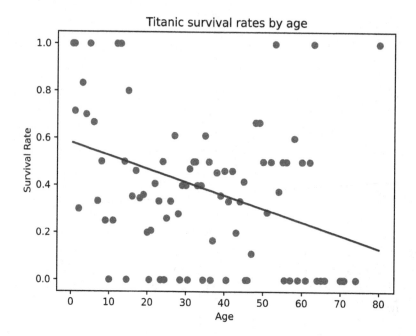

Figure 11.34: Adding a regression line (and labels) to Figure 11.33.

The result is shown in Figure 11.34. As indicated by the modest R^2 value, the fit in Figure 11.34 is OK but not great. Clearly, the correlation with age is far from perfect, and we found in Section 11.6 that both sex and passenger class had a significant effect on survival rates. We'll investigate these relationships further with more sophisticated learning models in Section 11.7.2.

11.7.2 Machine-Learning Models

In Section 11.6, we used pandas to discover an association between *Titanic* survival rates and the key variables of passenger class (**"Pclass"**), sex (**"Sex"**), and age (**"Age"**). In Section 11.7.1, we calculated a linear regression for survival rates as a function of age, but the predictive capability of the linear regression model was fairly modest. In this section, we'll look at significantly more sophisticated learning models that yield correspondingly better predictions.[34]

As in previous sections, we'll import the necessary packages and create the necessary DataFrame (shown without the REPL prompt for ease of copying):

```
import numpy as np
import pandas as pd
import matplotlib.pyplot as plt


URL = "https://learnenough.s3.amazonaws.com/titanic.csv"
titanic = pd.read_csv(URL)
```

There is a large variety of different models supported by scikit-learn that we might try. A detailed discussion of such models is beyond the scope of this tutorial, but here is a selection of the models we'll be considering in this section with links for more information:

- Logistic Regression (https://stats.stackexchange.com/questions/389395/why-uppercase-for-x-and-lowercase-for-y)

- Naive Bayes (https://en.wikipedia.org/wiki/Naive_Bayes_classifier)

- Perceptron (https://en.wikipedia.org/wiki/Perceptron)

- Decision Tree (https://en.wikipedia.org/wiki/Decision_tree)

- Random Forest (https://en.wikipedia.org/wiki/Random_forest)

These models were chosen as representative samples of different kinds of candidate algorithms. The only exception is Random Forest, which in the case of our dataset will turn out to be equivalent to Decision Tree, but was retained because "Random Forest" sounds really cool. (In all seriousness, seeing when and by how much Random Forest differs from Decision Tree is discussed in an exercise (Section 11.7.4).)

---

34. The analysis here is based in part on the article "Predicting the Survival of Titanic Passengers", which uses data from the popular Machine Learning from Disaster contest run by machine-learning site Kaggle (a subsidiary of Google). The Kaggle dataset includes both training and test data; the purpose of the contest is to use the training data to train models and then submit predictions based on the test data. Unfortunately, this step isn't clear in "Predicting the Survival of Titanic Passengers", which uses scikit-learn's **predict()** method to calculate predictions but then doesn't do anything with them. For participants in the contest, those predictions would be used to create the submissions required by Kaggle.

To use the various models on our training DataFrame, we first need to import them from scikit-learn, which is available via the **sklearn** package (Listing 11.24).

Listing 11.24: Importing learning models.

```
from sklearn.linear_model import LogisticRegression
from sklearn.naive_bayes import GaussianNB
from sklearn.linear_model import Perceptron
from sklearn.tree import DecisionTreeClassifier
from sklearn.ensemble import RandomForestClassifier
```

Note the similarity between these import statements and the one used for linear regressions in Section 11.7.1 (Listing 11.23).

At this point, we need to bring our data into the format required for input into scikit-learn's learning models. Because we've decided to focus on the effects of class, sex, and age on survival rates, our first step is to drop the columns that we won't be considering. For convenience, we'll spell out the corresponding column names in a list and then iterate over it, using the pandas **drop()** method to drop the corresponding column (which by convention is **axis=1**; the default value of **axis=0** would try to drop a row instead):

```
dropped_columns = ["PassengerId", "Name", "Cabin", "Embarked",
                   "SibSp", "Parch", "Ticket", "Fare"]

for column in dropped_columns:
    titanic = titanic.drop(column, axis=1)
```

Unlike things like histogram plots, which typically ignore Not Available values like NaNs and NaTs, the learning models will croak if given invalid values. To avoid this unfortunate circumstance, we'll use the same trick seen in Listing 11.20 and redefine our DataFrames to include only values that are *not* Not Available using the **notna()** method (seen before in Listing 11.20):

```
for column in ["Age", "Sex", "Pclass"]:
    titanic = titanic[titanic[column].notna()]
```

Another cause of model errors is raw categorical values like **"male"** and **"female"**, which the models don't know how to handle. In order to fix this, we'll associate each of these categories to a number using the pandas **map()** method we saw in Listing 11.12:

```
sexes = {"male": 0, "female": 1}
titanic["Sex"] = titanic["Sex"].map(sexes)
```

If **"Pclass"** were represented using strings like **"first"**, **"second"**, and **"third"**, we would have to do something similar for that variable, but luckily it's already represented using the integers **1**, **2**, and **3**. That means we're ready to move on to the next step, which is to prepare our data. The independent variables are class, sex, and age, while the dependent variable is survival rate. Following the usual convention, we'll call these **X** and **Y**, respectively:

```
X = titanic.drop("Survived", axis=1)
Y = titanic["Survived"]
```

Note that we've dropped the dependent **"Survived"** column from the **X** training variable because that's exactly what we're trying to predict.

Before applying the learning model algorithms, let's take a look at everything just to make sure the data looks sensible:

```
print(X.head(), "\n----\n")
print(Y.head(), "\n----\n")
   Pclass  Sex   Age
0       3    0  22.0
1       1    1  38.0
2       3    1  26.0
3       1    1  35.0
4       3    0  35.0
----


0    0
1    1
2    1
3    1
4    0
Name: Survived, dtype: int64
----
```

Looks good.

The original competition that inspired this example involved supplying training data for creating models, which was then applied to test data not available to participants in the competition. Because this section isn't part of that competition, we'll split the given data into separate training and test datasets ourselves. Using such separate datasets helps guard against overfitting, which involves using so many free parameters that the model doesn't have predictive value beyond the original datasets—as the great John von Neumann once reportedly quipped, "With four parameters I can fit an elephant, and with five I can make him wiggle his trunk." (We'll cover a second guard against overfitting called *cross-validation* as well.)

The main scikit-learn method for doing a train/test split is called, appropriately enough, **train_test_split()**, which returns four values consisting of a training and test variable for each of **X** and **Y**:

```
from sklearn.model_selection import train_test_split
(X_train, X_test, Y_train, Y_test) = train_test_split(X, Y, random_state=1)
```

Because **train_test_split()** shuffles the data before doing the split, we've set the **random_state** option so that your results will be consistent with those shown in the text.

At this point, we're ready to try the various models out on the training data and see how accurate their fits are when applied to the test data. Our strategy is to define an instance of each of the models imported in Listing 11.24, calculate the **fit()** on the training data, and then look at the **score()** of the model on the test data. We'll then compare the scores to compare the accuracy of the models.

First up is Logistic Regression:

```
logreg = LogisticRegression()
logreg.fit(X_train, Y_train)
accuracy_logreg = logreg.score(X_test, Y_test)
```

Next is (Gaussian) Naive Bayes:

```
naive_bayes = GaussianNB()
naive_bayes.fit(X_train, Y_train)
accuracy_naive_bayes = naive_bayes.score(X_test, Y_test)
```

Then Perceptron:

```
perceptron = Perceptron()
perceptron.fit(X_train, Y_train)
accuracy_perceptron = perceptron.score(X_test, Y_test)
```

Then Decision Tree:

```
decision_tree = DecisionTreeClassifier()
decision_tree.fit(X_train, Y_train)
accuracy_decision_tree = decision_tree.score(X_test, Y_test)
```

And finally Random Forest (using a **random_state** option as with **train_test_-split()** to obtain consistent results):

```
random_forest = RandomForestClassifier(random_state=1)
random_forest.fit(X_train, Y_train)
accuracy_random_forest = random_forest.score(X_test, Y_test)
```

Let's make a DataFrame to hold and display the results (again omitting the prompt for easier copying):

```
results = pd.DataFrame({
    "Model": ["Logistic Regression", "Naive Bayes", "Perceptron",
              "Decision Tree", "Random Forest"],
    "Score": [accuracy_logreg, accuracy_naive_bayes, accuracy_perceptron,
              accuracy_decision_tree, accuracy_random_forest]})
result_df = results.sort_values(by="Score", ascending=False)
result_df = result_df.set_index("Score")
result_df
```

The result appears in Listing 11.25.

Listing 11.25: The model accuracy results.

```
                    Model
Score
0.854749  Decision Tree
0.854749  Random Forest
0.787709  Logistic Regression
0.770950  Naive Bayes
0.743017  Perceptron
```

We see that Decision Tree and Random Forest are tied for the most accurate score, followed by Logistic Regression and Naive Bayes neck-and-neck, with Perceptron bringing up the rear. The models are close enough, though, that different values for **random_state** could easily affect their order (Section 11.7.4).

Once we've performed the **fit()**, we can look at how important each factor was in determining the results of the model. For example, for the Random Forest model, the importances are as follows:

```
>>> random_forest.feature_importances_
array([0.16946036, 0.35821155, 0.47232809])
>>> X_train.columns
Index(['Pclass', 'Sex', 'Age'], dtype='object')
```

Comparing the columns to the importances, we see that **"Age"** was the biggest factor, followed closely by **"Sex"**, with **"Pclass"** being a distant third (half as important as the second-highest factor). We can visualize the result as a bar chart as well:

```
>>> fig, ax = plt.subplots()
>>> ax.bar(X_train.columns, random_forest.feature_importances_)
<BarContainer object of 3 artists>
>>> plt.show()
```

Previous examples of **bar()** have gone through the pandas interface, but here we see that Matplotlib also supports bar charts directly. (This isn't surprising since, as noted in Section 11.4, pandas uses Matplotlib under the hood.) The result appears in Figure 11.35.

Cross-Validation

As previously noted, we split the data into training and test datasets as one guard against overfitting. Another common technique to avoid "fitting an elephant" (per von Neumann's quip) is known as *cross-validation*. The basic idea is to artificially break the original training data into new training and test datasets, train the model on the training data, and then use the model to predict the test data. If doing this on several different random choices for training and test subsets yields fairly consistent results, we can be more confident that the model actually works.

Because this is such a common technique, scikit-learn comes with a predefined routine for performing cross-validations called **cross_val_score**:

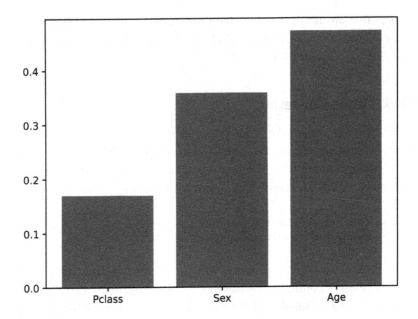

Figure 11.35: The importance of each factor in *Titanic* survival rates.

```
>>> from sklearn.model_selection import cross_val_score
```

This method implements so-called *K-fold cross-validation*, which involves breaking the data into K pieces, or "folds", using $K-1$ folds to train the model, and then predicting the values of the final fold to assess accuracy. The default value is **5**, which is fine for our purposes, so we need only pass the function the classifier instance and the training data. We'll use Random Forest since it was tied for first (and, as previously noted, has an especially cool name):

```
>>> random_forest = RandomForestClassifier(random_state=1)
>>> scores = cross_val_score(random_forest, X, Y)
>>> scores
array([0.75524476, 0.8041958, 0.82517483, 0.83216783, 0.83098592])
>>> scores.mean()
0.8095538264552349
>>> scores.std()
0.028958338744358988
```

With scores that are nearly 81% accurate on average with a standard deviation of just under 3%, we can reasonably conclude the Random Forest model is an accurate predictor of *Titanic* survival data.

11.7.3 *k*-Means Clustering

As a final example, we'll take a look at a *clustering algorithm*, which is but one of the many amazing things that scikit-learn can do.[35] We'll start by importing a utility method commonly used when demonstrating clustering algorithms called **make_blobs()**, in this case consisting of **300** points divided into **4** blobs:

```
>>> from sklearn.datasets import make_blobs
>>> X, _ = make_blobs(n_samples=300, centers=4, random_state=42)
```

Note that we've also passed a **random_state** parameter, which serves as the seed for the blobs and ensures consistent results (which can vary quite a lot).

We can see what's "bloblike" about the data created by **make_blobs()** by plotting the second column against the first:

```
>>> fig, ax = plt.subplots()
>>> ax.scatter(X[:, 0], X[:, 1])
>>> plt.show()
```

The result appears in Figure 11.36.

We can find a good fit for the **4** blobs using an algorithm called *k-means clustering*:

```
>>> from sklearn.cluster import KMeans
>>> kmeans = KMeans(n_clusters=4)
>>> kmeans.fit(X)
```

Note how similar the steps are to the model fits in Section 11.7.2. We can find the model's estimate for the center of each cluster using the **cluster_centers_** attribute:

---

35. See https://jakevdp.github.io/PythonDataScienceHandbook/05.11-k-means.html for more details.

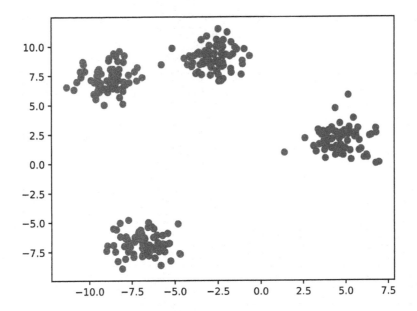

Figure 11.36: Some random blobs.

```
>>> centers = kmeans.cluster_centers_
>>> centers
array([[ 4.7182049 ,  2.04179676],
       [-8.87357218,  7.17458342],
       [-6.83235205, -6.83045748],
       [-2.70981136,  8.97143336]])
```

(Note the same trailing-underscore convention mentioned in Section 11.7.1 to indicate an attribute that is defined only after calling **fit()**.) The result is an array of points whose meaning we can interpret by plotting the second column against the first as we did with the original blobs:

```
fig, ax = plt.subplots()
ax.scatter(X[:, 0], X[:, 1])
centers = kmeans.cluster_centers_
ax.scatter(centers[:, 0], centers[:, 1], s=200, alpha=0.9, color="orange")
plt.show()
```

With the larger size, alpha transparency, and orange color, it's easy to see the estimated centers of the respective clusters on a scatter plot (Figure 11.37). The result is an

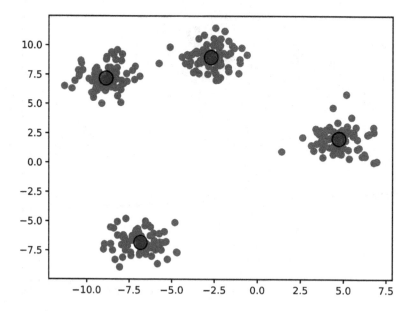

Figure 11.37: Clusters with their predicted centers.

excellent correspondence between the output of the clustering algorithm and what we expect based on an intuitive notion of "clusters".

11.7.4 Exercises

1. The **RandomForestClassifier()** function takes a keyword argument called **n_estimators** that represents the "number of trees in the forest". According to the documentation, what is the default value for **n_estimators**? Use **random_state=1**.

2. By varying **n_estimators** in the call to **RandomForestClassifier()**, determine the approximate value where the Random Forest classifier is less accurate than Decision Tree. Use **random_state=1**.

3. By rerunning the steps in Section 11.7.2 using a few different values of **random_state**, verify that the ordering is not always the same as shown in Listing 11.25. *Hint*: Try values like **0**, **2**, **3**, and **4**.

4. Repeat the clustering steps in Section 11.7.3 using two clusters and eight clusters. Does the algorithm still work well in both cases?

11.8 Further Resources and Conclusion

Congratulations—now you *really* know enough Python to be dangerous! In addition to the core material, you now have a good grounding in some of the most important tools for data science with Python.

There are a million directions to go from here; here are a few of the possibilities:

- The official pandas documentation includes 10 minutes to pandas followed by a large amount of additional tutorial material. The official documentation for NumPy, Matplotlib, and scikit-learn are also excellent resources. Finally, the SciPy and SageMath projects are worth knowing about; Sage in particular includes the ability to do symbolic as well as numerical computations (much like *Mathematica* or Maple).

- "Python for Scientific Computing": Although not for data science per se, this resource covers a lot of the same material needed for the subject. Among other things, "Python for Scientific Computing" was the inspiration for the section using Nobel Prize data (Section 11.5).

- *Python Data Science Handbook* by Jake VanderPlas: This book takes a similar approach to this chapter and is available for free online.

- *Data Science from Scratch* by Joel Grus: This book is basically the polar opposite of this chapter, taking a first-principles approach to data science that focuses on the foundational ideas of the subject. This approach is impossible in a space as short as ours but is an excellent way to go if you're interested in becoming a professional data scientist.

- Bloom Institute of Technology's Data Science Course: This online course is aimed at serious students interested in a career in data science.

- *Hands-On Machine Learning with Scikit-Learn, Keras, and TensorFlow* by Aurélien Géron: A much more advanced introduction to machine learning than Section 11.7, including Keras, a Python interface to Google's TensorFlow library.

For completeness, here are the general Python resources recommended in Section 10.6:

- Replit's 100 days of code: This is a guided introduction to Python programming using Replit's amazing collaborative browser-based IDE.

- Practical Python Programming by Dave Beazley: I've long been a huge fan of Beazely's *Python Essential Reference* and highly recommend his (free) online course.

- *Learn Python the Hard Way* by Zed Shaw: This exercise- and syntax-heavy approach is an excellent complement to the breadth-first, narrative approach taken in this tutorial. *Fun fact*: Zed Shaw's "Learn Code the Hard Way" brand was a direct inspiration for "Learn Enough to Be Dangerous" (https://www.learnenough.com/).

- *Python Crash Course* and *Automate the Boring Stuff with Python* from No Starch Press: Both of these books are good follow-ons to *Learn Enough Python to Be Dangerous*; the former (by Eric Matthes) has more detailed coverage of Python syntax while the latter (by Al Sweigart) includes a great many applications of Python programming to everyday computer tasks.

- *Captain Code* by Ben Forta and Shmuel Forta: Although this book is principally aimed at children, many adult readers have reported enjoying it as well.

- Finally, for people who want the most solid foundation possible in technical sophistication, Learn Enough All Access (https://www.learnenough.com/all-access) is a subscription service that has special online versions of all the Learn Enough books and over 40 hours of streaming video tutorials, including *Learn Enough Python to Be Dangerous*, *Learn Enough Ruby to Be Danger-ous* (https://www.learnenough.com/ruby), and the full *Ruby on Rails Tutorial* (https://www.railstutorial.org/). We hope you'll check it out!

Those are just a few of the incredible variety of options available to you now that you have learned the basics of Python and have developed your technical sophistication. Good luck!

Index

Photo by Marvent/Shutterstock

VIDEO TRAINING FOR THE **IT PROFESSIONAL**

LEARN QUICKLY
Learn a new technology in just hours. Video training can teach more in less time, and material is generally easier to absorb and remember.

WATCH AND LEARN
Instructors demonstrate concepts so you see technology in action.

TEST YOURSELF
Our Complete Video Courses offer self-assessment quizzes throughout.

CONVENIENT
Most videos are streaming with an option to download lessons for offline viewing.

Learn more, browse our store, and watch free, sample lessons at
informit.com/video

Save 50%* off the list price of video courses with discount code **VIDBOB**

Register Your Product at informit.com/register

Access additional benefits and save up to 65%* on your next purchase

- Automatically receive a coupon for 35% off books, eBooks, and web editions and 65% off video courses, valid for 30 days. Look for your code in your InformIT cart or the Manage Codes section of your account page.

- Download available product updates.

- Access bonus material if available.**

- Check the box to hear from us and receive exclusive offers on new editions and related products.

InformIT—The Trusted Technology Learning Source

InformIT is the online home of information technology brands at Pearson, the world's leading learning company. At informit.com, you can

- Shop our books, eBooks, and video training. Most eBooks are DRM-Free and include PDF and EPUB files.

- Take advantage of our special offers and promotions (informit.com/promotions).

- Sign up for special offers and content newsletter (informit.com/newsletters).

- Access thousands of free chapters and video lessons.

- Enjoy free ground shipping on U.S. orders.*

* Offers subject to change.

** Registration benefits vary by product. Benefits will be listed on your account page under Registered Products.

Connect with InformIT—Visit informit.com/community

 twitter.com/informit

 Pearson

 informIT

Addison-Wesley • Adobe Press • Cisco Press • Microsoft Press • Oracle Press • Peachpit Press • Pearson IT Certification • Que